RACIAL TRAUMA RECOVERY

HEALING OUR PAST USING RHYTHM AND PROCESSING

EACH ONE
TEACH ONE
PUBLICATIONS

DAVID ARCHER

First Printing: September 2022
Second Printing: November 2023

ISBN: 978-1-7774504-7-2

David Archer

3420 AVENUE WILSON

SUITE 101

MONTREAL, QUEBEC, H4A 2T5

CANADA

david@archertherapy.com
www.racialtraumarecovery.com

David Archer is available to speak at your business or conference event on a variety of topics. Send an email to david@archertherapy.com for booking information.

WHY READ THIS BOOK

My intention is to share an integrative clinical framework designed to solve the mental health consequences of racial trauma.

Where my first book, **Anti-Racist Psychotherapy,** was designed to raise consciousness regarding the effects of anti-Black racism, **Racial Trauma Recovery** expands on this mission. Once again, the primary focus will be on the mental health consequences of anti-Black racial trauma, and because all other socially constructed oppressions are linked, the strategies described in this book are easily applicable to the full spectrum of identity-based issues including gender, sexual identity, indigeneity, culture, nationality, class, caste, ethnicity, disability and other historically excluded or systemically marginalized groups.

Theories relating to memory reconsolidation, motivational interviewing, structural dissociation, polyvagal theory, and EMDR therapy's Adaptive Information Processing theoretical model will be used to explain how racial trauma survivors can recover rapidly, efficiently, and permanently.

Learning **Rhythm and Processing Strategies** will help you to become a better anti-racist practitioner and inspire hope during this challenging time in our collective existence. This new clinical framework includes the use of novel therapeutic interventions in combination with online video conferencing software and video streaming websites.

Our journey will involve confronting the systemic injustices that are endemic in societies plagued by the psychological warfare of white supremacy/insecurity. The goal is to eradicate the negative cognitions that fuel the internalization of anti-Black racism.

The world must heal and recover. And toward this purpose, I pass on all that I know to you. Let us have courage, be open-minded, and create change in our global community.

ABOUT THE AUTHOR

David Archer is an anti-racist psychotherapist, an EMDRIA certified EMDR practitioner, a certified Brainspotting therapist, a clinical social worker, a couples and family therapist, and a mindfulness meditator from Montreal, Canada (Tiohtià:ke). He is an expert clinician who works in private practice with diverse clinical populations.

Archer provides both individual and group consultations to other therapists in training. He specializes in efficient psychotherapeutic interventions that are designed to maintain long-lasting changes. He previously authored the highly acclaimed book called Anti-Racist Psychotherapy: Confronting Systemic Racism and Healing Racial Trauma. His second book is entitled Black Meditation: Ten Practices for Self-Care, Mindfulness, and Self-Determination. Both publications exist in paperback, hardcover, eBook, and audiobook format.

Having co-presented the ground-breaking plenary discussion Elephant in the Room: Racism and Psychotherapy, Archer led anti-racist workshops at both the EMDRIA and ISSTD world conferences, as well as participated in numerous panel discussions and peer supervisions in local community circles. He has years of experience working with a range of clients who suffer from racial trauma, child abuse, anxiety, depressive disorders, relational conflict, addictions, and eating disorders. In addition to extensive work with immigrants and people of diverse racial origins, he spent several years as a counselor in the Indigenous community of Kahnawake, where he cultivated a deeper understanding of culture, community, and the spirit of resilience.

Archer provides expert consultation to professionals regarding anti-Black racism, trauma resolution, and minority stress. When not writing about these topics, he enjoys listening to deep house music and roots and culture reggae while cruising on the highway. He believes that therapists do not always need to take themselves so seriously. He enjoys eating spicy food like it's his day job, and generally in between reading and writing about psychotherapy, he enjoys playing very difficult indie/Japanese anime video games. His current favorite game is Guilty Gear Strive, which is the wickedest fighting game out right now, just in case you were wondering. He believes that people learn best while having fun—even when approaching challenging topics.

After reading this book, you will gain a greater understanding for how to help people recover from racial trauma using a trauma-informed and neuroscience-inspired approach to healing. I hope this experience will be as inspiring as it will be thought-provoking.

To invite David Archer as a speaker at your next event or conference, email him at David@archertherapy.com **or visit** www.racialtraumarecovery.com

ADVANCE PRAISE FOR RACIAL TRAUMA RECOVERY

"Mr. Archer has written a book that is a must-read for any practitioner in the field of trauma treatment. Get your copy!"

Resmaa Menakem, MSW, LICSW, SEP
Bestselling author of My Grandmother's Hands

"David's model for working with individuals who have experienced racial trauma offers practitioners an innovative and highly responsive way to support clients to transcend the space of coping with racial harm and move towards deep healing and thriving. This book is an essential read for anyone engaged in liberatory therapeutic practices!"

Kamilah Clayton, MSW
Owner of ADWO Counselling & Consulting Services Inc.

"Mr. Archer's latest literary offering imparts a ground-breaking therapeutic model that not only gets to the root cause and effects of psycho-racial harm but also other types of trauma. It is a thought-provoking, challenging read that is entirely accessible in language and form."

Michael Bowe
Equity Consultant, Principal, Bowe and Associates Inc.

"Very practical and a synthesis of the most current methods of the third wave of cognitive and behavioral therapy. This therapeutic model is a must in your arsenal against human suffering."

Marco Goupil, CD, Inf, TCF, MAP
General Director of Clinique de thérapie conjugale et familiale

"Mr. Archer's model offers a new paradigm in the treatment of racial trauma. Every therapist needs a copy of this. Mr. Archer's model perfectly addresses the needs of BIPOC and responds to their unique experiences."

Radamis Zaky, Ph.D.
Part-Time professor at the University of Ottawa

"Mr. Archer's important work to address the mental health consequences of racial trauma is an essential read for mental health professionals."

Thomas Zimmerman, Ms.Ed., LPCC
EMDR Therapy Trainer, Developer of Four Blinks Approach

"On many occasions, I have thought about many of the realizations David Archer has in his book but could never find the words to express them. What David has written here is a must read by any practicing clinician who is venturing into doing anti-racist practice, stemming from the way he has articulated and framed racial trauma and its treatment. David's personal and professional examples, conversations and understandings of therapeutic practice in treating racial trauma are unique, insightful, and hard hitting. Not only am I a better Clinician and Teacher due to reading his book, but a better person in what I can offer to my community."

Tom Caplan, MSW, MFT
Adjunct Professor at McGill University's School of Social Work
Consultant to the McGill Domestic Violence Clinic
Founder of the Montreal Anger Management Centre

"With this new offering, David Archer reveals himself as a true gift to the field of Psychotherapy. I had the pleasure of participating in a small group introduction to Mr. Archer's new therapeutic methodology of healing trauma. It was a transformative experience that I was immediately excited about bringing into my private practice as the primary modality to address chronic issues resulting from anti-Black Racism, racial trauma, and PTSD. Mr. Archer's new book, Racial Trauma Recovery, provides a revolutionary new paradigm in the treatment and healing of racial trauma. During this global demand for racial justice and social change, we need more than just talk, we need healing."

Kimberly Cato, RP
Registered Psychotherapist
CEO / Founder of True Roots Counselling Services

PREFACE

— ❦ —

THE IMPERATIVE FOR RHYTHM AND PROCESSING

The Problem

B ack in the day, when I would tell people what I do for a living, they would question it. Some racially oppressed people would think I couldn't possibly be serious. Some would doubt my effectiveness, telling me that therapy is "white people stuff" or question whether "it even worked" on Black people. Some professionals also had concerns about learning some of the approaches I am trained in, wondering whether it would work for their own communities or populations of interest.

I used to think, "Hey, why don't they trust the science?" They would question whether new approaches would work, despite coming from a person with all the necessary degrees and certifications. The qualifications of a mental health practitioner were not enough to convince them fully.

And rightfully so. As I gained experience, I learned to empathize with their concerns. The vast majority of psychotherapies are not designed with diverse racial groups in mind. Anyone who questions this should simply ask, regarding the questionnaires we administer during our assessments, "Is their validity established for all racial groups? Can the results be replicated when assessing recent immigrants? Have they ever once been tested for reliability in Indigenous communities?"

When people state that therapy *does* work, we have to ask for whom? Does it work for "them" or does it work for "us"? In a nation-state where the country's flag carries so many divergent and politicized meanings, there can never be a "we." The client who has been denied racial equity knows that "we" are not all the same. To assess what works, researchers need subjects. In most cases, those subjects will be people whom the researchers can easily reach. In practice, this means that our standard psychotherapy tools and approaches have mainly been tested against white university or college attendees. The kind of clients that I meet rarely find requests to participate in research studies in their email inboxes.

With such a whitewashed pool of research participants, the findings and assessments are bound to be skewed to favor predictable results for a small white minority who do not resemble the global majority. Because I identify as an anti-racist psychotherapist, I expect that elements of what I propose in this book will be rejected. There will be people who will cast doubt on my findings and closed-minded old fogies who will reject any possibility of technological advances in our field. But the history of scientific study is full of ideas that were rejected at first, only to be celebrated later. Glass ceilings and moving goalposts carry no surprises for me.

The history of psychology is rooted in the conservation and protection of whiteness. The standard measures of intelligence that psychologists adopted in the early twentieth century—at the height of European imperialism and the American Jim Crow era—were developed by eugenicists to promote ideas of white supremacy (White, 2000), and psychologists played important roles in establishing beliefs of a racialized human hierarchy through their studies of racial disparities. The American Psychological Association only in 2021 acknowledged its role in helping to fuel and sustain racial injustice based on skewed interpretations of race-based data and its abject silence throughout the civil rights era.[1]

Psychiatrists have only recently reckoned with the fact that inequitable—or non-existent—treatment of Black, brown, and Indigenous Peoples has been built into their systems and procedures. The American Psychiatric Association finally admitted, again only in 2021, to the harms caused to communities of color by race-based theories, including differential diagnoses for schizophrenia that continue to this day. As the apology acknowledges, modern psychiatric practice has been marked by "abusive treatment, experimentation, [and] victimization [of Black and Indigenous people] in the name of 'scientific evidence'." The apology concedes that racist concepts and practices are "ingrained in the structure of psychiatric practice and continue to harm BIPOC [Black, Indigenous, and People of Color[2]] psychological well-being even today."[3]

---

1 https://www.apa.org/about/policy/racism-apology

2 The term BIPOC (and even the phrase "people of color") is outdated. Terms like these attempt to lump diverse people into the same category and are frequently used by diversity, equity, and inclusion people to justify one blanket approach to very different racial/cultural groups. Black, Indigenous, and people of color experience systemic racism differently. So you won't see me using it in any further publications. Middle Eastern people do not experience racism in the same way as people from the Caribbean. Even Asians differ in their experiences, hence the differences in income and representation between East Asians and South Asians in the United States. See this link for more information: https://medium.com/@SilleckConsultingServicesLLC/how-using-the-term-people-of-color-masks-anti-black-systemic-racism-f595da1a0eca

3 https://www.psychiatry.org/newsroom/apa-apology-for-its-support-of-structural-racism-in-psychiatry

Who do these approaches work for? What if the tentacles of anti-Black racism have already descended into the institutions that train the therapists? I will never know how many theories or approaches in my field I was prevented from knowing or having access to because of the atrocities of structural racism. I wonder how many Black researchers were prevented from graduating because a white supervisor had a racialized grudge against them. How many Black students have failed because they refused to go along with the white guilt and implicit racist beliefs of white instructors or students? Was I the only one who noticed that the few mentions of race in my undergraduate psychology classes were ill-intentioned? Whenever they mentioned Black people, it was always in reference to a supposed deficit in them. Quite apart from the hidden racism that revolves around comparing the results of IQ testing of racial groups (Gillborn, 2016), even studying "neutral" topics in biology, sensation, or perception always seemed to involve sneaking in a comparative analysis of white and Black people, as if Black was the only racial group to study.

Consider, for example, one study (Dwyer & Stanton, 1975) that focused on a burgeoning concern at the time that because Black and white people are different "colors," they may even perceive chromatics differently. Spoiler alert: no, your race is irrelevant to how you perceive colors. This was the predominant way race was mentioned in my psychology undergraduate program, always as something incidental; a "by the way, you're Black" statement that intruded on my learning and created awkward communications with so-called "experts." With time, I realized that the intention behind this "accidental" racism was to mask my white instructors' own insecurities. Thankfully my social work experience, and ultimately my couple and family therapy master's degrees, largely made up for this color-blind learning experience. Even there, however, I encountered the same "accidental" racism whenever my social work or therapy training collided with psychiatric and psychological theories saturated in racism and classism. Indeed, I am convinced that no university discipline that concerns the psyche precludes the possibility of perpetuating, either directly or indirectly, the racial and class oppressions that have fuelled the history of education in the West. James McGill, the founder of my alma mater, owned enslaved people after all, and his statue graced the lawn of its downtown campus until 2021.

Although I'm grateful for my academic training—as it is the foundation of my psychotherapeutic writing and practice—the fountainhead of my approach lies outside the institutions. My family and my ancestors provoke the rhythm of my heartbeat. I would never have written a thing about anti-racism or developed a practice centered around overcoming racial trauma had it not been for the family members who helped me to be a proud Black Jamaican African Canadian in a white nationalist province with all of the additional complexities that being an anglophone in Quebec brings with it. I could not have written this book or any of my others if I weren't determined that my son and his descendants should have an easier time in this world than I did. I write for the future generations of unborn Black children.

The Purpose

I wrote this book knowing that there are many theories that I have probably been prevented from learning because of invisible barriers. During my studies, Black people were only mentioned in the context of "disadvantaged," so I am unaware of how many more anti-racist theories, therapies, or clinical frameworks I was unwittingly prevented from knowing about. In my training as a social worker and psychotherapist, how many approaches never made it into my course materials because some unknown non-white, anti-racist students in training had been prevented from contributing their alternative, Black-positive ideas at conferences or even prevented from graduating at all?

To my unknown predecessors,
I dedicate this approach to racial trauma recovery to you.

The cover of this book is an artistic representation of the reconsolidation of traumatic memories. Trauma survivors are often plagued by reexperiencing the past as if it were the present. Thus, the two Black women depicted on the cover symbolize this encounter in the trauma therapy context. One woman sits with a protective animal of her imagination while facing her mirror image, also accompanied by an imagined spiritual creature. The women appear to be reflections of each other, but which of them is the past version and which of them exists in the present?

In an anti-racist approach, the goal is to develop resources that will help to protect clients from the burdens and traps based on a past history of oppression and present-day, ambiguously defined identity constructs. The cover was inspired by several of my Black female clients who, without knowing, chose similar animals such as lionesses or black panthers to protect and lead them toward victory. Inspired by the inspirational recovery of my clients, the ultimate goal is to bring our resources to bear on confronting and overcoming our past. When we think about our traumatic episodes, we revisit the lack of compassion, the absence of a hug, or the paucity of wisdom that could have helped us make peace with our suffering. While we cannot change the past, we now have the technology to perceive our memories differently and give our past selves the resources we possess in the present. In this way, we can heal our past trauma. We can effectively rescue ourselves.

*In consideration of all of the above, without pridefulness or ego,
I dedicate this book to the past version of myself.*

In the past, I wish I could have answered and told them, "Here is your therapy. This therapy is ours." I wish I could have told them that there already was a therapy taught by a Black man who cares about your future. I wish I could have explained that the foundations of this therapy cover anti-racist psychotherapy, motivational interviewing, genograms, memory reconsolidation, EMDR therapy, structural dissociation, polyvagal theory, technological advancements in the practice of telehealth services; and hey, that he even threw YouTube videos up in there, he wrote a book about an approach that integrates all of this for us and for the world.

Well, we now have a framework that is designed to heal the psychological complexities of racial trauma, and I have worked hard to be able to say this to my current and future clients. I have learnt from mistakes along the way. And somehow, through the grace of God, through the synchronicities of the universe, I managed to become the therapist I always wanted to meet. Just like the cover, I offer the gift of this resource to my past self. I hope this resource can change the way we all see therapy. I desire to see those who are historically excluded being permanently exalted. The time has come to rescue ourselves.

The Plan

For those who would like to know what to expect in this book, you are in luck. This section of the preface will cover the outline. Here is the general structure of the book: it starts with the general mindset and principles that I follow as an anti-racist psychotherapist, then it covers interventions that promote the possibility of healing from traumatic experiences; and it ends with practical instructions and informative discussions regarding the implementation of racial trauma recovery.

The name of the integrative clinical framework that is the subject of this book is **Rhythm and Processing (RAP)**. Rhythm refers to the collaborative interaction between client and therapist. Processing represents the transmutation of suffering into wisdom. RAP is designed to address socially constructed forms of suffering in general, but special attention is given to racial trauma in particular. RAP improves wellbeing by utilizing highly effective therapeutic interventions (or strategies) from different modalities. The goal is to empower all trauma survivors who come from diverse backgrounds, cultures, and identities.

If you'd like, I could get even more specific. Chapter one describes the foundational principles of Anti-Racist Psychotherapy and clarifies why we need a new approach to treat the complex issue of racial trauma. The second chapter discusses the Fundamental Africentric Dimensions that encourage strong working alliances with racially oppressed people, as well as a discussion of theories that have influenced the development of Rhythm and Processing. Traumatology is covered in the third chapter alongside the neurobiological impacts of stress, and the biopsychosocial effects of structural racism. The fourth chapter discusses a new theoretical explanation for how traumatic material becomes dysfunctionally stored in our minds and how we can recover by using transformative interventions. Next, chapter five explores essential clinical interventions for starting off on the right foot, as well as mindfulness-based interventions that are designed to inspire hope for change. Ambivalence is discussed in the sixth chapter, and I describe ways of addressing limiting beliefs that could surreptitiously derail clinical progress. Chapter seven provides a short explanation of the theory of structural dissociation, complex trauma symptoms, and the resource integration strategy. The eighth chapter explores the Rhythm and Processing technique through the use of transcripts and guided instructions. Chapter nine highlights polyvagal theory, the importance of safety and the legacies we inherit through our family tree. The tenth chapter describes the Racial Trauma Target History process as well as treatment plans that make use of computer software for addressing identity-based stresses. Chapter 11 is a guided demonstration of the RAP technique, which takes into account information from all of the previous chapters, and the twelfth chapter summarizes the book's content and concludes with a discussion of how therapists can embody the philosophy of anti-racist psychotherapy, both inside and outside of the clinical environment.

Through reading this book, it is my hope that you, the reader, also learn ways of rescuing yourself while supporting people of all races, ethnicities, sexualities, bodies, and identities. Welcome to the anti-racist psychotherapy approach to racial trauma recovery.

TABLE OF CONTENTS

CHAPTER 1

Racial Trauma Recovery and Anti-Racist Psychotherapy 1

    A Conversation 2

    The Global Context 3

    The Pandemic 4

    The Therapist 7

    Anti-Racist Psychotherapy 8

    The Trauma of Whiteness 10

    The Binary Complex Trauma Cycle 13

    The Internalization of Anti-Black Racism 15

    A New Approach to Treating Racial Trauma 16

    Summary 18

CHAPTER 2

Principles and Rationale for Rhythm and Processing Strategies 19

    The Worldview 20

    Fundamental Africentric Dimensions 21

    Rhythm and Processing's Family Tree 24

    Adaptive Information Processing 25

    Brainspotting 27

    Memory Reconsolidation and Taxing Working Memory 27

    Summary 30

CHAPTER 3

The Problem: neurobiological consequences of Trauma 31

    An Overview of the Problem 32

    What Is Trauma? 32

    A Brief Summary of the Neurobiology of Trauma 34

    The Stress Response System 35

    The Biopsychosocial Effects of Stress 37

    Structural Violence and Racial Segregation 40

    Summary 45

CHAPTER 4

The Resolution: Memory Reconsolidation 46

    Changing the Course of Trauma Histories 47

The Cycle of Consolidation 47

Memory Reconsolidation 50

Therapeutic Reconsolidation Using Rhythm and Processing 51

Healing from Echoes of Suffering 59

Summary 60

CHAPTER 5

Getting Started: Intake and Mindfulness-Based Strategies 62

Starting Off on the Right Foot 63

Initial Client Request 63

Setting Expectations 63

The Presenting Problem 65

The Four Cores of Anti-Racist Psychotherapy 66

The Client's Opportunity to Ask Questions 69

Questionnaires and Assessments 74

The Initial Client Session 75

Mindfulness-Based Interventions 76

Summary 81

CHAPTER 6

Ambivalence and The Advantage of The Disadvantage 82

Being on the Fence 83

Addictions and the Underlying Source of Suffering 83

EMDR Approaches to Substance Abuse Treatment 84

Associating Problems With Positive Affect 86

The Motivation for Ambivalence 87

Implementation of the PROS/CONS Balance Sheet 89

Summary 96

CHAPTER 7

STRUCTURAL DISSOCIATION AND RESOURCE INTEGRATION 98

Putting the Pieces Together 99

Structural Dissociation: The Effects of Severe and Chronic Traumatization 99

Mental Levels, Substitute Actions, and Integration 102

The Skill of Resource Integration 104

The Process of Installing the Resource 106

Integrating with the Resource 108

Fine Tuning the Resource 109

Summary 110

CHAPTER 8

The Rhythm and Processing Technique 112

Check the Technique 113

Precursors to the RAP Technique 113

The Flash Technique...113

Zimmerman's Four Blinks Approach 115

The Setup: RAP Initialization 117

The Process: Using the RAP Technique 122

Deepening the Experience 124

Summary...126

CHAPTER 9

Polyvagal Theory and Legacies through Genograms 127

Our Interdependent Existence 128

The Social Context's Harm to Indigenous People......................................128

A Brief Summary of Polyvagal Theory 131

The Ladder Metaphor of Polyvagal Theory..132

The Need to Connect...133

Tracing Our Roots: Using the Genogram..134

Genogram Considerations and Suggestions...135

Anti-Racist Psychotherapy Recommendations...139

Summary...141

CHAPTER 10

THE RACIAL TRAUMA TARGET HISTORY...143

Planning the Path Toward Recovery...144

Creating the Racial Trauma Target History...145

Special Considerations 146

Trauma History Questions:...151

Completing the Trauma History 156

Color Coding the Trauma History...159

Final Notes on Racial Trauma Target Selection 160

Summary...162

CHAPTER 11

A Session in Rhythm and Processing 163

Rhythm and Processing in Action 164

Setting the Stage for Recovery..164

Reconsolidating the Traumatic Memory...166

Accessing the Target 168

Initiating the Transformation 171

Verification of Target Completion 177

Closing the Program..183

Summary...184

CHAPTER 12

Wrapping it up: Anti-Racist reflections 185

   Final Thoughts Relating to the Protocol 186

   Insights and Challenges Between Sessions...186

   Sharing Our Screen to Address Phobias..188

   Working with Instead of Against our Client..189

   Summarizing our Work Together..190

   Final Reflections on Racial Trauma..192

   The White Person's Internalization of Anti-Black Racism 194

   The Social Construction of Suffering...196

   Be About It 198

   Summary..200

APPENDIX I

Black Meditation scripts 201

   Skill #3: Guided Earth Meditation 203

   Skill #4: Mindful Color Breathing 205

   Skill #6: Five Grateful Things Exercise..207

APPENDIX II

Racial Trauma Recovery: Summary Sheets.. 209

   The Binary Complex Trauma Cycle 210

   The Cycle of Consolidation 211

   The Internalization of Anti-Black Racism..212

   Rhythm and Processing Technique 213

   RAP Technique: GeneralScan 214

   RAP Technique: DeepScan...215

REFERENCES 216

INDEX..224

OTHER BOOKS BY THIS AUTHOR...229

LET'S WORK TOGETHER...230

CHAPTER 1

RACIAL TRAUMA RECOVERY AND ANTI-RACIST PSYCHOTHERAPY

A Conversation

The first white colleague I shared the title of this book with reacted with a question. "Why do you need to call it *racial* trauma recovery?" he asked. "I mean, it's meant for *everyone*, right?" To him, the term *racial* implied exclusion. Seeing the word as an epithet is an attitude that proliferates in any society that supports anti-Black racism. This is how I responded:

Archer:	There are two reasons. First, race is something that everyone has, but at the same time, it is a fiction. White people conveniently forget both these facts. There is no scientific basis for racial classifications. They are a social construction based on political presuppositions. Take the concept of being a man. We've all heard people talk about being a "real" man, haven't we? But who is a real man? Is it the man who owns the big truck? The man who has the big beard? The concept is not based on science. It is a fabricated concept based on someone else's imagination. Race exists in the same way. Because of your perceived racial identity, certain things are more likely to happen to you. These identities are imaginary concepts, but they have very real consequences.
White colleague:	Oh, wow. I've never actually thought about that. And the second reason?
Archer:	That's simple. I have always wanted to write the books I have always wanted to read.

The Global Context

Millions of people have lost their lives to the COVID pandemic. An invisible disease has spread its suffering, ravaging the land with profound consequences for economies, cultures, and social norms. The mental health effects have been gigantic. In my practice, as in many others, requests for therapy have far exceeded what I am capable of managing. Referrals to other therapists have been almost futile; they are mostly in the same dilemma.

Many of those coming to me for help have been racially oppressed people seeking therapy for the first time in their lives. Traditionally, these historically excluded people have tended to shy away from psychotherapy, viewing it (with a good deal of justification) as a "luxury" meant for rich white people. But something has changed because of the social strain of the pandemic. Increasing numbers of people are now willing to forsake the cultural taboo on sharing family secrets—to save lives and livelihoods.

This change has coincided with another important one. Over the past several years, one of the most interesting things that I've observed has been the awareness of systemic racism becoming mainstream. People now dare to say the words *white supremacy* on television. Corporations suddenly want to be seen as caring about Black people, and it appears as if the mainstream culture really is moving away, at last, from its complicity in anti-Black racism.

But let's be clear. This change only happened because of a global surge in anti-racist militancy and mobilization unmatched by any other popular protest and largely facilitated by social media. Not all social institutions or media have had a change of heart, of course. And definitely not all police departments. In the three months after the murder of George Floyd in May 2020, police officers in the United States killed almost another 300 people, and although Black Americans are about 13 percent of the U.S. population, they were approximately 20 percent of the victims. Despite global protests over the George Floyd murder, racist police violence did not slow down. In some states, the rate of violence even increased.[4]

During that time, while I was treating Black people recovering from racial trauma, some white colleagues confided in me that they were seeing

---

[4] https://www.cbsnews.com/news/george-floyd-killing-police-black-people-killed-164/

more and more white clients becoming radicalized by far-right internet influencers who espoused anti-Semitic, racist, or xenophobic conspiracy theories. But these white therapists dared not speak publicly about this. Our professional workshops and zoom conferences were only highlighting the sufferings of Black people, never the possibility that white people had a problem too.

The inevitable "whitelash" soon occurred. When a colleague of mine asked to present at a conference about race and mental health last year, they were informed that all presentations on race had been stopped about a year earlier. After the January 6 insurrection at the US capital in 2021, the rest of the year was focused on preventing children from being exposed to the very scary tenets of Critical Race Theory. Chants of "CRT" and the "war on woke" could even be heard north of the border and beyond. The unconscious material of white racism had become conscious to the public, but the drive to suppress the resulting internal conflict was already well underway.

The Pandemic

The pandemic has taught us many lessons. One is that we have the ability to mobilize professionals from all continents and create vaccines for vast numbers of people in a short amount of time. When countries and nations unite in the face of a global emergency, we can create drastic changes to defend vulnerable populations. In Canada, at the time of this writing, over 80 percent of the population is at least double-vaccinated. More than 80 million doses have been administered in this country alone.[5] The public health response in the North has been both extraordinary and unprecedented, but the same cannot be said for the countries of the Global South, which have been chronically underfunded and neglected since even before the pandemic. Even the waiving of patents to allow more equitable access to the vaccines in developing countries was intentionally halted. All for the sake of the almighty dollar. Make no mistake, the system has not broken down. The gears of racism, sexism, and classism continue to operate as planned. The cycle of suffering is a well-greased machine in our world,

---

[5] https://covid19tracker.ca/vaccinationtracker.html

and COVID has been, if anything, a magnifier of the injustices that take place due to a person's racial identity.

Early in the pandemic, people used to say "we're all in this together," but somewhere along the way, that changed. As early as March 2020, the CDC was aware of racial differences in hospitalizations for COVID-19.[6] Research later that year and in 2021 confirmed disproportionately high rates of hospitalization of African Americans, Hispanic, Alaskan Indian, and Alaskan Native (Indigenous) populations in all states that recorded race-based data (Karaca-Mandic et al., 2021). Researchers also found higher rates of COVID-related mortality in the Black population of the Bronx in New York (Golstaneh, et al., 2020). Three major systemic factors explain these racial disparities. The aforementioned racial groups faced greater disadvantages based on having:

1. a greater number of untreated comorbidities

2. higher levels of undiagnosed comorbidities

3. a higher risk of exposure to COVID-19 due to residential overcrowding, frontline occupations, and reliance on public transportation.

All these factors arise out of a system that has discriminated against Black people for several centuries. The lack of universal health care in the United States effectively denies health care to poor and low-income people, who are disproportionately Black and brown people, while historical neglect and exploitation by medical researchers and health providers has led to widespread distrust of public health initiatives among Americans of all racial groupings.

COVID-19 has had an especially disproportionate impact on women from diverse racial groups. They are more likely to work on the frontlines as nurses and hospital support staff in close physical proximity to people infected with COVID. Their low levels of job security and benefits threaten what has been called a global "she-cession." Researchers are predicting that

---

[6] Centers for Disease Control and Prevention. Hospitalization rates and characteristics of patients hospitalized with laboratory-confirmed Coronavirus disease 2019—COVID-NET, 14 States, March 1-30, 2020. Published April 17, 2020. Accessed August 29, 2022. https://www.cdc.gov/mmwr/volumes/69/wr/mm6915e3.htm

female poverty may rise by ten percent worldwide due to the influence of the pandemic (Fisher & Ryan, 2021). There has also been a disproportionate impact on trans and non-binary communities. A study based on data from 76 countries found numerous documented cancellations and delays of gender-affirming surgeries due to prioritization of COVID treatment, lockdowns, and other measures. This has led to increases in recorded cases of depression, anxiety, and suicidality.

The pandemic caused many countries to lock down whole regions and cities for weeks and months at a time and to close down their borders or enact highly restrictive travel measures. These containment measures also disproportionately affected vulnerable populations. One study found that women faced increased risks of violence and mental health problems as a result of lockdowns (Piquero et al., 2021). The researchers explained this by increased male unemployment and family financial insecurity, the stresses of home-schooling, and maladaptive coping strategies for dealing with stressors. Moreover, women's own rates of pandemic-related unemployment were found to be four times those of men. Survivors of domestic abuse faced even greater social isolation because they could no longer reach out to support groups or shelters. The study concluded that "declining mental health and negative economic impact combined with trauma of violence exposure [is] expected to have long term effects on parents and children" (p. 8).

The intersection of gender with race further increased the risk of violence faced by women during the pandemic. The disproportionate impact of the pandemic on Black and brown people intensified the financial and emotional stressors they already faced, and the toll of managing the unpredictability of it all led to sharp increases in domestic violence. Gun violence increased throughout the United States but increased most in areas with high levels of poverty. Homicides in 2020 increased by 30 percent across the board, but for Black men the increase was 34 percent and for white men it was 22 percent. The rate at which Black women and girls were killed increased by 33 percent,[7] a much higher increase than any other group and more than double the increase that white women experienced (15%).

---

[7] https://www.theguardian.com/world/2022/jun/25/homicide-violence-against-black-women-us

Hence, while gender plays a role in violence, the combination of race and gender had especially terrible consequences during the pandemic.

The cumulative effect of all these inequities is incalculable. Had our societies been more equitable at the start of the pandemic, an enormous amount of mental and physical suffering could have been avoided, and millions of lives could have been saved.

The Therapist

The pervasiveness of racial disparities demonstrates that the problem is both widespread and systemic. Psychotherapy, despite its image as a "helping profession," cannot be immune to these problems. The American Psychiatric Association recognized its complicity and apologized for its decades-long role in standing idly by while the scourge of racism allowed for the misdiagnosis and mischaracterization of many of my Black brothers and sisters.[8] In some cases, they actively promoted our mistreatment. The American Psychological Association also apologized for "perpetuating, and failing to challenge racism."[9] These apologies are a good start. They mean that it's no longer taboo to state that institutions can make "mistakes," but more important than any apology is reparative behavior and actions.

We need to do more than offer "thoughts and prayers" after these great tragedies. We need to rethink our assumptions and theories, reform our practices, and revolutionize our way of helping people. This book is a step in that direction.

The distinguished Black chair of Social and Behavioral Sciences at Harvard's Chan School of Public Health, D. R. Williams, succinctly laid out the fundamental truth that motivates the decolonization of psychotherapy. Discussing the impact of cultural racism and how it relates to clinical practice, he pointed out that "even the most well-meaning and consciously egalitarian individual who holds a negative stereotype of a social group will likely discriminate against a member of that group when s/he has an encounter with that individual. These are universal processes and all persons are capable of them" (2018, pp. 11–12). Therapists come from a racist

---

[8] https://www.psychiatry.org/newsroom/apa-apology-for-its-support-of-structural-racism-in-psychiatry

[9] https://www.apa.org/about/policy/racism-apology

society, so there is always a risk that they will either consciously or inadvertently reactivate their experience of racial trauma in their clients. The therapist emerges from a social system that even managed to make COVID variants look racist by disproportionately targeting Black, brown, and Indigenous people. Because we are supposed to help people recover and heal all aspects of their complex and intersecting identities, we have a responsibility to engage with anti-racism. The remainder of this chapter reviews some essential concepts for decolonizing therapeutic practice.

Anti-Racist Psychotherapy

The goal of anti-racist psychotherapy is to enable both therapist and client to understand, confront, and deconstruct the mental health and social consequences of racial trauma. Racial trauma includes both objective and subjective experiences of racial discrimination. In either case, the trauma is real; it leaves a "mark" on an individual's nervous system, self-concept, and sense of self-worth. Thus, it is not about the intent of the racists, whether they are overtly racist (Klan members or Proud Boys, for example) or "closeted" (like fair-weather white liberal "allies"). What matters is the impact of the statement or gesture—or the underlying social structure—from the perspective of the racial trauma survivor.

I want to highlight three phenomena that are vital to recognize for an anti-racist psychotherapy. First, racial trauma has a multigenerational impact. It is passed down through time. Mental health vulnerabilities and multigenerational alterations in stress response systems appear to exist in the descendants of survivors of the Holocaust (Yehuda et al., 2016) and of the Rwandan genocide, for example (Perroud et al., 2014). Moreover, the effects of trauma are not limited to race. Research has shown that when pregnant women encounter sufficiently traumatizing experiences, enough to produce a diagnosis of PTSD, there are changes in DNA methylation that result in genetic changes in later offspring. If a pregnant person is carrying a daughter, the female fetus has all of her eggs from the beginning of her development in the womb. It is possible, therefore, that through genetic transmission, the eggs can also receive genetic vulnerabilities from indirect traumatic exposure. We are impacted by the actions of our ancestors, and we can impact at least three generations in the future because of the actions we take today.

Second, present-day impacts can occur through a host of social microaggressions. When individuals are exposed to perceived racial discrimination (PRD), especially at key developmental stages (such as adolescence), cortisol changes are demonstrated that lead to an increase in the impact of later racial injustices on adult stress biology. In a longitudinal study, researchers found that the influence of PRD on an adult's diurnal cortisol rhythm is greater and more pervasive for Black than white people (Adam et al., 2015). This study lends support to the idea that the experience of PRD at vulnerable periods can cause changes to neurobiological functioning.

Microaggressions can be intentional or unintentional. In some cases, they can link back to an event in one's history of racial trauma. In much the same way that "triggers" do not need to be identical to the original stored memory to cause a chain reaction with implicit memory systems, microaggressions function as "pointers" to memory addresses that cause harm even if offenders shrug them off as jokes. Obvious forms include "blackface" parties, but there is also a subtler and much more prevalent use of "digital blackface" ranging from social media images of Michael Jackson eating popcorn to Kanye West being Kanye West. In a society that privileges whiteness, the Black face can convey exaggerated or unnecessary emotionality or be used to serve as comic relief.

The third phenomenon is simply the widespread social acceptance of forms of injustice that disproportionately affect equity-denied racial groups. Foreigners visiting the United States are often shocked to learn how rarely the North American media covers important world events in any depth, or at all in many cases. Even for Canadians, there is a largely "American" ethnocentric focus in the media and news we get. This focus that may be intentional: to either highlight American exceptionalism or to control and direct focus away from the exceptionalism of others. A similar strategy affects public awareness of racial trauma.

This paradigm accounts for the fact that statues of generals and political leaders who tried to destroy the United States in order to preserve slavery still stand in prominent locations in American government buildings and public spaces. Another example is the recent discovery of numerous unmarked graves of Indigenous children who died at residential schools.

These schools, a collaboration between church and state, were explicitly designed to "kill the Indian in the child" and have traumatized generations of Indigenous survivors and their communities. There has been little detailed coverage of the systemic abuse, sexual mistreatment, and cultural harm that priests, nuns, teachers, and government officials inflicted over many decades in and through these schools. Racism is part of the fabric of the flags flying over our most cherished institutions. Racism is normal and accepted.

An anti-racist psychotherapy needs to be aware of these three enabling factors, alert to their deep and lasting effects across generations of racialized communities, and capable of helping clients understand, confront, and recover from them. Racial trauma is significant not only because it is often imperceptible even to the trained eye, but because its multigenerational effects, microaggressive daily-life features, and the public's acceptance and neutrality toward its effects make it one of the most complex issues a therapist can deal with.

The Trauma of Whiteness

I would like to take a moment to address the racial trauma that exists in the white body and mind. I have previously written about this in *Black Meditation: Ten Practices for Self-Care, Mindfulness, and Self-Determination* (2021). It is important in anti-racist therapy because it helps to explain the thrust of white insecurity. In *Black Meditation*, I explained that:

> Race is a social construct—meaning that it was created. It was not created for the benefit of Black people. It was created for the benefit of white people. The creation of whiteness occurred at the same time as the creation of Blackness. This occurred despite the fact that Black Nubian and Egyptian civilizations were up and running for millennia, way before "Europe" existed. Generally speaking, the earliest known "human" refers to mitochondrial Eve, who was the first woman of our species recorded in Africa. She would have been the first ancestral mother of humanity who lived approximately 200,000 years ago. She was a dark-skinned Black woman. In Europe, Africa, and the other continents,

"racial" diversification only started 25,000 years ago within the Homo sapiens species. Before that all human beings were dark-skinned and "Africoid" in physical appearance (Bynum, 2021). This means two things; first, that we all share a common ancestor and we are all cousins, aunties, and uncles. Secondly, and this is important, is that we are all one people—all people: Black, brown, red, white; all of us are descendants of Africans.

Whenever someone says that Blackness started with the enslavement of African people, they deny the breadth and historical significance of the entire African continent.

Racism, however, is not based on reality. White people could not have existed before Black people in such a warm climate, but this stirs up white fear and discomfort. For the white person, the internalization of anti-Black racism reflects a deep fear of the eradication of the imagined privilege that comes from whiteness. Additionally, the word *race*, both in itself and as a general concept, is also problematic. It is a pseudo-scientific term that has primarily been used to justify European expansionism and colonization (Rutherford, 2020), while also creating hierarchical divisions to ensure optimal conditions for chattel slavery (Trudel, 2013). Therefore, the accumulation of wealth from Black labor and the theft of land from Indigenous people are deeply linked to the oppressive nature of these made-up categories.

There is a myth-making element that is essential for understanding "race." For a number of reasons, we should abstain from uttering the term *Caucasian* ever again. It is not only unscientific, but it also reflects a white supremacist racial hierarchy. The word originated with the eighteenth-century race theorist Johann Friedrich Blumenbach, who believed that the Garden of Eden must have been in the Caucasus region that traditionally marks the geographical boundary between Europe and Asia. Through his powers of "deduction," and without any actual evidence, Blumenbach decided that all white people must have originated from there. It might seem that it could not get any stranger than this, but there's more. Because white people originated in the Garden of Eden, Blumenbach concluded that all other people were morally degenerate forms of God's perfect creation. But even within the supposed Caucasian category, there was a racial hierarchy. Nordic people stood at the top and at the bottom lay the Jewish people. Somehow even anti-Semitism was wrapped up in Blumenbach's idiotic theory (Moses, 2017).

No "Caucasian" culture exists (Mukhopadhyay, 2016). Many white North Americans may identify as Caucasian, despite never visiting their supposed homeland. People of the Caucasus region do indeed have a diverse and rich history, but the use of the modern usage of *Caucasian* refers to white people who come from any part of the world. Logically, it would make more sense for us to use the term European American for white people in the Americas, just as we use African American for Black people, but this would require the use of logic.

As a Black person who considers himself a citizen of the world, I have been surprised over the years to see how many of the cultural traditions of different Black peoples resemble those of my Jamaican upbringing. There are Black people in the United States that have traditions that began in Africa. And although I am a Black Jamaican African Canadian, I share a lot of common experiences with the African American community across the border. The same cannot be said for whiteness. White people from Russia, France, and Canada do not share similar cultural origins, traditions, or history. All of my future publications will therefore put the term *white* in lowercase (except when it comes at the beginning of a sentence). I am not alone in this. AP has explained that they will continue to capitalize the word Black but that "capitalizing the term white, as is done by white supremacists, risks subtly conveying legitimacy to such beliefs."

I would love to be able, like the great American educator Jane Elliot, to completely do away with the words *white* and *Black* and instead see us all as one race, but I acknowledge our unity in a different way. I acknowledge that race is not real, but we still must tend to its very real consequences. Diversity and equity initiatives that try to prevent white people from using racist language at work will never be an adequate anti-racist action. The trauma of whiteness is not stored in the part of the brain that manages decision-making. Racism is a survival response, and it must be dealt with in this way. The internalization of anti-Black racism by white people implicates the limbic system, the use of vehement and systemic actions, and dissociative processes meant to erase any prospect of a mixed and multiracial future where whiteness loses all significance.

The Binary Complex Trauma Cycle

A consideration of equal importance in anti-racist psychotherapy is the binary complex trauma cycle (see Appendix II, page 225). When we look honestly at the violent origins and commodification of human life in the history of North America, we naturally have a negative reaction. Among white people, this can fuel an aversion to discussing these realities or their consequences. Shame, guilt, and an almost phobic response to enacting the original "trauma" leads to a suppression of discussions that come too close to revisiting past harms or that would require accountability or reparations for those harmed. In some cases, what may appear bizarre is in fact strategic. There are concerns for the burdens of the next generation, which are well warranted due to the growing impacts of climate change, worsening economies, and endless wars fueled by statecraft and geopolitical interests. Yet, such valid fears for the fate of our children are frequently displaced onto calls to ban textbooks, even math textbooks, from a fear that they might be dangerous due to "unsolicited strategies of indoctrination" in relation to critical race theory.[10] Imagine worrying that children's math texts are going to discuss concepts taught only in graduate-level law programs. This is not logic; it is psycho-logic. And we know that it is not critical race theory that people fear when they also target books that discuss Dr. Martin Luther King Jr.[11] In other words, "critical race theory" is code for Black.

The binary complex trauma cycle explains and predicts these kinds of deflections and obsessions. As a concept, race is generally organized around trauma or psychological injuries from the past. White supremacy is a concept steeped in insecurity and phobic fears of self-annihilation (because of the drive to appear supreme in the face of insecurity, I will henceforth use the terms *white supremacy* and *white insecurity* interchangeably). White supremacy generates a self-inflicted double-bind scenario in which white people, while continuing to benefit from systemic racism, harbor orientalist, othering

---

[10] https://www.politico.com/news/2022/04/18/florida-critical-race-theory-math-textbooks-00025918

[11] https://www.mediamatters.org/critical-race-theory/banning-books-about-martin-luther-king-jr-and-opposing-school-district

beliefs (for example, irrational anxieties about immigration) and live in fear that their own policies will insidiously lead to their irrelevance. To alleviate this cognitive dissonance, whiteness must dissociate itself from its undesirable characteristics in order to maintain a semblance of self-esteem. To manage the pain of this dissociative experience, it projects its discomfort onto Blackness. We use the term "soul murder" for this.

Leonard Shengold, an American psychiatrist well known for his studies of childhood abuse and trauma, defines soul murder as "a certain category of traumatic experiences—those instances of repetitive and chronic overstimulation alternating 'with emotional deprivation that are deliberately' brought about by another individual." (1975, p. 533). Cultural genocide, discriminatory policies, and news media cycles that depict the Black experience through dehumanizing stereotypes are all forms of collective soul murder deeply entrenched in our society. They create an ongoing categorization that delegitimizes the spirit of the Black individual and associates Blackness with trauma. Unable to emancipate itself from this tormented society where racial conflict is etched into the foundation of its creation, the Black body becomes a recipient of rejected "parts" of the white body. Thus, Black men, for example, are identified with hypersexuality despite the white enslavers sexually assaulting countless women and girls. Similarly, Black people are seen as lazy despite their ancestors being worked nearly to death by idle thieves. The list of denials and mental trickery goes on and on.

Gaslighting is, of course, essential for maintaining a cycle of oppression and violence. There was even a time when an enslaved Black man who ran away to find freedom was considered mentally ill. The "condition" even had a scientific-sounding name: *drapetomania*. Arguably, more than 150 years later, the Black desire for freedom is still being gaslit as a delusion or a perversion. Systemic anti-Black racism cannot survive unless whiteness maintains this abusive relationship.

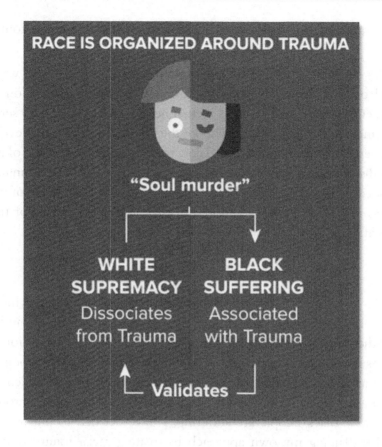

From Anti-Racist Psychotherapy:
The Binary Complex Trauma Cycle

The Internalization of Anti-Black Racism

When a Black person accepts the lies, internalizes the inferiority, and equates more melanin with less self-worth, they validate the myth of white supremacy. The internalization of anti-Black racism entrenches the experience of Black suffering (see Appendix II, page 227). When everyone buys into the idea of white perfection, white people do not need to confront any of the glaring logical fallacies in their image of themselves. In such a scenario, Black people would no longer need to recover their own ways of knowing. We could all be satisfied with a status quo that bails out the Wall Street tycoons while renovictions kick our brothers and sisters out on the street. I profoundly oppose this state of affairs. We *have* to create something new.

Our current social structure treats people in radically different ways that depend on their identities. This book comes with the assumption that a fundamental part of our work, as mental health practitioners who serve the public, includes staying informed about the world around us and developing tools to eradicate the ongoing social construction and proliferation of mental health disorders. In a world where the status quo is so deeply unjust and misguided, I have decided to bring together my own knowledge of what is around me to help provide a more effective and efficient way of treating people affected by racial trauma.

A New Approach to Treating Racial Trauma

Many different frameworks have been proposed to address the racial dimensions of mental health. In my case, writing about anti-racist psychotherapy has led me to some answers, but also to more questions from my consultees, supervisees, and presentation attendees. This book is my attempt at addressing some of the concerns my colleagues and clients have raised. Rather than creating another framework, model, or fancy acronym to explain why Black people are suffering, I have decided to put my energy toward explaining my own approach to treating racial trauma and other forms of mental health problems. In the spirit of my Jamaican ancestors— who developed patois as a way of communicating with one another even though they all came from different parts of the world—I have tried to do the same in my approach from my own readings and research across various theories and disciplines. I call my approach Rhythm and Processing Strategies. It is a therapy that is designed to eliminate the binary complex trauma cycle.

This approach is based on the principle that, instead of navel-gazing in our individual professional silos, specialists from all of the fields of science should come together to address the problems that threaten our collective well-being. Rather than generate another therapy that celebrates the ego of an individual, this therapy is designed to be taught to others so that it will exist even after I cease to. After completing this book, if you do so with an open mind, I am confident you will be in a better position to reduce the impact of unresolved traumatic material in your clients' lives. Your therapy will become more streamlined and easier to understand for both you and your clients, and in the process we will all improve the technology of our ways of healing.

This book is divided into three sections. The first section (Chapters 1 to 4) introduces the concepts and outlines the development and implementation of the Rhythm and Processing approach. The second section (Chapters 5 to 10) explains the different strategies that make up the main components of this approach, and the third section (Chapters 11 and 12) concludes with a descriptive transcript of the Rhythm and Processing technique in session as well as a call to action to build a more consistent anti-racist society that takes mental health seriously and treats people of all backgrounds with more consideration.

Summary

In our contemporary society, we face multiple struggles involving political strife, social injustice, and global health and environmental concerns. The limitations of our ways of managing underlying issues such as anti-racism are insufficient. Racism is systemic. It concerns more than just interpersonal factors. Anti-racist psychotherapy is a framework designed to explain the impact of racial trauma from a trauma-informed perspective. It employs a unique definition of the impact of racial trauma, addresses the binary complex trauma cycle, and explains how Black people become unintentionally implicated in white insecurity and its vain attempt to maintain relevance and significance. Rhythm and Processing is designed to treat the trauma that underlies the fear of insecurity at the core of whiteness and the internalization of oppression at the core of Black suffering. The next chapter will introduce Rhythm and Processing, and the rest of this book will explain how to use it.

CHAPTER 2

PRINCIPLES AND RATIONALE FOR RHYTHM AND PROCESSING STRATEGIES

The Worldview

I have developed an integrative framework for racial trauma treatment that uses models and methods that have proved their value in my practice. This chapter explains the foundational ideas and principles behind the change we seek through racial trauma treatment.

Many clients come into therapy seeking not only concrete methods that will help them but also explanations for why change has happened or failed to happen for them. In *African American Psychology: From Africa to America*, Faye Belgrave and Kevin Allison in 2018 provided the first comprehensive survey of theory and research on the African roots of Black American psychology and the need to integrate an African worldview into therapies for racial trauma. They compiled a list of seven fundamental dimensions of Africentric culture that need to be taken into account in any effective therapy for African Americans.

➢ Spirituality
- There is a higher power and a greater meaning in human life.

➢ Collectivism
- Human beings are interdependent. Family and kinship are the foundation of all human relationships.

➢ Time
- Past, present, and future are of equal value. Time is malleable.

➢ Orality
- Knowledge comes ultimately from oral tradition and narrative.

➢ Affect and Emotion
- Consideration for others depends on sensitivity to one's own emotional state and awareness of the factors that determine it.

➤ Balance and Harmony
  - Life is made meaningful by finding one's place in nature, not trying to master it. Spiritual imbalances are responsible for most of our physical, emotional, and mental challenges.
➤ Verve and Rhythm
  - There are many ways of knowing and learning. Top-down learning is only one way. Learning from the bottom up is at least equally valid.

Let me now briefly explore the relevance of each of these dimensions in the context of my own Rhythm and Processing (RAP) Strategies.

Fundamental Africentric Dimensions

Spirituality in the Africentric worldview is not something reserved for those who are "religious." I have many agnostic or atheist clients who still believe in phenomena beyond their conscious awareness or knowledge. Many others follow conventional religious paths but still feel unsatisfied or troubled. In either case, RAP taps into clients' spiritual understanding by connecting them to a dimension that exists beyond the physical plane and by highlighting their capacity for infinite creativity in relation to this spiritual dimension.

This opens an opportunity to find or create a higher meaning behind the suffering they have endured. In the process, they realize that the imagination is limitless and can exceed all their previous expectations when it is empowered with the appropriate context. Many clients present to therapy with a belief that they are "broken." They have internalized various kinds of negative cognitions, perhaps inherited from a society that commodified the bodies of certain people, perhaps a result of traumatization by early attachment figures or retraumatization by social interactions that mimic and replicate earlier experiences of lack, rejection, and isolation. RAP enables these traumas to come into consciousness and be comprehended and overcome.

Collectivism refers to the idea that there is no person who exists independent of their relationships to others. From a family systems perspective, the idea of bi-directionality is especially significant. We take actions, but we are also acted upon. If we are unable to change our environment by changing ourselves, we can effect change in our interactions with the environment. In this way, we are all connected. Even in therapy, the client is connected to the therapist, and collaboration and coregulation are active parts of the process of change (Dana 2018).

The time orientation of an Africentric worldview considers what happened to a person in the past, what is happening to them presently, and what may take place in the future as all having an equal importance. When considering a person's mental health concerns, it is essential not to avoid the etiological forces that have set the stage for the mental health concern. For example, a person with an eating disorder may have had an initial trauma that set the course for the disorder. Similarly, someone suffering from anxiety, depression, or other emotional problems may have experienced an initial psychological injury (or an accumulation of injuries) that led to the present experience of distress.

It is also not enough to help clients feel better in the present. There also needs to be a focus on future interactions. Concerns about the future are as important to treat as concerns about the past. Both dimensions of time impact the person's experience in the present.

Orality foregrounds the importance of the client's individual story. While maintaining a healthy skepticism, we have to trust the client's own narrative of what has happened to them. In particular, we have to avoid judging a client's explanation of their own origin. When creating genograms that represent a visual form of the client's experience, we must always respect the client's own account of their race or other characteristics, their personal pronouns, and their origins.

In relation to affect and emotion, we acknowledge not only that transference and counter-transference are natural occurrences in therapy but that there is always a racial, sexual, cultural, age-based, or other undercurrent to the reason for the therapy. Clients choose therapists for largely unconscious reasons beyond the therapist's knowledge. The therapist in many cases ends up meeting and experiencing specific clients for reasons outside of their own immediate knowledge. Being attuned to the client and cultivating a therapeutic relationship that emphasizes honesty and safety is a necessary safety net for a person who is bravely confronting the history of their trauma and the challenges that the trauma poses for their nervous system.

To move toward the balance and harmony with nature that therapy from an Africentric perspective seeks to achieve, we have to help clients cultivate self-appreciation, self-acceptance, and self-love. One of the goals of RAP therapy is to establish a new homeostatic pattern that works toward integration rather than isolation or rejection of the client's fragmented personality. According to the Kemetic principle of *Ma'at*, we achieve balance by removing the weights of suffering from a person's heart. In line with the Twi principle of s*ankofa,* we can only advance if we aware of what has passed (Archer 2021b). In healing from the past, we take steps in the present to advance toward the future. The path will rarely be linear; all paths in nature swerve, lead up or down, or vary in other unpredictable ways. Rather than encouraging clients to focus on the desired end point, we need to enable them to appreciate the journey in all of its bumps and twists.

Verve and rhythm are perhaps the hardest dimensions of Africentric therapy to conceptualize or capture in words. These dimensions begin from an appreciation that there is a rhythm to life that is fundamentally unknowable and immeasurable. Like nature, with which it is entwined, life is never a clear path. It possesses its own twists and turns and ups and downs, but there is a beginning and an end to all things. Rhythm refers to the natural flow of existence. After we breathe in, we must exhale. After we experience suffering, we experience recovery. Levelling up is also a rhythm. When we heal from certain patterns, we "level up" and no longer need to suffer from those patterns. Only when people in abusive relationships become conscious of the patterns that create these relationships can they separate themselves from these patterns. For those of us experiencing multigenerational trauma, only when we become conscious of the causative patterns can we bring about change and break free from the cycle of unconscious replication. The basis for all therapy is this rhythm of existence. Thus, there are uncountable means and mechanisms for healing and recovery that exceed what the therapist is conscious or aware of. In my approach, we therefore engage with the potential for limitless progress that exists in all people who seek to recover.

Before I was a psychotherapist, I was an addictions counsellor, and before that an English teacher working with new immigrants in Montreal. Before that, I was a software engineer specializing in reverse-engineering desktop applications and designing websites, and before that I was a hip-hop emcee battling rappers and speaking about social issues. As a young child, I was an artist. Now, as an adult and a father, I am still all of those past things.

But I am more. All of us are more than the sum of our experiences, but too many clients identify with their suffering and label themselves "depressed" as if this word is the sum and end point of everything they have been. We are more than what has happened to us, no matter how deep an imprint those past events have left. We can exceed whatever labels we or our social structure ascribed to us. We can remove the marks that past oppression has left upon us.

Rhythm and Processing's Family Tree

Rhythm and Processing utilizes the evidence base of other models, while at the same time emphasizing the importance of practice-based evidence. It is informed by what has worked for the majority of my clients and by the feedback they have given me. As a pragmatist, my focus is on the advancement of psychotherapeutic technologies to eliminate suffering in the world, and my approach has benefitted from the work of many other therapists.

One of the most important is the work of Dr. Francine Shapiro, a psychologist in New York City who developed eye movement desensitization and reprocessing (EMDR) therapy. Her model of psychotherapy changed my life and the lives of many of my clients. EMDR is an evidence-based approach that has proved highly effective in the treatment, in particular, of post-traumatic stress disorder.

In the 30-plus years since EMDR's first pilot study, numerous randomized controlled studies have confirmed its effectiveness as an evidence-based psychotherapy (Shapiro 2018). The practice guidelines of the International Society for Traumatic Stress Studies designated EMDR therapy as an effective treatment for PTSD in 2000. Other organizations have followed suit, including the Departments of Veterans Affairs and of Defense in the United States and the World Health Organization.[12] Organizations

---

[12] https://www.who.int/news/item/06-08-2013-who-releases-guidance-on-mental-health-care-after-trauma

that recognize EMDR as a recommended form of treatment for PTSD include the British Association for Psychopharmacology (Baldwin et al. 2014), the National Institute for Health and Care Excellence,[13] also in Britain, and the Phoenix Australia Centre for Posttraumatic Mental Health.[14] Many others agree; this a non-exhaustive list.

EMDR therapy has changed the lives of many people afflicted not only with PTSD, including complex PTSD presentations, but also with anxiety and depressive disorders. Nevertheless, at the time of this writing, the American Psychological Association still recommends EMDR therapy only "conditionally."[15] As a therapist who has been told by many clients that EMDR is the only approach that has been able to help them, I am perplexed by the lack of recognition of Dr. Shapiro's work by the APA. I hope it will eventually recognize the value of EMDR, but as of 2022 it still lists EMDR as conditionally recommended only.[16]

What this suggests to me, as a clinician who uses this model, is that even when the results are life-changing from the perspective of the client, outsiders can still view what you do as lacking evidence. To my mind, it is a tragedy that Dr. Shapiro did not receive the recognition she deserved for this revolutionary treatment model before she passed away in 2019. Even to this day, people remain skeptical about the efficacy of EMDR despite being supported by copious research. EMDR therapy deeply informs the work that I do, and the clinical framework discussed in this book is based on it. I would now like to take some time to outline the theory—adaptive information processing or AIP—that explains EMDR's positive effects.

Adaptive Information Processing

Although EMDR has the word *desensitization* in its name, its goals go well beyond making the client feel *less* of something. EMDR is based on the adaptive information processing model, which theorizes that desensitization

---

[13] National Institute for Health and Care Excellence (NICE). Post-Traumatic Stress Disorder; National Institute for Health and Care Excellence (NICE): London, UK, 2018.

[14] Australian Guidelines for the Prevention and Treatment of Acute Stress Disorder, Posttraumatic Stress Disorder, and Complex Posttraumatic Stress Disorder; National Health and Medical Research Council: Canberra, Australia, 2020.

[15] https://www.apa.org/ptsd-guideline/treatments/eye-movement-reprocessing

[16] Ibid.

is a by-product of the brain's natural ability to adapt to information and reprocess pathogenic mental associations.

The AIP model explains how pathogenic memory associations occur as well as how they are resolved (Solomon & Shapiro 2008). We process new information by integrating it into previously established neural networks. As long as our brains have sufficient resources to metabolize our experiences, we can continue to adapt positively and move forward. However, when experiences are unable to be metabolized, we change in ways that hinder rather than help us; "Maladaptive behaviors, cognitions, or personality characteristics result from unprocessed, dysfunctional memories, cognitions, and events" (Archer, 2020, p.133). The memories are then stored in a corrupted format that differs from how other memories are stored in long-term memory (Archer 2021a). The AIP model predicts that the mind's (and body's) natural way of reprocessing, reorganizing, and restructuring pathogenic memories can be brought back online through forms of bilateral stimulation.

The three principles of the AIP model can be summarized by paraphrasing the standard EMDR therapy protocols (Leeds 2016) as follows:

➤ Principle 1
All people have the innate capability to recover from trauma.

➤ Principle 2
Trauma is encoded in a maladaptive form in our memory system.

➤ Principle 3
Dual attention to both the memory of the trauma and bilateral stimulation reengages our adaptive information processing.

These principles are important because they both explain the simplicity of the procedure and also predict what can take place. As I gained experience with EMDR therapy after the basic trainings, I encountered instances where pathogenic memory associations did not reprocess efficiently. After more advanced training—and through my own path toward becoming a consultant myself—I learned more and also grew more curious. I became increasingly interested in learning more about what it was that actually brought about change and if there were ways of improving not just EMDR therapy but any other psychotherapy.

Brainspotting

I attended numerous trainings and workshops looking for a way to build on EMDR therapy's means of resolving trauma. I learned not only from other clinicians but also from my clients, whom I encouraged to correct and redirect me when I went in a wrong direction. In the process, I discovered Brainspotting (BSP), an approach developed by the American psychotherapist Dr. David Grand that enables survivors of trauma to process traumatic material and install internal and adaptive resources by focusing their attention on specific visual access points. Dr. Grand's approach demonstrated the efficacy of having clients listen to bilateral beats while attending to an unmoving visual stimulus.

This demonstrated the importance of sound and vision in processing and suggested how modern technology could assist in focusing attention. While the method had different hypothesized mechanisms of action, using it led me to conclude that the AIP's third principle was valid but also that there were multiple methods for reengaging the adaptive nature of the nervous system. However, while Brainspotting appeared in some cases to clear a smoother path toward processing traumatic material and to have less abreacted potential (in my practice), I encountered challenges with some of my clients who could not stay within their window of tolerance with resourcing from EMDR therapy or BSP.

Memory Reconsolidation and Taxing Working Memory

I wondered if perhaps this was because Brainspotting did not enable these clients to access multiple memory networks due to the active bilateral stimulation so characteristic of EMDR therapy. I then read about Bruce Ecker and colleagues' theories of memory reconsolidation (Ecker et al. 2012). Their ideas dramatically changed the way I looked at therapy. I had finally found an explanation of why experiential therapies work and why both EMDR therapy and BSP change how processed memories are retrieved when the procedures are successfully completed.

However, the challenge of keeping complex PTSD clients within their window of affect tolerance still presented itself. Some clients also felt insufficiently resourced to risk using either method. While researching this problem, I learned about Philip Manfield's EMDR-based Flash Technique (FT) and found that his techniques of bilateral tapping, eye flashing, and actively recalling moments of positive, engaging focus enabled many more of my clients to *maintain* a positive focus. This meant I could help them get "unstuck" when using EMDR therapy or BSP.

A further problem remained. Clients who were unable to recapture a positive and engaging focus due to presently challenging past events, severe developmental trauma, or attachment injuries were unable to contain their disturbances. I tried various combinations of techniques to optimize the effectiveness of my emerging hybrid method. Then the COVID pandemic arrived and pushed many therapists toward an even greater reliance on technologies such as video conferencing software. As I had previous training with computer systems, I was well placed to use these technologies to support my practice rather than hinder it.

Learning about Ad de Jongh and Suzy Matthijssen's EMDR 2.0[17] was helpful at this time because their approach also maximized the use of technology and showed me once again that the third principle of AIP is not always bilateral. Their method maximizes the use of techniques that deliberately tax a client's working memory. Through counting and spelling exercises, and similar tests, the client's retention limits are challenged, which then mobilizes some of the principles of memory reconsolidation. In my practice, however, perhaps due to my not having mastered their techniques, some clients found the approach too bizarre and internalized their inability to perform the complex memory tasks as failure. I continued my research, looking now for approaches that both utilized technology and were also person-specific, yet not too random for my clients' personalities or my own.

In sharing my screen with clients, I made various adaptations to enable exposure-based therapies online. For example, if a client had a phobia for household appliances, they would bring them into the therapy session and show me their fears. Then, through EMDR therapy, they would show that the appliances no longer caused them fear. Similarly, if a client had a phobia for snakes, we could test whether the fear was resolved by googling an image

---

[17] https://www.emdria.org/course/emdr-2-0-an-enhanced-version-of-emdr-therapy/

of a snake and checking their reaction. I had a number of successes with such methods. I also experimented with applications of the Flash Technique. For clients with these difficulties, I asked them to look at photographs or videos on their cellphone, such as images from their favorite vacations, and by looping these videos, we were able to see positive improvements. Still, some clients remained unable to contain their negative affect. Further refinements needed to be made.

Around this time, I was able to meet with Thomas Zimmerman and get a direct explanation of his Four Blinks approach to Flash Technique. By studying his developments and refinements of the technique, I began to feel that I was nearing the answer. Through further experimentation, I found that combining a simplified EMDR-derived approach (resource development and installation) with bilateral stimulation—through hand tapping rather than eye movement—and the client's choice of nature scenes and music videos on YouTube (or similar platforms) amounted to a veritable revolution in addressing stubborn treatment resistant issues. The work of further developing and refining this approach will continue, of course. I regard this breakthrough as a beginning, not a culmination. Nevertheless, this is the developmental path, so far, of my Rhythm and Processing Strategies.

With each therapy style I learn and incorporate into my practice, it is my clients who show me its strengths and limitations. As a result, my practice is constantly evolving, and it is highly likely that my current approach to Rhythm and Processing will not be the final framework that I propose for change in the world. At the moment, however, this is the approach that I think is most worth sharing.

My goal is to show the world that we can *all* recover. And moreover, that recovery does not need to be limited to the therapist's office. Even though I teach Rhythm and Processing Strategies to other therapists, my hope is that clients will learn the method for themselves and awaken the inner therapist we all have within us. Ultimately, my goal is to make effective therapy so accessible that therapists are no longer required. I firmly believe that we will achieve the true goal of psychotherapy only when the professional therapist is obsolete and clients no longer see themselves as a "problem" or a "patient" but value themselves for their infinite creativity, wisdom, and innate capacity for healing.

Summary

Rhythm and Processing Strategies are informed by practice-based evidence. Approaches that achieved limited progress with clients helped determine the necessary course corrections. Approaches that were more helpful have been stripped down to their essential characteristics to make them as accessible as possible. Because my formal therapeutic training was so limited in its understandings of race or culture, I have had to do a lot of research and experimentation of my own in order to incorporate the missing Africentric dimensions into my practice and develop an authentic anti-racist psychotherapy. Through a long series of challenges and successes, with each approach building on the others, from EMDR therapy to Brainspotting to EMDR 2.0 to Flash Technique and up to the most recent inclusion of the Four Blinks approach, and with constant input from clients, I have been able to find both a framework for understanding racial trauma and a method of permanently resolving it. But before going into the practical details, we need to dive deep into the neurobiological aspects of this treatment. Thank you for joining me on this wild ride.

CHAPTER 3

THE PROBLEM: NEUROBIOLOGICAL CONSEQUENCES OF TRAUMA

An Overview of the Problem

T
rauma is the proverbial domino that sets the cascade of mental health concerns in motion. While it is true, of course, that some disorders are more organic in nature, many struggles that our clients experience result from an internal or external emotional experience. In this chapter, I offer a brief review of what we know about the impact of stress from a biopsychosocial perspective with a focus on how structural racism contributes to differential health outcomes for historically excluded groups.

What Is Trauma?

In biomedicine, trauma refers to a severe injury to the body. In our field, when we refer to trauma, we are talking about its psychological forms. These are also injuries, but the damage is to the person's sense of self and personality structure. Like physical forms of trauma, psychological trauma also leaves "scars"—but on the brain. Trauma is an inevitable component of both the cause and exacerbation of mental health stressors.

The timing of the traumatic event is important. Traumatogenic events experienced during vulnerable periods such as childhood or adolescence, when identity structure is being developed and a person is still learning to differentiate between their own needs and those of others, usually have deeper and more long-lasting effects. The term trauma is overused, however, especially on social media. All people experience difficulties, but not everyone becomes traumatized, even by very serious stressors. In other words, "traumatic events" are not always traumatizing (Van der Hart et al., 2006). When I use the term trauma, I am therefore referring to damage that has left an alteration on the individual's nervous system and/or sense of self.

The level of significant injury depends on two related factors. As Van der Hart and colleagues (p. 34) explain, "the extent to which an individual will become traumatized is due to two sets of interacting factors: the objective characteristics of the event and the subjective characteristics that define the individual's mental energy and mental efficiency (components of integrative capacity)." For example, after mass disasters such as a floods or earthquakes, most of those who experience the disaster will not necessarily have lasting psychological problems. Most people are resilient.

Likewise, despite the massive scale of the COVID-19 pandemic, merely having contracted the illness, even suffering severe physical effects, is insufficient in itself for a diagnosis of PTSD (Pfefferbaum & North, 2020). The social and political contexts of the pandemic have been stressors for everyone, but some groups (for example healthcare workers, people confined to their homes for extended periods, small-business owners, laid-off workers, children unable to go to school, and the bereaved) have been more vulnerable to these stressors than others (Brooks et al., 2020). Shifting or contradictory information and regulations from health and government sources have also been more stressful for certain groups. There are protective factors such as internal (psychological) and external (social) resources that reduce the risk of traumatization and protect against retraumatization from potential future triggers, but these vary from person to person.

Infants are a special category. Whether they experience "subjectively" traumatic events (small-t trauma) or "objectively" devastating ones (large-T trauma), their helplessness makes virtually any traumatogenic event an existential threat, and their means of coping can be drastic, prioritizing survival of the organism above all else. In learning from the initial experience of suffering, the child adopts a pattern of hypervigilance to fend off other possible conditioned responses, whether perceived or actual.

Childhood trauma thus creates risks for the later exacerbation of problems such as depression and schizophrenia; "apart from being at increased risk of depression, people with a history of childhood emotional trauma are also more likely to have an early onset, and increased chronicity and comorbidity" (Giotakis, 2020, p. 163). The hypervigilance that survivors of childhood trauma adopt is meant to protect against future stressors, but in reality it taxes the nervous system and creates even more vulnerabilities. Almost all mental health concerns are a problem of conditioned associations either to our inner, subjective experience (thoughts, reflections, or distorted memories) or to our external experience (social stressors, perceived threats, or the actions of attachment figures).

If they fail to receive compassion and support from those around them, some survivors resort to what are known as substitute actions (Van der Hart et al., 2006). Substitute actions (covered more in depth in chapter 7) can manifest as substance abuse (ingesting socially accepted poisons as a means of dulling the pain of the caregiver's absence) or self-harm practices (such as cutting or disordered eating to regain a sense of control). These are counterproductive methods of coping with emotional overwhelm and the absence of a reliable caregiver. They fill the gap created by that absence and provide a temporary sense of relief, but this occurs at the cost of severely harming and further damaging the trauma survivor.

Trauma eats away at the spirit. The survivor learns to trust their trauma more than their own intuition. The emotional part of the self is unable to distinguish past from present and is therefore primarily concerned with its own survival. Thus, the client's presenting problem often precedes the substitute action. These detrimental actions are only surface-level symptoms intended to cope with the injury stored at a deeper level of consciousness. Whether the substitute actions actually serve an adaptive purpose or end up being life-threatening, they are secondary concerns.

Anti-racist psychotherapy recognizes that mental health concerns are largely due to an initial psychological injury or cumulative traumatic injuries. In either case, long-lasting impacts on the neurobiological functioning of the individual result. These difficulties are self-regulating in that the challenges of attaining mental efficiency lead to substitute actions that are both intrapsychic and interpersonal. The struggle of maintaining balance in one's life by avoiding traumatic reminders or by coping though maladaptive strategies explains the large majority of mental health problems.

A Brief Summary of the Neurobiology of Trauma

Post-traumatic stress disorder (PTSD) is a condition in which discernible and identifiable stressors (whether consciously or unconsciously experienced) have caused lasting changes in a person's sense of self. This makes PTSD especially interesting for the practice of anti-racist psychotherapy because racial trauma can also arise from either internal or external events. In racial trauma, the catalysts for the formation of pathogenic memory associations are identity-based stresses due to interpersonal interactions, structural violence, exposure to media imagery, or just the general consequences of living in a race-based social structure (Archer 2021).

The Greek psychiatrist Orestis Giotakos (2020) explains that PTSD, as an anxiety and memory disorder, is best understood as the inability to integrate trauma into consciousness. This is why it is associated with intrusive thoughts, the desire to avoid reminders of the trauma (triggers), an altered and negative mood state, and persistent hypervigilance (American Psychiatric Association, 2013). Giotakos also posits that PTSD can cause physiological changes to the brain, as can any chronic and prolonged stress. The effects of acute stresses are largely reversible, but chronic stress causes a structural remodeling to occur. Dendrites atrophy in the prefrontal cortex and hippocampus, and this leads to hypertrophy of the amygdala, which later atrophies as well (McEwen, 2006, p. 367). Damage can also occur to the orbitofrontal cortex and hippocampus, obstructing the encoding of autobiographical memory, while a hypersensitive amygdala causes alarm responses to benign stimuli. The frequent activation and overstimulation of these systems cause the neurological circuits to become "undifferentiated," leading to chaotic internal messages that can assault a person's mind and render the individual emotionally numb or cause spontaneous abreacted responses (Giotakis, 2020).

The Stress Response System

But how exactly does this happen? Let me give a simplified explanation of the stress response system based on an article from Harvard Medical School.[18] When an individual encounters difficulties, the brain interprets the information from the senses in order to understand the danger. The parts of the brain responsible for interpreting the sensory inputs relay the data to the amygdala, which is responsible for "ringing the alarm" when a person is confronted with stress. The amygdala interprets the data, and if it determines that the situation is dangerous, it relays that message to the hypothalamus.

The hypothalamus is the brain's command center and communicates with the body through the autonomic nervous system, which in turn controls

---

[18] https://www.health.harvard.edu/staying-healthy/understanding-the-stress-response

involuntary body functions such as breathing, blood pressure, and other bodily systems necessary for survival. The autonomic nervous system is composed of two different systems: the sympathetic nervous system and the parasympathetic nervous system. The sympathetic nervous system is responsible for the fight or flight response. Like pressing the gas in a car, it gives the body the ability to move and react, driven by the instinct to survive at all costs. The parasympathetic system is like the brake. It gives the body the ability to rest, relax, and digest. After the danger has passed, it enables the body to calm down, but it also has an emergency brake function: the freeze response. When a danger is too serious to either fight or flee from, the parasympathetic nervous system can cause the body to "play dead." That freeze response is also designed for survival.

Our ability to mobilize and respond to danger is also based on two systems: the sympathetic adrenal medullary (SAM) system and the hypothalamic-pituitary-adrenal (HPA) axis. The SAM is responsible for responding rapidly (using bursts of adrenaline) and subsequently returning to homeostasis. If the danger does not subside, the HPA is responsible for releasing the stress hormone cortisol. The SAM responds in milliseconds while the HPA can take longer. The two processes work in tandem to enable us to take individual, specific actions as well as mobilizing the entire body to defend itself and remain hypervigilant if needed (Dana, 2018, pp. 19–20).

When the amygdala sends a stress response to the hypothalamus, this triggers a cascade of other responses that cause the sympathetic nervous system to release epinephrine (i.e., adrenaline). Epinephrine in the blood causes the heart to beat faster, extra blood to rush to the muscles, and breathing to become more rapid. It also leads to the release of glucose and fats and the flushing of nutrients through the arteries and veins. These effects enable a burst of extra energy. The process is so rapid that it occurs outside of conscious awareness before even our visual centers have any knowledge of it. This is why we are able to jump out of the way of a speeding vehicle, for example, before we are "consciously" aware that it is heading in our direction.

The next phase of the stress response system is activated by the hypothalamus. After the original flow of epinephrine diminishes, the HPA axis is activated. This consists of the hypothalamus, pituitary glands, and adrenal glands. The hypothalamus releases a corticotropin-releasing hormone (CRH), which travels to the pituitary gland and triggers the release of adrenocorticotropic hormone (ACTH), which makes its way to the adrenal glands. From there, the release of cortisol takes place. This keeps the pedal to the metal and the body ready to respond to additional threats. When the danger passes, the parasympathetic nervous system applies the brake, and the stress response subsides. Although even this much-simplified explanation of the stress response system required several paragraphs, the actual phenomenon, complex as it is, occurs in a split-second.

The Biopsychosocial Effects of Stress

The system does an excellent job of triggering the appropriate survival response in a real emergency. However, repeated activations of the system cause problems. Repeated epinephrine surges, for example, damage the circulatory system, leading to elevated risk of high blood pressure, heart attack, and stroke (Mays et al., 2007). Persistent high cortisol levels contribute to increased fat storage and weight gain. This is a major reason for the higher risks of these same health problems faced by Black Americans as a result of living in environments where the stresses of racism are prevalent. These socially constructed stresses impact more than the individual, they also threaten the next generation as well. For example, regardless of their socio-economic status or education levels, Black women in the United States are at higher risk for preterm births.

One of the proposed explanations for the impacts of psychological stress on physical health is allostatic load. McEwen (2006) suggests that the mind seeks balance (homeostasis). Maintaining a state of homeostasis requires allostasis (equilibrium), which depends in turn on the continuous management of challenges by adaptation to stress. Chronic stresses place heavier demands on the HPA axis, leading to the prolonged secretion of stress hormones. As I have stated elsewhere (Archer, 2020), because our stress response system is designed mainly for managing acute stress, chronic and prolonged stressors can push the relevant biological systems beyond their expected capacities and cause an allostatic overload. The resulting biological dysregulation produces neurological changes, and it is these that culminate in mental health disorders such as PTSD, as well as creating additional vulnerabilities to further environmental stresses. At the neurobiological level, there is evidence to suggest that the excessive release of stress hormones and subsequent changes in neurophysiology can even prevent the integration of experience that is essential for resolving the effects of traumatic stress (Nijenhuis et al., 2010). Therefore, stress response must be addressed if we are to achieve any resolution of trauma.

In a 2018 review of research on the impacts of race-related stressors on Black Americans, David Williams (2018) draws several conclusions relevant to the impact of socio-political forces on diverse racial groups in our society. He notes, for example, the worsening mental health challenges facing Black youth in particular. Although suicide remains the leading cause of death for all children between the ages of 5 and 11 in the United States, between 1993 and 2012, the suicide rate reduced for whites, remained stable for other groups, but *doubled* for Black children.

Elections and political polarization in the United States also impact mental health differently depending on race. Williams's review found that the election of the first Black president, Barack Obama, in 2008 led to increases in social media animosity but so did the subsequent election of Donald Trump, widely seen as a white supremacist sympathizer. Not surprisingly, Trump's win triggered far more concern about the future among Black and brown students than white students, while his anti-immigrant rhetoric was a major source of anxiety and distress for Latino and Arab children in particular.

Racist immigration policies have an especially negative impact on the mental health of recent immigrants, but there is also a spillover effect for American-born Latinos. A quasi-experimental study reported in the *International Journal of Epidemiology* (Novak et al., 2017) analyzed the effects of an immigration raid at a large meat-packing plant in the Midwest. The raid was one of the largest single-site enforcement operations ever carried out in the United States. It deployed 900 Immigration and Customs Enforcement (ICE) officers, using military tactics that included a Black Hawk attack helicopter to arrest 389 employees. The study analyzed all births in the vicinity of the raid over the following 37 weeks and found that Latina mothers, both American-born and immigrant, had a 24 percent higher risk of preterm low birth-weight births. White mothers experienced no increase. Being born preterm can have many adverse consequences for the developing child. If a baby is born before 31 weeks, the ventral vagus (an integral part of the autónomic nervous system) does not develop fully. This can lead to difficulties in self-regulating, co-regulating, and coping with distress in general (Dana, 2018, p. 31).

State-sanctioned violence by police officers also has an impact on the nervous system of trauma survivors. Black Americans are more likely to be killed by police than white Americans—more than three times more likely according to a recent study in *The Lancet* (Bor et al., 2018). In another confirmation of the indirect effect of traumatic events, the article reported that, when police officers kill an unarmed Black man, there is a mental health spillover effect even on Black Americans who only learn about the killing from media coverage. In the aftermath of the event, there is, for example, an increase in sick days taken by Black workers, pointing to a need to cope with the vicarious traumatization, whereas White Americans do not need to take as many sick days. Indeed, Black Americans are much more affected by police killings regardless of the victim's race. What was surprising about the study is that white Americans were comparatively (and practically) unaffected by police killings regardless of the victim's race.

Note:

Some of my white readers will refuse to believe these findings despite the study's publication in one of the world's most authoritative medical research journals. This denialism relates to the binary complex trauma cycle identified in Chapter 1. Many white people dissociate from the harsh reality of state-sanctioned racist violence as a largely unconscious defensive reaction to protect their deservedly fragile self-esteem. Black people face the additional burden of this avoidance. I cover why that occurs in more depth in Anti-Racist Psychotherapy: Confronting Systemic Racism and Healing Racial Trauma (2021). But, if you are one of those incredulous readers, you can also just read the article by Bor and colleagues. They also explain why this phenomenon happens.

Structural Violence and Racial Segregation

The context of racial trauma involves physical and mental health concerns and the systemic injustice that maintains them. Yet when so many thousands of people are impacted by social stressors, it is too simplistic to dismiss an effect as an allostatic load problem of people seeking racial equity. Some researchers inadvertently contribute to an atmosphere of victim blaming by emphasizing the individual trauma survivor's coping difficulties. When there are such widespread problems, however, they must have a common source.

The prominent American sociologist Douglas Massey (2017a) has proposed a model that incorporates the concept of allostatic load but accommodates an expanded view of the problem. Massey's model explains that structural racism plays a key, though not an exclusive, role in the increased mental health risks faced by Black and brown people, especially those who live in mainly African American and Latino neighborhoods. He explains that one of the primary reasons for Black economic and social disadvantage is segregation and notes that more than half of all Black metropolitan residents live in conditions of "high" racial segregation and one third in conditions he calls *hypersegregation*. No other group of Americans is as racially segregated as Black Americans. At the same time, residential segregation of people living with higher levels of poverty concentrates poverty, increases danger, and deepens the disadvantage gap with other groups. When people are suffering but unable to escape their circumstances and prevented from accessing resources they would have if they lived elsewhere, an endless cycle of suffering is created.

Segregation is a key part of America's structural racism. It is fundamentally the result of political decisions designed to prevent certain groups from being able to participate fully in a society that privileges whiteness. Massey explains that the concentration of disadvantage in segregated neighborhoods predicts higher rates of violence, crime, exposure to environmental hazards, and overall poorer health and well-being.

The neurobiological consequences of the chronic stress exposure inherent in segregation include:

➤ Increased allostatic load

- Leading to an increased risk of hypertension, cardiovascular disease, diabetes, and other physical and mental health concerns.

➤ Shortened telomeres (DNA sequences that protect chromosomes)

- Leading to increased risk of genetic deterioration, morbidity, and mortality throughout life.

➤ Gene-environment interactions specific to disadvantageous environments

- Leading to increased risk of genetic vulnerabilities to both physical health concerns and emotion dysregulation due to influence on DNA methylation.

Massey (2017, p. 158) sums up his theoretical model as follows:

> Segregation produces concentrated poverty, which in turn undermines health, cognition, and well-being in three ways: by shortening telomeres and thus foreshadowing a life of ill health ending in premature mortality; by increasing allostatic load and thereby contributing to elevated rates of cardiovascular disease, allergic reactions, autoimmune disorders, and cognitive impairment; and by affecting gene expression so as to produce higher risk phenotypes determined to social, psychological, and physical well-being, most notably by causing those who are genetically sensitive to environmental effects to wither rather than thrive.

In a society that privileges whiteness over all else, our nervous systems can end up working against us. The experience of being in a hostile environment, of witnessing social defeat, and of being denied access to spaces that could allow us to heal maintains the cycle of suffering. A key goal of therapy is to enable the client to recognize that they themselves cannot possibly be the source of suffering when inhabiting a sick system. The social construction of mental illness is a top-down process.

At the same time, it is important to understand that the Black experience is no monolith. When we point out that Black people are disproportionately impacted by poverty, we are looking at the overall numbers. This does not mean that all or most Black people live in poverty. In fact, according to the latest United States Census (2020) 72.3 percent of the "Black alone" population do *not* live in poverty. The racial nature of poverty is revealed, however, when we look at *disparities* in the rates of poverty. These reveal that 86 percent of white people, 91.6 percent of "Asian alone," and 76.9 percent of "Hispanic (Any Race)" are not in poverty. Overall 83.9 percent of all Americans are not in poverty.[19]

Moreover, policies that only look at financial corrections for anti-Black racism, while helpful, cannot be the end goal of reparations. Black maternal mortality is higher across the board. For example, within the first year of giving birth, Black women mostly die from complications relating to cardiomyopathy and cardiovascular conditions, whereas white women die primarily as a result of mental health conditions.[20] Black women suffer constant social stressors and are more than three to four times more likely to have a pregnancy-related death from any cause than white women. (Howell, 2018). These are issues that go beyond the common refrain of income inequality. The "running program" of racism is a feature, rather than a bug, in a social system such as ours.

---

[19]
https://www.census.gov/content/dam/Census/library/publications/2021/demo/p60-273.pdf

[20] https://www.cdc.gov/reproductivehealth/maternal-mortality/docs/pdf/MMR-Data-Brief_2019-h.pdf

Fear of Annihilation and White Racial Trauma

If as Massey's model posits, the most detrimental effects on mental and physical health are due to segregation, two questions arise that the research discussed in this chapter does not address: Who are we being segregated from? And why?

Why is it that so many white people feel the need to be so segregated from others? Why do "sundown towns" exist, for example? These are towns or neighborhoods with largely white populations that have been created by deliberately excluding racially oppressed people. Such places are not just relics of the past or confined to the South. They still exist throughout the United States and, in fact, are now more common in the Midwest (Onibada 2021). There may be many reasons white people self-segregate, but very few of them are anti-racist in nature. These substitute actions may be related to the fear of self-eradication. White people are a minority in the world.

In this book, and in any other material I write in future, I will no longer use the term *racial minority* to describe certain racial groups. "In 2018, for the first time, the combined non-white population [of the United States]— blacks, Hispanics, Asians, persons identifying as multiracial, and other races—comprised the dominant share of the population under the age of 15 (50.1% compared with 49.8% in 2017), with Hispanics accounting for more than a quarter of this youth demographic."[21] Thus, white people under the age of 15 are the true "minority." In the period from 2010 to 2020, we see a similar situation. The Brookings Institute explains that "since the 1970s, white population growth has shown continued declines—plummeting to just 1.2% in 2000 to 2010 and now to a -2.6% loss (or over 5 million people) for the 2010s."[22]

These decreases in the white population have various causes such as lower fertility, aging, and fewer births than deaths during the 2010s. It is projected that the white population will decrease further in the coming decades. Additionally, there has been more immigration, as well as an increase in multiracial marriages, leading to more people identifying as other

---

[21] https://www.brookings.edu/research/new-2020-census-results-show-increased-diversity-countering-decade-long-declines-in-americas-white-and-youth-populations/
[22] Ibid.

than just white. More people than ever before are identifying as two or more racial groups. The growth of Latino, Asian, and other racially diverse groups is largely responsible for the increase in the nation's youth population. The declining white youth population is being countered by gains in racially diverse youth; "Were it not for these race-ethnic groups, the last decade's decline in the [overall] youth population would have been substantial."[23]

The terms *minority* and *majority* confer power and even validity, but they are not based on global population demographics, or even, as just discussed, on the reality in the United States. These terms are only used to enhance the political leverage of whomever is termed the majority; the so-called minorities rarely receive their due.

The population trends noted above are not just taking place in the United States of America; they are also occurring in European countries. Indeed, the white population decline is a global process. The future will be racially diverse. We therefore need approaches that are as diverse as our populations are becoming. We need policies that promote equity in education and services for families and that provide housing that people can actually afford and mental health support for people of all ages.

It is no coincidence that in the United States decisions have recently been made to withdraw the right of abortion. While there may be other factors in play such as the organizational power of the Christian religious right, taking away the right to choose will disproportionately harm Black and brown women who may not be able to relocate to states where abortion remains legal. Some underlying explanations for these drastic and sweeping restrictions could be linked to preventing further changes to racial demographics. No matter the cost. Even at the cost of a woman's freedom. Even at the risk of ending the woman's life who carries the child. Even in cases of sexual assault. White insecurity pushes the goal of its absolute survival even at the expense of the lives of others. All measures must be taken to prevent the possibility of whiteness becoming the minority.

The conditions that create injustice are not accidental. They are created intentionally. Our social identity and political context impact our everyday

---

[23] https://www.brookings.edu/research/new-2020-census-results-show-increased-diversity-countering-decade-long-declines-in-americas-white-and-youth-populations/

experience. The fear that created and sustains these conditions, based in a past history of hatred and oppression, continues to echo into the present. Here it lies, deeply entrenched, hidden from scrutiny; unquestioned; unquestionable; an accepted part of the status quo.

Summary

Trauma involves both the presence of suffering and the absence of compassion. When intensely distressing events happen, they leave a mark on us, especially when they happen during key developmental periods. Trauma can leave physical scars, but more often than not, its scars are imperceptible to the senses. Nevertheless, these emotional scars have deep effects on our minds, bodies, and spirits. They affect multiple parts of the brain and the sympathetic and parasympathetic nervous systems. Chronic and prolonged stresses lead to allostatic overload, increased vulnerability to future threats, and an ever-present hypervigilance. Rather than blaming these consequences solely on the nervous systems or the circumstances of people from diverse racial groups, let us remember that much of what forces people into dire conditions are policy decisions. Looking at Massey's model, we can see that the fundamental factor is segregation, leading to a domino effect that penetrates right down to the genetic material of its victims. In our next chapter, we will begin to talk about how to heal from this suffering.

CHAPTER 4

THE RESOLUTION: MEMORY RECONSOLIDATION

Changing the Course of Trauma Histories

As stated in the previous chapter, when we talk about trauma, our neurobiological functioning must be part of the discussion. It is critical to understand that neuroplasticity is a reality and epigenetics an everyday occurrence. Suffering is *not* our destiny.

Negative associations happen very quickly in our minds. It is possible to become traumatized by a single past event. We can eat at a favorite restaurant ten times, but let us get sick just once and we'll never return. Even if we catch the stomach flu from someone else while there, our brain can associate getting sick with the smell of the food at the restaurant and create an aversion to the place that will be difficult to shake off even when we know better. This ability to make associations is essential for survival. Our ancestors could not risk getting poisoned more than once. When we escape harm, our nervous system can remember this to ensure continued survival. The important thing is that this accelerated form of learning not only concerns traumatogenic events, it can also catalyze our recovery. Healing does not need to take forever. With the right approach it can take place within a clinical hour.

Before explaining the specifics of this rapid form of recovery, we need to reflect more on our understanding of how it comes to pass. Let us first discuss the nature of memory and how we can resolve issues for which there are no words. I will start with a metaphor. The symptom cycle metaphor is helpful in understanding how problems are connected and why we need to focus on the process rather than the content of the client's presenting problem. The problem lies in the process through which the cycle of consolidation connects to the road. This explains the majority of client complaints stemming from identity-based forms of suffering.

The Cycle of Consolidation

The target of our interventions is located in the hub (see Appendix II, page 226). The hub contains the distorted belief that one holds about oneself and the negative feelings that correspond to that belief. A feedback loop is essential to maintain any recurring thought. Whenever you feel bad, this activates a negative internal dialogue about yourself, and when you engage with the discouraging assumptions that underlie the discomfort, this triggers a bad feeling again. The hub of the wheel causes our internal narrative to impact our feelings and vice versa. This internal spiral causes the symptom as a whole to "spin." The spokes connect this interplay of mental energy, which is both preconscious and unconscious, to the outer section (the tire) of the wheel, which carries all of the near-endless reminders and traumatic memories that connect back to the negative self-attributions.

As the tire spins, it comes into contact with external events (the road), including all the microaggressions, racial profiling, gender barriers, and ableist, heterosexist, or other identity-based stressors—all the endless forms of discrimination that exist in our society—that prevent access to resources. The external environment has a near limitless number of potential stressors. When the road comes into contact with the wheel, this triggers a cascade of reminders that link to previously held schemas in the internal memory, the near-endless memory addresses and connections to the hub where the preconscious and implicit memories that fuel the suffering are stored.

The wheel analogy is appropriate because the centrifugal force that causes the wheel to keep moving in contact with the road is analogous to the way the core trauma material causes the survivor to continually come into contact with trauma triggers and external stressors. And just as the centripetal force of a spinning wheel engages with the center of the wheel, our society pushes certain members of our society to internalize specific negative beliefs about themselves. The reminders and external stressors of a discriminatory environment lead back to the core material and produce a continuous consolidation of the cycle of negative cognition and negative somatic experience. Both the centrifugal and centripetal forces work in tandem to propel the wheel forward and trap the traumatized client in a seemingly endless cycle of symptoms.

Rhythm and Processing seeks to rectify the traumatic material that causes the cycle of consolidation to generate symptoms. Therapies that prioritize talking only about the symptoms can drive clients in circles. There are endless amounts of stories and events that have caused their suffering, so rather than talk around the problem, Rhythm and Processing addresses it directly. Rather than targeting every possible traumatic memory on the outermost edge of the wheel, it mainly concerns itself with trauma targets that relate directly to the hub. The therapist's objective is to change how clients feel about the problem by clearing the hub at the center of all symptoms. This prevents the wheel from being as disturbed by memories, triggers, or other external events.

A client plagued by negative thought loops once told me that when she felt triggered by external events or internal self-critical thoughts, she would find herself overwhelmed by numerous other negative thoughts. I explained that this was part of how her memory networks were organized. The negative thought she experienced had activated movement from the entire wheel. Her beliefs about herself had then connected to many other negative thoughts, memories, and judgments that would invariably reinforce the negative cognition of self. The solution, then, is not to target every endless thought but only whatever sets off the feedback cycle in the first place. The place where we keep our suffering

We store information in two categories of memory: explicit and implicit (Levine, 2015). The explicit category is made up of declarative and episodic memory. We can generalize and say these are information-based categories. They store facts, stories, and autobiographical information that serve our need for a place where we can store instructions, explanations, and recollections of events so that we can relay them to others. The implicit category stores emotional and procedural memories. It is where we store material that is essential for survival such as fixed action patterns and emotions that can be experienced as physical sensations. Physical sensations cannot be explained by words alone, but examples of this category include the soothing feeling in the chest that occurs when your attachment needs are met and the negative sensations experienced in the gut when you experience a betrayal. These body sensations and representations of intrapsychic distress vary widely between people and may even be culture-bound. Procedural memory refers to automatic impulses, instinctual responses, and tendencies for approach or avoidance. Implicit memories are more difficult to consciously retrieve or examine than explicit memories.

This explanation may sound clear-cut, but in practice it is difficult to say where one category ends and another begins. Additionally, there may be more categories than these; our knowledge of the brain is still developing. Generally speaking, however, we can say that implicit memories are less likely to be recalled in regular conversation and are not usually the target of many psychotherapies. However, if we want to efficiently address trauma, survival responses, and urges to act, we must find a way to   readjust our focus to the issues that have no name: the maladaptive procedural and emotional memories that drive pathological relationships to self and others.

Memory Reconsolidation

Tronson and Taylor (2007) discuss how new memories become stable. The initial learning of a novel experience is called consolidation. This is the process through which memories are stored. When we attempt to retrieve a stored memory, it assumes a labile state. This renders the memory in question susceptible to alteration, or updating. It is this process that is called memory reconsolidation.

Our understanding of memory has changed significantly in recent years. Previously, it was thought that each time we remember something, there is a reference to the original stored experience. In our current understanding, however, as Alberini and LeDoux (2013) explain, "memories are susceptible to change each time they are retrieved. The next time the memory is activated the version stored during the last retrieval, rather than the version stored after the original experience, is called up" (p. R747) Memory reconsolidation refers to this idea: that each time we retrieve a memory we are potentially altering it. Alberini and LeDoux go on to explain that this function, which is shared by a number of other species, is adaptive in that it allows for organisms to respond flexibly to changing environments.

Lee and colleagues (2017) explain memory consolidation using the example of a man who is terrified by a barking dog. This leads to the formation of a long-term and emotional memory. If in the future he encounters any cues that relate to that memory, for example, a dog's red collar, this will activate the memory and cause it to become destabilized. Memory reconsolidation then occurs, causing the memory to return to a stable state. During a time-sensitive window, updates can take place by extinction, counter-conditioning, or interference, processes that update the memory or get in the way of allowing it to be stored in the same state. This prevents the memory from being retrieved in the original state. It no longer has the original negative emotion attached to it. The memory has been updated.

Ecker, Ticic, and Hulley's *Unlocking the Emotional Brain: Eliminating Symptoms at their Roots Using Memory Reconsolidation* was the first study to make me aware of the idea of memory reconsolidation. It explains how to target the emotional learning that underlies mental health concerns. Rather than "counteractive" therapeutic interventions meant to provide an extinction response to a negative cognition, mental health practitioners can use more than words to enact change. Where some approaches may address a person's negative belief that, for example, "I'm not good enough" by having them yell "I *am* good enough" into the mirror until year's end, we do not try to install a *competing* memory or belief. This would be an approach focused on the surface-level *content* of the presenting problem. Instead, we address the *process*, the *how* they came to experience the negative feelings, thoughts, and behaviours in the first place. In effect, we are reconsolidating the deepest content of where the memory points to.

The therapeutic reconsolidation process has three parts:

1. The accessing sequence
    *   Identifying the presenting symptom
    *   Retrieving the emotional learning underlying the symptom (A)
    *   Presenting disconfirming knowledge (B).

2. The transformation sequence
    *   Reactivating the emotional learning
    *   Activating the disconfirming knowledge (B), thus prompting a mismatch with the emotional learning.

3. Repeating the pairing of A and B
    *   The verification phase
    *   Verifying that there is no further reactivation of symptoms
    *   Change is maintained without the need for ongoing maintenance.

Therapeutic Reconsolidation Using Rhythm and Processing

In its current form, Rhythm and Processing has similarities to EMDR therapy's standard protocol. Thus, although the RAP technique can be used on its own (see Appendix II, page 228), it can also be used in conjunction with other trauma-informed psychotherapies. To demonstrate RAP's integrative nature, therapeutic reconsolidation will be presented and illustrated using EMDR therapy's phases 3 to 8. Here is an example. The client (let's call him Imari) has been conditioned to fear white police officers by exposure to violent social media posts and the "copaganda" that typically frames Black people as inveterate offenders, and state-sanctioned violence as having few or no consequence for its perpetrators. Imari seeks to address his internalization of anti-Black racism. The symptoms are hypervigilance and negative self-evaluation; he identifies the negative cognition as "I am a problem." The positive cognition he does not *yet* believe about himself is "I am free."[24]

The Accessing Sequence

This is the part of the RAP protocol that may most closely resemble EMDR therapy's phase 3, known as "Assessment." The session begins with Imari explaining how he feels about police officers while simultaneously retrieving explicit memory information and negative cognitions that relate to the neural network of police violence. A "trauma target" is elicited that may or may not relate to the presenting problem but houses the core negative somatic experience (this is because the content and process of the discomfort are often different). Through a series of questions, the negative cognition "I am a problem" is elicited. It is a belief that points to a "tight" feeling in the stomach for which there are no words but that is associated with an action tendency (fight or flee) and an ever-present hypervigilance. In our example, this is registered as the emotional learning (A). Before engaging with the stressful memory, the client is presented with options. They are provided with visual and/or auditory stimuli that provide disconfirming evidence and can also, if they choose, tap from left to right on their shoulders. More than just "knowledge," disconfirming information is both the presentation of a

---

[24] As an aside, the process of memory reconsolidation does not require any discussion of negative or positive beliefs. The installation and associated visualizations related to positive beliefs and resource states is more of a stylistic inclusion in RAP (and a nod to EMDR Therapy). Alterations in negative/positive cognitions are a natural byproduct of the process. After using the RAP technique, it can be quite impressive for clients to hear that the negative beliefs they held at the beginning of the session no longer carry any familiarity or resonance. Thus, discussions of positive/negative cognitions are primarily intended to demonstrate discrepancy and increase motivation. There is no need for them to be explicitly defined in order for transformative change to take place.

stimulus initiated by the therapist (or client) and the client's nervous system's response to this stimulus. In Rhythm and Processing, we call the result of this dynamic "overturning information."

Overturning information prompts a mismatch with previously stored patterns and traumatic material. If the result of being presented with a video of a baby goat wearing a party hat is that the person reports feeling calm— or if they start laughing—their response is mutually exclusive from the dysfunctional stored belief "I am a problem" located in their neural network. Hand taps are a neutral, predictable rhythmic action that engages the person's attention but does not necessarily bring about feelings of elation. However, rhythmic hand tapping still meets the necessary conditions to assist in reconsolidating traumatic material. The solution does not need to have a logical connection to the "problem" as long as it allows the client to access something different. By doing something different, they experience thoughts and sensations that are different. This different, even unexpected, response is used to counteract the emotional learning behind the symptom. This is what we use to change the course of the cycle of consolidation. This disconfirming knowledge or overturning information is labelled as (B).

The Transformation Sequence

While EMDR therapy in the form of bilateral stimulation of the eyes is well supported, eye movement is not the only method that encourages the reprocessing of information. Leeds (2016) explains that "central to the EMDR therapy approach to psychotherapy and the treatment of post-traumatic stress syndromes is the principle of a dual focus of attention to the *selected target memory from the past* to be reprocessed and to the sensory *stimulation in the present* provided by bilateral eye movements, taps or tones" (p. 29). Even a dual focus may not always be necessary, at least not actively and consciously attended to. The mind is very complex and can process parallel streams of information by just lightly attending to them. It is thus possible to treat multiple problems (general: having a bad day) and multiple aspects of a problem (specific: my boss yelled at me; I was late; my colleagues saw that I was embarrassed) by simply accessing and activating the corresponding memory address. To resolve the problem, it is not necessary to focus on it directly or even to talk about it.

Much of EMDR therapy's research and evidence support is based on eye movement. Shapiro (1994), however, showed that bilateral hand taps and auditory tones also appeared to be effective as clinical alternatives. Some researchers have questioned this, arguing that eye movements grant a larger reduction in the vividness of negative memories than auditory beeps or other forms of bilateral stimulation. In Rhythm and Processing, eye movements are not the main method of memory reconsolidation, although they could be. The "butterfly hug" tapping approach, which Lucina Artigas was one of the first to be recorded using in EMDR therapy, can be highly effective, as can EMDR therapy online and at a distance, which Michelli Simpson was one of the first to use.[25]

After the initial identification of the problem and activation of the neural network connected to the specific stressor event, it is necessary to prime the target, which can be done by hand taps. This is the RAP protocol that may most closely resemble EMDR therapy's fourth phase, called "Desensitization." From an EMDR therapy perspective, using open palms to tap alternate shoulders initiates the process of information processing. In RAP, this step is also included to increase the potential of generalizing therapeutic benefits to additional spokes in the cycle of consolidation, leading to a reduction in the number of trauma targets and consequently the number of sessions that are required.

If the client has sufficient adaptive information stored in their own neurology, there is a chance that hand taps alone can create enough overturning information to trigger the transformation sequence. Because I have been seeing clients only virtually during the COVID pandemic, I have stopped using any of my technical equipment for EMDR therapy, including light bars, tactile pulsators, and other remote-controlled devices. This has led me to rely strictly on hand tapping. Many of my clients have had no problem reprocessing targets in this way (of course, with additional alterations and advanced adaptations to the procedure). Therefore, hand taps on their own would resemble any of my average EMDR therapy sessions. In practice, however, some clients who are further along the spectrum of structural

---

[25] Artigas and Simpson are Black and brown women who do not get the recognition they deserve, but I am proud to acknowledge them here. Both my techniques of working online and my use of tapping for EMDR therapy have been developed thanks to their pioneering work.

dissociation can become overwhelmed by negative thoughts or emotional parts of their personality that override the client's ability to tolerate distress. Hand taps can not only connect to adaptive information; they can also drag a person down a rabbit hole of unlimited "spokes" and "tires" that deepen their descent into the abyss, with the risk of unexpected abreaction or the dreaded experience of retraumatization. In my experience, then, hand taps are useful but limited. A more reliable form of disconfirmation is necessary.

While working virtually, I've noticed that sharing my screen with others, a functionality that most video conferencing software now has, creates a different dynamic in the experience of psychotherapy. Rather than the client having something done to them, the therapy is done *with* them. This shared experience is received quite differently from that of looking at a stimulus on one's own. Following the collectivist nature of this approach, the client holds the decision-making power. They are instructed to search online for a video of their choice on any streaming platform (YouTube, Vimeo, Twitch, etc.). The choice is always theirs. The therapist then brings up the video the client has chosen. On its own, this process encourages the client's self-efficacy as well as prompting a role reversal in which the client is now instructing the therapist. The video chosen by the client can then be used either as auxiliary support or as the main method for processing the traumatic material. In Rhythm and Processing, we call this the COM (Calm or Motivating) video.

Using procedures that I will explain more fully in later chapters, the sequence centers around lightly checking in with the client regarding their subjective unit of disturbance (SUD), which reactivates some aspect of the emotional learning, before quickly moving to clear the client's mind of the somatic and emotional material relating to this stressor from immediate focus, then redirecting attention to the COM video while the therapist instructs the client to blink rapidly at set intervals. Using RAP, the process of desensitization can in some cases take place in between 10 and 20 minutes. The repetition and alternation creates a sense of mismatch, and the presentation of overturning information is repeated very rapidly.

How can one suffer while at the same time feeling so calm? After the target memory assumes a labile state, the disconfirming experience in the present moment updates the material stored in the dysfunctional memory network. The trauma survivor's prediction of discomfort from the retrieval of the memory becomes overturned. The fear and concern about accessing the memory is thus replaced. The hub of the wheel no longer carries the feedback loop of suffering and no longer leads to the further consolidation of additional spokes connecting to other memories. The memory has been reconsolidated at its core.

The Verification Phase

Returning to the SUD, the therapist verifies that there is no perceived discomfort in the body of the client. Several methods can be used to review this. The client's assessment of the SUD being at zero is a clear indication that they no longer "feel" discomfort in their body or their mind about the problem. But what is even more convincing is the client's own narrative. The therapist asks the client to repeat the negative cognition and determine how true these words feel to them.

As in our example above, the therapist would ask our client, Imari, "When you look back to the original target, and you say the words, 'I am a problem,' what do you notice now?" It is essential that the therapist ask this question for further confirmation of change. When the SUD has been reduced down to a zero and the negative cognition has become invalidated, we typically get responses such as "Nah, that doesn't sound like me," "that is completely false," or "it's *their* problem, not mine."

In addition to uninstalling the negative belief, it can be helpful to install a positive belief in its place[26]. This is the RAP protocol that may most closely resemble EMDR therapy's fifth phase, called "Installation." In EMDR therapy, typically the positive cognition is elicited at the same time that the negative cognition is first elicited (during the assessment phase). When using RAP, however, the positive belief can be determined either at that moment or once the target has been reduced to a SUD of zero and the negative cognition is no longer supported by the client. To initiate the installation of the new positive cognition, whether it was determined before desensitization or afterwards, the therapist must first verify whether the positive belief is still

---

[26] The elicitation of negative or positive beliefs is not required from the perspective of Ecker and colleagues' research on memory reconsolidation but these steps can be helpful for developing discrepancies and improving motivation. Remember, the target of our interventions is *implicitly* stored information. Still, eliciting *explicit* information can later be recalled in order to improve motivation by developing discrepancies while simultaneously making the client conscious of prediction errors and overturning information.

valid or must be changed as a result of the desensitization process. We ask, "Now that we have reduced the intensity of this event, when you think back to the original target, are the words 'I am free' still what you would like to believe about yourself, or is there something else that you feel would be more worthwhile to believe about yourself today?"

Whether the client confirms their prior choice or selects a new one, the outcome is the same. A process unfolds that allows for the installation of the positive belief. From that point onwards, the memory address no longer holds a negative cognition cycling through a negative somatic experience. The client has replaced the negative physical sensation with a positive feeling and the negative cognition with a positive belief of their choice. Once the positive belief has been successfully installed, the memory content is irrevocably changed. The past has not only been cleared, but permanently resolved.

The client is now asked to confirm that the positive belief is 100 percent true for them in this present moment and that a scan through their entire body finds no indication of discomfort. Staying with our example, the therapist provide Imari with the following instructions: "As you think about the original target and this new belief, 'I am free,' I would like for you to scan through your body. With your eyes open or closed, I would like for you to scan from the top of your head down to the bottom of the toes. Check to see that there's no remaining discomfort and that all parts of your body and mind are clear on this new belief, 'I am free'."

During this scan, the therapist and client may engage in gentle, slow butterfly tapping. This is to ensure that there are no remaining disturbances preventing the client from fully accepting the new perspective. About 30 seconds to a minute elapse. At this point, the client may express a feeling of being "present" and able to think about the past event without getting absorbed and lost in it. The client experiences clarity, a felt sense of safety and calm in the present moment.

The final component of Rhythm and Processing relates to *future integration*. This is the RAP protocol that may most closely resemble the "Future Template" stage of EMDR therapy's three-pronged protocol. In RAP, it is designed to verify whether the client can envision a future where the positive cognition holds up in the face of adversity. In the case of Imari, for example:

Therapist:	So now we want to make sure that, if there is anything in the next few days or the next few weeks that challenges you in relation to the negative belief, you will be able to handle it. We're going to use something called future integration.
Imari:	OK.
Therapist:	The way we will do that is by creating a resource for you. When you think about this positive belief that we just installed—the positive belief of "I am free"—what is the image that comes to your mind that represents the *essence* of those words for you?
Imari:	Hmm...I can see my ancestors. Like, a whole group of them, guiding me and protecting me.

The client creates a visualization inspired by the positive cognition and then visualizes integrating with it. When their visualization moves from a third-person perspective to a first person perspective, the client gains a heightened experience of their positive cognition.

In the future, this mental imagery can be called forth at will, enabling the client to feel more confident outside the session. To complete the process, the client is instructed to practice integrating with their constructed, positive visualization until they feel perfectly comfortable with it. After the client accepts their visualization, the therapist checks the viability of the positive belief (whether it can stand up to scrutiny) represented by the newly integrated image by contrasting it with potential future triggers or reminders of the negative cognition.

Once again, an SUD is established to determine the intensity of a future threat that corresponds to the negative belief. This can be any foreseeable danger, adverse thought intrusion, stressful physical experience, or associated discomfort. The client is instructed to "overlay" the positive image while simultaneously calling up the imagined challenge. Because the positive cognition was previously stated as being completely true and is now attached to an integrated image that brings about positive feelings, this once again activates overturning information. The feelings brought up by the integrated image and the perceived threat are likely to be mutually exclusive. This prompts a further mismatch.

The process is repeated until the client no longer anticipates distress from a possible future event. The therapist then instructs the client to imagine being able to "move through the world" fully integrated with the positive belief, rehearsing how they would respond to future stressors associated with the reconsolidated belief. This enables the client to rehearse their future success and reduces any anticipatory anxiety. The verification phase is now complete. We have ensured that the previous target memory can no longer be experienced in the same way. The client, as a survivor, "owns" their feeling of calmness about an experience that has been tormenting them perhaps for years or decades. Moreover, they now have irrefutable, experiential evidence of their ability to repair their nervous system and recover their dignity.

Healing from Echoes of Suffering

Because these changes can often occur without any overwhelming cathartic response such as tears flowing or fists pounding the client's computer table, it is not surprising that, in the following session, the client may downplay the significance of change. Quite recently, one of my clients successfully reprocessed a long-standing trauma target relating to sexual assault. The presenting issue was a feeling of being unable to respond to any physical affection from their partner—or even a compliment—without flying into a rage. In the session after reprocessing, they were talking about a separate event when they had been triggered by a conflict with a male coworker and their partner consoled them with a hug. I asked, "Hold on a second, your partner was able to give you a hug?" They casually responded, "Yeah, that's not a problem anymore." We call this the *apex effect*. The client no longer attributes the radical change to therapeutic intervention but feels as if it "just happened." After repeating the experience of integrating with the positive belief and envisioning a future where there is no disturbance based on the negative belief, clients naturally and freely move through the world with dignity and increased self-worth.

Because Rhythm and Processing does not "look" like therapy, clients may question whether the change they experience is really or fully attributable to the procedure. This is why therapists are advised to keep thorough notes. In the following session, we can use these to remind a client of their negative and positive cognitions and determine whether any new insights have been gained in relation to the previous target. In some cases, clients laugh off the previous negative cognition as "melodramatic," but in others, there may be a need to reinitiate the therapeutic reconsolidation process with the target.

When the SUD has been reduced to a zero and the positive belief is reported as 100 percent true, the problem usually does not recur, but there can be exceptions. In some complex cases, it can take up to four sessions before identity-based trauma or severe attachment disruptions are fully resolved. But in each session after the initial one, the brain becomes more adaptive at reprocessing further difficulties, and change generally comes about with fewer and fewer obstructions. When the client is able to state the negative belief without disturbance and the positive cognition with confidence, the target has been cleared. The problem is very unlikely to return again.

Summary

This chapter began with the metaphor of the wheel, which I used to represent the structure and operation of traumatic memory. The hub of the wheel stores the negative belief, which creates a feedback loop with the negative feelings and cognitions about the self that the belief generates. The spokes connect to triggers, memories, and reminders of the negative spiral, and the problems of the trauma survivor are often stored in implicit memory systems. Through the use of therapeutic reconsolidation, we can update the survivor's memories with adaptive information. Rhythm and Processing enables the body to reengage its natural ability to recover. Rather than reexperiencing dysfunctionally stored memories as if they are happening in the present, the client, using Rhythm and Processing Strategies under the guidance of the therapist, is empowered to reconsolidate the memory and place it "back on the shelf." The target becomes stored the way it was meant to be, in the distance with the rest of our long-term memories.

CHAPTER 5

GETTING STARTED: INTAKE AND MINDFULNESS-BASED STRATEGIES

Starting Off on the Right Foot

Now that we have discussed the major theories and principles behind Rhythm and Processing Strategies, it is time to devote a chapter to the initial session. Here, as elsewhere in this book, I use anonymized client data and composite narratives to provide examples of the different phases of treatment. In many of the models I have learned from, the emphasis was on implementation of a specific technique with little or no attention to what surrounds the cognitive restructuring, reprocessing, or clearing of dysfunctional material. My approach will be different. Progress in later phases of treatment can become stagnant without a proper strategy. This chapter provides some suggestions on how to ensure that the recovery process begins on a sound footing using the Rhythm and Processing approach.

Many of the problems I see novice therapists encounter result from lack of proper assessment or insufficient case conceptualization. This chapter includes some recommendations on how to avoid such problems when doing Rhythm and Processing, but it is important to note that all mental health professionals have an obligation to practice due diligence and make complete assessments in accordance with the standards of their professional organizations and their own commitment to excellence.

Initial Client Request

In June of 2021, a year after the racial justice protests that rocked the world, Aaliyah contacted me by email seeking psychotherapeutic services to cope with self-doubt and internalization of anti-Black racist beliefs. We agreed on an initial phone session that fit our schedules. The 20 to 30 minute phone call set our expectations, delved a little more into Aaliyah's presenting problem, and gave her an opportunity to ask questions.

Setting Expectations

There is important information to gather at this point. We need to know whether the client is currently seeing any other therapist and whether there is presently any youth protection or child protective agency involvement, any domestic violence or risk of it, and any ongoing involvement with legal or judicial entities. This is because responsibility for the structure of this and future sessions lies with the therapist, who needs to be aware of any outside influences that might compromise sessions or prevent the completion of treatment (e.g., violent partners). And since the motivation for treatment is the responsibility of the client, the therapist also needs to know if any external factor (e.g., a court order) is the client's primary motivator. Such factors might not prevent the work from taking place, but knowing about them before starting can undermine the therapy if they are not discussed in advance.

There are advantages and disadvantages to working virtually and working in person. One upside of meeting clients in a physical office is the protection it gives against tracking by potentially violent partners or family members. But an upside of working virtually is the opportunity to be mobile and even conduct sessions in one's car, for example, or in a park or other location where privacy can be maintained. In either case, care must be made to ensure safety when talking about challenging topics. If other professionals are involved, whether therapists, lawyers, or the courts, letters of consent to release information may be needed or the therapist's work may have to be coordinated with theirs.

It is essential that the client give informed consent to memory reconsolidation-based approaches and understand the experimental nature of Rhythm and Processing Strategies. Even approaches supported by large-scale clinical trials may not all have been tested with the client's specific issue, and clients must be made aware of this. Although professional ethics require disclosure statements that clearly outline the benefits and risks of treatment, some clinicians skip this step when working with our clientele. There are also situations where the timing may simply not be right for starting the journey of recovery.

While it is expected that clients will be able to heal from their suffering, they must be made aware of the possible consequences of doing so. For example, if external entities that may rely on witness testimony are, or could become, involved, we need to make it clear that, after targeting some material, the client may not be as emotionally charged during a hearing or court case. This could work against the client's and lawyer's goals; for instance, tears or other signs of overwhelming emotion may be advantageous on the stand. We must be aware of who may be implicated both inside and outside our sessions.

The Presenting Problem

The second and third tasks in the initial session are designed to help clients clarify their reason(s) for seeking therapy. During this conversation, they usually provide details that not only improve the therapist's understanding of the treatment request but also reveal any third parties that may be motivating the request. A teenage client, for example, may be under pressure from a parent and have no interest themselves in being helped, sometimes rightfully so; in some situations, family therapy is preferable. Sometimes, treating the young client alone can shield the parents from needing to address their own dysfunctional dynamic. In such a case, individual therapy would be contraindicated; it would only address the symptom rather than the underlying source of the problem.

In other cases, the client may have a motive for proving that your therapy doesn't work. Secondary gain issues will be covered in Chapter 6, but this initial conversation about the client's motivation can in some cases bring a greater awareness of the underlying motivation. Some clients may want therapy, but a part of them may feel that they benefit from maintaining or even nourishing the problem. And sometimes there is just a bad match between therapist and client; not every client needs to be seen by every therapist.

It is not always easy to know what questions to ask at this early stage. Every client is different. Systemically themed questions can therefore be helpful in gathering initial information. Such questions help to broaden the focus and bring other related issues into the field of vision. The client's problem often involves more than one specific issue. Both during and after this initial consultation, when questions arise or there is ever a lack of conversation, the Four Cores of anti-racist psychotherapy are especially helpful. Let's now have a closer look at these.

The Four Cores of Anti-Racist Psychotherapy

The illustration and table below represent what I call the Four Cores of anti-racist psychotherapy. These should be used to guide our information gathering and give us a better picture of the inner workings of the client. We do not need to ask every one of these questions in one session; they are directions to assist in understanding the individual. Talking about race and racial trauma extends far beyond just microaggressions, so it is essential for the therapist and client to have a shared understanding of the complexity of racial trauma.

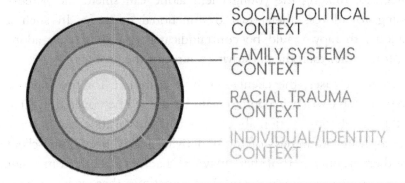

ANTI-RACIST PSYCHOTHERAPY: FOUR CORES

SOCIAL/POLITICAL CONTEXT

FAMILY SYSTEMS CONTEXT

RACIAL TRAUMA CONTEXT

INDIVIDUAL/IDENTITY CONTEXT

Four Cores	Examples
The Social Context	The social climate for people with the client's unique or intersectional identity (racial, gender, class, sexuality, etc.) Q→ How do you feel society views you as a person? How do you view this society?
The Family Systems Context	The relational systems the client interacts with (more than just the immediate family) Q→ **What (negative or positive) legacy do you carry from your family history?**
Racial Trauma Context	The role the client's identity plays for them Q→ **In what ways do you feel that your identity worsens or protects against the presenting problem?**
The Individual Context	Resources for resolving the presenting problem Q→ **What beliefs about yourself, your self-care strategies, and your positive peer groups can help you to deal with the presenting problem?**

When communicating with clients about clinical material, we need to use a systemic lens. Many clients who experience socially constructed difficulties present with an individual perspective and a deficit model of their problem. In the initial phase, we are trying to understand their problem using a heightened conceptual frame. We therefore attempt to elicit connections between their experience and the context that surrounds it. Even though the initial phone call may only last 20 or 30 minutes, in my practice I will most likely ask about one or two of the Four Cores. This is because I want the client to realize that their problem is more than just an individual one. Asking about some of the Four Cores at this point also provides an opportunity to form a therapeutic alliance because it enables the therapist to demonstrate validation and comprehension of the client's intricate situation from a systemic perspective.

Whenever we ask a Four Cores question, after the client responds, the therapist makes one reflective listening intervention. This can take the form of a comment such as "It sounds like you. . . " or a paraphrase ("So what you're saying is . . ."). The intervention verifies a shared understanding up to that point. Maintaining a shared understanding is vital for the recovery process because people with stigmatized identities have historically been excluded (especially by people in positions of authority) and therefore have a tendency to feel misunderstood. The client's narrative is the only truth we can work with in individual therapy, so we need them to correct us if our validating statement is even slightly inaccurate. At the same time, we also want to make sure that, in validating them, we do not feed into their negative cognitions, as many authority figures have a tendency to do. Only after the shared understanding has been confirmed should the next question be asked.

Here is an example of a terrible reflective listening intervention.

Client:	Life sucks.
Therapist:	So, what you're telling me is that your whole life is garbage.

This intervention is likely to feed into negative cognitions. A better example would be any of the following:

Client:	Life sucks.
Therapist:	So, what you're telling me is that things are kinda rough right now.
Or:	
Therapist:	It sounds like you've been going through some challenges.
Or:	
Therapist:	Tell me more about what's been making it so tough for you.

After several such interventions have been made, summarizing again can further assist in ensuring that the gist of the client's story is understood by both client and therapist. Many people feel that the effects of identity-based oppression are incomprehensible to others (especially when the therapist's own identity differs from them in any way). The client always gets the final say in how their problem is understood. Give the client power. We therapists don't need so much of it anyway.

The Client's Opportunity to Ask Questions

Although most clients know why they are consulting a therapist, the initial phone call provides an opportunity for the therapist to gauge the client's level of insight into the presenting problem as well as for the client to get a basic understanding of the therapist's style of operation. Some people may understand the rationale for an experiential psychotherapy more than others. Others will completely misunderstand it, but this is not their fault. It is the fault of our field, so it is our responsibility to clear up any misconceptions. Clients who have misconceptions about what to expect benefit greatly from being able to ask questions before committing to treatment.

Thus, after getting as much client information as is necessary to start with, we give the client the opportunity to question the therapist. We say something like this:

> Therapist: Now I think we have a shared understanding of the reason you are seeking sessions. But I would like you to have the opportunity to ask me some questions so you can make sure that this is the right therapy for you. Do you have any questions about Rhythm and Processing therapy?

The therapist should welcome any and all questions. Questions about the therapist are fine, provided they are relevant and any self-disclosure is measured and intentional. It is fair for clients to ask questions about why the therapist uses a particular therapeutic approach. Clients have a right to make informed decisions about treatment options. For this reason, therapists must stay up to date on the latest research and feel comfortable talking about memory reconsolidation.

Understandably, clients often ask about the goal of my approach or what to expect from reprocessing memories. A typical dialogue might go like this:

Client:	So what is this EDM, or ERDM, or whatever you call it? (Most clients do not know or care about all of our acronyms, by the way. Even if a client says they know what to expect, the therapist is advised to provide information regardless.)
Therapist:	Let me give you an example of what our work will be like. When we think of the proverbial example of PTSD, we think of a soldier who goes off to war. There, he experiences traumatic experiences. He may see, hear, or feel things that cause him to internalize the negative belief "I am not safe." So when he gets back home, even though he is no longer in the warzone, he may behave in ways that are better suited to the battlefield. He hears a loud noise, thinks "I'm not safe," and dives under his desk at work. He gets upset with his partner due to not feeling safe, all of that. What we are trying to do, now that the soldier is home, is to reprocess his negative belief from the warzone. Whenever he thinks about anything that reminds him of the warzone, he goes back to that belief. So in our therapy we will use various techniques to reduce the impact belief of "I'm not safe" and change it to a positive belief like "I can be safe," or "I survived," or "my life is important." So, after reprocessing, when he runs into a potential trigger, instead of his mind going back to the warzone and the negative belief, it will no longer go back to that place. This will change his beliefs and actions in the present.
Client:	So what can *I* expect?
Therapist:	Well, if you choose to accept this approach, I will send you a questionnaire. This is just so that I can get a baseline, see where you're at. Doing that will help me to

help you. You will also be getting the contract. Make sure to read through it so you know what to expect, the cancellation policy and all of that. After you complete all of that, we'll be able to have our first session. In our first few sessions, we will not be talking in depth about your trauma, that all comes later. In the first session, I will be clarifying some information from your questionnaires and making sure we're on the same page. For the next few sessions, I will be teaching you different visualization techniques and meditations, so that you learn some skills to care for yourself without the need for a therapist. The next few sessions after that will involve learning a little bit about your family, making a list of the trauma targets that have impacted you throughout your whole life, and finally we will reprocess each of them one at a time.

Client:	Oh, OK, great. Also, I had one more question. How many sessions does this all take?
Therapist:	Ah! [smiles] That's a common question. People ask me this all the time. And I always wonder, are y'all the same people who go to the fitness instructor and ask how many sessions will it take to get a six-pack?
Client:	[laughs]
Therapist:	Nah, I'm joking, It's a good question. But because everyone's brain and everyone's trauma is unique, people do 20, 30, or even 40 sessions. Some even come back after a few years for regular check-ups. What I've found is, you get from this what you put into it. Therapy is more than just one hour of the week, it's everything you're doing outside the session too. So instead of this being like me analyzing your brain and you just sitting around chillin', let's look at this like training. Both of us are working toward you recognizing your awesomeness.
Client:	OK, that's cool. And how often do we need to meet?
Therapist:	Sometimes I'll meet people weekly, some people I'll meet every two weeks. I even do intensives because reconsolidation therapies don't require homework, so some people book me multiple times a week. But give me a heads-up before you do *that*, so I can make sure the schedule is good for all of my other clients too. I have some clients who see me just once a month, but that can be tough because it requires extra motivation. The most important thing is that when we get to reprocessing trauma, the sessions have to be closer together so we can follow up with each other closer in time…

(Aiming to keep the phone call between 15 and 20 minutes, the therapist proceeds to wrap up the phone call.)

Therapist:	So, any other questions?
Client:	Great, that sounds good. Nah, I don't think I have any other questions.
Therapist:	So, would you like to select me as your therapist? If this sounds like the right therapy for you, send me your email, and I can send over all the documents, and then we can do our best to make a change for you.

Clients usually appreciate being able to interview a therapist in advance like this. Because some therapists might have political leanings that can be anti-Black, anti-LGBTQ, or otherwise problematic, I encourage all people seeking therapists to make sure they can be comfortable with whoever they are sharing secrets with. Therapists are not neutral; they're people too. And on that note, even when I meet a client who shares the same racial identity as I do, or if they identify any social issues of concern as part of what maintains their problem, I respond like this:

Therapist:	Even though I am an anti-racist psychotherapist and you and I share the same race, my experience as a Black Jamaican African Canadian may be different from yours. And because I am a hetereosexual, able-bodied male, there may be times where I get things wrong or slip up. Always know that you always have permission to check your therapist. I am still learning and trying to be a better human, one day at a time.

Therapists need to humble themselves. When using an anti-racist psychotherapy, the therapist is not the only expert. A client's lived experience may not always grant them an Ivy league graduate diploma, but they still have a lot to teach us.

The initial phone call is also important as an opportunity for the therapist to assess whether they are the best person to assist a particular client. Are there any contraindications to using memory reconsolidation-based therapies with this individual? Knowing that sometimes things get worse before they get better, is there an active risk of suicide or a history of attempts? Is the client currently abusing substances or struggling with anorexia nervosa or any other concern that poses an immediate risk of harm? Are there psychiatric issues requiring additional medical follow-up and collaboration with external actors that have not already been arranged? Whenever a presenting issue arises that is outside of my specialty, I will consult other trained therapists who specialize in the problem. As well as ensuring that the client is given the appropriate support, this provides another opportunity for my own growth. It is not that some clients cannot be assisted, but that we may need to manage our expectations for client progress and humble ourselves. We cannot take full credit when things go absolutely well. And when life gets challenging, we have both an ethical and legal responsibility to ensure the best possible client care.

Questionnaires and Assessments

For the first session after the phone call, the therapist should have the results of questionnaires and screening tools that were sent to the client after the phone consultation. (It is preferred that these be sent electronically with results being stored on secure HIPAA-compliant servers). These allow for a baseline understanding of what the client is struggling with. They also help to give an idea of how best to direct the initial sessions and especially how much to focus on stabilization before beginning to explore trauma history, much less family history. The questionnaires that I recommend, all freely available, include:

> PTSD Checklist for DSM-5 (PCL-5):
>   • used to assess for PTSD symptoms. It is important to know how much memories of the past impact the client in the present.
> Generalized Anxiety Disorder Questionnaire (GAD-7):
>   • used to assess their experience of anxiety, worry, or irritability over the past 14 days.

> ➢ Center for Epidemiologic Studies Depression Scale (CES-D):
>   - used to determine the client's level of sleep disturbance, general sadness, and the degree to which negative cognitions have been prominent over the past week.
> ➢ Multidimensional Inventory of Dissociation 60–item version (MID-60):
>   - used to assess the client's experience of the spectrum of structural dissociation. Questions range from forgetfulness and somatic disturbances to hearing voices or experiencing multiple personalities. This relates to the entire lifetime of the client.
>   - Discussing the results of the MID-60 can be very important in early sessions to help the client understand structural dissociation as well as to explain that these phenomena are automatic, unintentional responses that arise from emotional parts of the personality as an attempt at self-protection.

At this point, we also let the client know that the extent of their difficulties, as recorded by the questionnaires, is a reflection of what they have survived but that they are more than any label or diagnosis. We don't have to overdo this point, just mention it.

The Initial Client Session

The function of the initial intake is not to pathologize the client. There are ways to use the results of the questionnaires that normalize the experience of mental health concerns on a spectrum of concerns rather than as a checklist of "disorders." Therapists should begin by explaining that anxiousness, sadness, and the effects of trauma influence all people to some degree. Our role in the initial session is to hear from the client and then very quickly reflect with them on the results of the questionnaire as a way of validating their experience.

During the first part of the initial session, we ask about previous therapy experiences and medical issues, and guided by the Four Cores of Anti-Racist Psychotherapy, seek clarifications on the presenting problem. The guiding principles of the first session are learning the "rhythm" of the client (see Chapter 2), avoiding any inappropriate judgments, avoiding microaggressions (mansplaining, whitesplaining, etc.), and cultivating safety. Applying these principles takes practice and is not always as straightforward as it sounds, but when done correctly, an atmosphere of reciprocity develops through which the client and therapist, in a relationship of trust, embark on a journey of mutual self-reflection and beneficial change.

Mindfulness-Based Interventions

The second part of the first session is devoted to guided meditation. Depending on how much time is left, one or two practices from my *Black Meditation: Ten Practices for Self-Care, Mindfulness, and Self-Determination* (2021) can be introduced, for example, Skill #3: Guided Earth Meditation (Appendix I, page 218) and Skill #4: Mindful Color Breathing (Appendix I, page 220). Both of these skills are designed to help the client learn to use their body to calm their mind, and their mind to calm their body. The guided earth meditation is designed to help the client to non-judgmentally notice different parts of their body, and it ends with a visualization meant to encourage a belief of being well supported by the natural environment. It also serves a secondary purpose of assessing the client's capacity to be soothed through the use of visualization and breath awareness. Clients typically report feelings of relief and calmness after its use. The mindful color breathing technique, as I explain in *Black Meditation*, "is very helpful for people who need mild relief from stress. It involves the acknowledgement of suffering and its corresponding opposite" (p. 56). The implementation is similar to what Shapiro (2018) calls the "light stream technique," an EMDR therapy interpretation of an ancient yoga technique. The light stream technique benefits clients who are experiencing chronic physical and emotional pain (Levine, 1991). When using this technique, bilateral stimulation is optional but not necessary to gain a benefit.

The language of meditative scripts is vague, but this is intentional. If we put too many words into a visualization, we put boundaries on the client's experience. If we use the *right* kinds of words, we can enhance their creativity. The following dialogue gives an idea of how this might typically be done after the therapist has used the guided earth meditation and the client has expressed calmness.

Therapist:	I would like for you now to scan through your body and let me know if are there any parts that hold any pain or tension or any kind of suffering at this moment?
Client:	Uh…yeah, my shoulders have been a little tense since this morning.
Therapist:	Ah, OK, let's see what we can do about that. I would like to ask a different kind of question.
Client:	OK.
Therapist:	On a scale of zero to ten, what is the level of discomfort in your shoulders?
Client:	Maybe . . . three?
Therapist:	I'd like to ask another question. What would be the emotion that is in that three?
Client:	Oh…I never thought of that… tired.. is tired an emotion?
Therapist:	Sure, let's go with that. My next question is, what is the color of this tired feeling in the shoulders?
Client:	Oh, a color?
Therapist:	Yup, the first one that comes to your mind.
Client:	Uhh.. yellow?
Therapist:	OK great. So my next question is, if yellow is the color of suffering then what is the color of healing?
Client:	Hmm… blue!

> **Therapist:** OK, fantastic . . . So now we will practice breathing in again, but this time, I would like for you to breathe in the color of healing on the inhalation. And on the exhalation, breathe out a different color. Wanna give it a try?
>
> **Client:** OK sure.
>
> **Therapist:** Ok, great, let's breathe in and breathe out again, breathing the color of healing into the parts of the body that need it.
>
> **Therapist and client:** [inhaling and exhaling]

In this situation, the client who identifies one side of the coin of suffering can often identify its opposite. An example: If I ask someone not to think of elephants, they will have difficulty not thinking of a certain large, four-legged mammal. However, if I ask you what you have been afraid of, I will get an answer that tells me what you need more courage for. In using mindful color breathing, after asking about the color of the problem, we then ask about the color that represents healing. The open-endedness of this question gives the client the freedom to come up with whatever color feels right to them.

Being vague and working with colors works great here. Introducing too many limiting factors can induce a self-sabotaging intellectualization, but when the client's options are not shut down, they can often surprise themselves even on the first or second try by calming their body using the opposite color of whatever bothers them The dialogue can then continue like this:

Therapist:	OK, now take one more, even deeper breath [inhales]… and let it go… [exhales]
Therapist and client:	[inhaling and exhaling]
Therapist:	OK, great. Now on a scale of zero to ten, what's the level of stress in your shoulders now?
Client::	Oh, wow, it's like a one now . . . but it never goes down to zero.
Therapist:	OK well what's the color of it now?
Client:	Hmm! That's funny, now it's like a pale purple…
Therapist:	And what's the color of healing for pale purple?
Client:	Umm… Maybe a darker blue?
Therapist:	Great, so let's try this again.
Client:	[resumes breathing]
Therapist:	And this time, I would like for you to tune into your infinite creativity. Not only will you breathe in the color of healing, I would like for you to breathe in an *extra special* healing quality. It can be visual, auditory, or even a sensory experience. Some people like to breathe in hearts, others rainbows or unicorns. It's up to you. But breathe in the color of healing with that extra something special to it [inhales] . . . and let it go [exhales]. Continue doing this for a few moments.

When the client practices this exercise, even if 95 percent of the time there is no previous reduction in their discomfort, the prompt to use their infinite creativity will provide the extra creative room they need to try something new. Notice the open-endedness of the instructions. The client identifies the intensity of discomfort, the color of the problem, and the color of the solution for themselves. If they succeed in reducing their discomfort, they will have demonstrated self-efficacy and created at least some small hope for change.

Therapist:	And what's the intensity now?
Client:	Zero.
Therapist:	Isn't that great? Good work. Can I ask what was the extra quality you ended up breathing in?
Client:	I imagined breathing in some waves and a little bit of sun from the beach!
Therapist:	Ain't that something? Understand that there is no skill I *gave* you. All I did was provide a context for you to access your inner gifts. That is the work we will be doing together. And just so you know, as your therapist, I never would have been able to guess in a hundred years that breathing in some waves and a beach would help to relieve stress in your shoulders.
Client:	[laughs]
Therapist:	The important thing to know is that there are resources that you have had all along that can exceed both of our expectations. My job is just to help you realize that you have what it takes to recover.
Client:	Thank you.

After completing the exercise, the therapist gives the client a homework assignment to practice additional breathing exercises until the next meeting as well as to study Skill #6: Five Grateful Things Exercise from *Black Meditation* (see Appendix I, page 222). Five grateful things is a cognitive exercise of journaling and listing five things the client can be grateful for. It is designed not only for self-monitoring and self-reflection, but to get the client used to the positive feelings that gratitude engenders. When we list reasons for gratitude, we are taking into account the past, present, and future and making statements that empower us to feel positive in the present moment. The positive feeling is what the exercise seeks to reinforce through practice. It cannot be underestimated. It is the client's first recognition that they are able to do things for themselves to change the previously entrenched pattern of hypervigilance and threat detection. This is the beginning of the journey toward recovery.

Summary

This chapter explains pre-session and initial session requirements. Clients who may never have been to therapy before are owed an explanation of what to expect from their sessions. More experienced clients must be able to ask questions to determine if yours is the right approach for them. The therapeutic alliance is affected even by these initial communications. Where necessary, the therapist must seek outside consultation to ensure adequate service delivery as well as attending carefully to the myriad of comorbidities that can either obstruct later trauma reprocessing or must be prioritized in advance. In seeking to understand the full reality of the client's inner world, the therapist should always be guided by the Four Cores of anti-racist psychotherapy, adopt a lens of validation, and work recursively toward a progressive understanding of the mental health concerns from the client's perspective. In the initial session, through guided meditations, we can inspire hope for change and practice the first stages of overturning information with them. The next session continues with the orientation to therapy and also gives the client their first exposure to the Rhythm and Processing technique and an explanation of how it can be used.

CHAPTER 6

AMBIVALENCE AND THE ADVANTAGE OF THE DISADVANTAGE

Being on the Fence

Clients who seek healing encounter many obstacles, but their own ambivalence about therapy is perhaps the major threat to clinical progress. The observant therapist will watch carefully for any limiting beliefs about change that a client may have. Usually, the ever-lurking threat of ambivalence will have made its entrance by the second session if not in the initial phone call or first session. If it is not dealt with, ambivalence is often the culprit when treatments become stagnant.

Ambivalence is a part of any decision we make. Let's say we decide to go to a restaurant. We can choose between two places we know—one where the food is well-seasoned and delicious or another where it is less tasty but more nutritious. We will always weigh our options and ask ourselves questions. Is this one the best choice for me? How did the food taste last time? Will it taste as good again? How did I feel afterwards? What did my doctor just tell me about my cholesterol again? And so on before making our decision. Some of us will decide quickly. Others may struggle with the choice. But there will always be some degree of ambivalence. Whenever we make a choice, we never enjoy 100 percent certainty about the decision. It is usually a decision that has been weighed against the other options, and so we end up with a *degree* of certainty rather than absolute confidence. The same is true for a person who chooses therapy in order to recover from trauma.

Addictions and the Underlying Source of Suffering

For a period of five years, I was employed as an addictions counsellor in a community setting. The more I worked with individuals suffering from addiction, the more I realized that the conventional ways of discussing substance abuse with clients did not appear to enable much progress. There was a part of every client that sought to recover and a part that was reluctant to relinquish the addiction. After a therapy session, a client would sometimes take actions that jeopardized not only the gains made in the session but their very life. They did not always reveal these actions openly in later sessions. Over time, I saw that not every substance abuser carried the same goals.

Certain types of personalities got something out of their drug use that others did not.

Patterns became apparent. Cocaine abusers, for example, use a drug that gives them a temporary feeling of power. This addresses a need of those who normally feel powerless. Opioid consumers, on the other hand, seemed to self-medicate to address an unending pattern of deep-rooted suffering. Those who were addicted to alcohol would regularly drink to the point of blacking out with the intention (usually unconscious) of nullifying a painful part of their life and dulling negative cognitions that plagued them. In all cases, however, consuming harmful substances that undermined the goals of their careers, families, and relationships appeared counterintuitive to say the least. Recognizing this helped me see that there was always, from the client's point of view, an advantage to their disadvantage.

EMDR Approaches to Substance Abuse Treatment

Ambivalence is an especially prominent theme in addictions. This has led to great interest in the field of substance abuse treatment. There are various approaches to treating addictions through EMDR therapy. As I learned more, I found several that were especially helpful. The Desensitization of Triggers and Urge Reprocessing (DeTUR) model developed by Arnold Popky, a founder of the EMDR Institute, was one of the first that I was introduced to. Although DeTUR can be used to treat addictions, it can also assist in cases of self-harm and in severe personality disorders (Annesley et al., 2019). The person who self-harms uses that self-inflicted violence for a benefit in the same way that an alcohol abuser or someone addicted to nicotine consumes substances that offer temporary relief at the cost of critical and chronic health concerns.

The Feeling State Addictions Protocol (FSAP), developed by Robert Miller while working in a U.S. naval hospital, is another approach I have found useful as a basis for treating addictions in my practice. Miller's theory of behavioral addiction suggests that associating positive experiences with certain behaviours creates a "feeling-state" (Miller, 2012). This refers to the psychophysiological arousal of the body in connection with a particular action. As Miller observes,

> This arousal includes emotions and feelings such as excitement, satisfaction, and power, along with any accompanying sensations. [Feeling-state theory] proposes that the combination of the feelings, sensations, and the behavior compose the FS that causes the impulse-control problems. There is a large variety of FSs because any desired emotion or feeling can become fixated with any behavior. Once created, the FS continues to exist, with the same feelings and behavior associated with it as when the FS was originally formed. (pp. 160–161)

The presence of any intense desire (to belong, to be strong, to be seen as special), if followed by a highly charged positive experience that satisfies this need, engenders a feeling-state. When a person who has such a feeling-state encounters a trigger (internal or external), the desired feeling is activated and an urge to execute the behaviour arises. The need to execute the behavior becomes a near uncontrollable priority that supersedes the needs of the client's health, well-being, or attachment relationships. Even when the substance abuser shows up in the session, a part of them would much rather prefer to drink or drug themselves into oblivion as soon as they leave the office. The advantage of the disadvantage can obstruct therapeutic progress at the least and be unpredictably lethal at its worst. When working in the field, it is not unnatural to hear of people who have literally drunk their lives away.

The result of the feeling-state, then, is a compulsive behaviour that repeats whenever an appropriate trigger is encountered. For example, a client I worked with some years ago (I'll call him Karim) told me how, as a youth, he had an absent father and was continually bullied by other boys. He grew up with no real connection to other young men or paternal figures. He was rarely praised and often criticized. All these elements combined to solidify his low self-esteem. One day, when Karim was in his late teens, he ran into his older brother, Jamal, in a shady part of the city. Jamal invited him into a bar to play the video lottery machines at the back. Sitting on a stool, the young boy pulled the lever and a foundational event took place. He won the jackpot.

The machine blasted out loud music, beeped, shook, and flashed its lights. His brother grew as animated as the machine and hugged the young boy. At that moment, the association was made, and the cycle of consolidation started to etch itself into existence. The behavioural addiction to gambling was imprinted into Karim's mind. Even when he later lost thousands of dollars, the association in his mind between pulling the lever and attaining a sense of belonging and self-worth would drive him to a cycle of suffering. It was not the winning, but the possibility of winning that led him down a reckless path of sabotage, theft, and bankruptcy after bankruptcy.

Associating Problems With Positive Affect

Many therapeutic approaches to change target the compulsive behaviour but avoid any discussion of the original precursor. This keeps the client on the fence about change. We will not move an inch unless we can target the etiological events that set the wheel of pathological associations in motion. There are many protocols to address addiction, depression, anxiety, and other mental health disorders, but in all cases, we must direct our attention to the original association where a lack and confirmation of the lack converge. We cannot succeed until we direct our attention to the first association. The pathogenic associations made in people's minds that have led to compulsive or maladaptive behaviors are not always evident or explicitly stated by the client. Some disorders can be labelled as "treatment-resistant" by mental health professionals. In the case of these intractable difficulties, there is often an unexamined benefit to the status quo. A client can be on the fence even if it is not in their short- or long-term interest to stay there. I mentioned EMDR-based theories above because, in some instances, what leads these associations to be made can be trauma or deficit-related. However, to create these associations, we do not always need life-threatening or completely negative affects.

Mosquera and Knipe (2017) discuss the use of EMDR therapy in the treatment of ambivalence with women who are survivors of domestic violence. They explain that there are forms of dysfunctional positive affect that can prevent the resolution of traumatic material. Even under the threat of extreme violence, some women have difficulty leaving their violent partners. Once again, there are advantages for them in maintaining a dangerous status quo. There is a degree of positive affect associated with the abuser and fuelled by psychological defenses. Thus, as Mosquera and Knipe (2017) write:

> successful avoidance of a traumatic memory can be experienced with affect of relief; idealization of a perpetrator can contain distorted and unrealistic positive feeling. In such instances, the post-traumatic material cannot be fully accessed, and therefore cannot be fully resolved through standard EMDR procedures. (p. 57)

Having a psychological defense against bad feelings is adaptive. There is a function to resisting change; it prevents the harm of needing to leave. The concept of dysfunctional positive affect explains avoidance, co-dependent relationships, procrastination (Knipe, 2005), and many other common forms of self-sabotage (Knipe, 2009). From an EMDR perspective, it is possible, because of the adaptive information processing facet of the psychotherapy, to reduce the salience of positive affect relating to certain advantages of the disadvantage. For the great majority of mental health concerns, these are the first steps to healing from the cycle of suffering.

The Motivation for Ambivalence

Shapiro (2018) admonishes therapists to explore the possibility of secondary gain issues during the preparation phase of EMDR therapy, cautioning that "until these fears are resolved, no other significant therapeutic effects can be expected or maintained" (p. 67). Freud's concept of secondary gain has multiple definitions, but generally "the concept can be used to describe an unconscious mechanism with an intrapsychological reward . . . or to describe a conscious aim to attain an external reward irrespective of any previous disorder. All variants between these two extremes are also possible" (van Egmond, 2003, pp. 145–146). Secondary gains thus relate to the advantages of maintaining the disadvantage. While the symptoms may be troublesome, there are unconscious and conscious advantages to the dire circumstances that drive them. By adding that all variants between the extremes are possible, Shapiro means that while some advantages may be completely outside the client's awareness, others may be known and able to be discussed. There is a special category of secondary gain material that is also *pre*conscious, meaning that asking the right questions can bring this material to the client's awareness.

With every maladaptive pattern of behaviour, we need to get real about the pros and cons. The PROS/CONS balance sheet is a Rhythm and Processing strategy that is designed to clarify the motivations for maintaining vs changing the status quo. This balance sheet has been heavily inspired by my work using what Miller and Rollnick (2012) call motivational interviewing. We all have the ability as therapists to either encourage the client through our interventions or to create resistance. To build motivation for change, Miller and Rollnick stress the importance of asking open questions, listening reflectively, affirming the client's effort, summarizing as a means of demonstrating collaboration, and eliciting change talk. The therapeutic frame of collaboration is especially important when using Rhythm and Processing.

The decision to change always involves a conflict. This is true for everyone. There are things that we desire (what we want to approach) and things that are undesirable (what we want to avoid). Kurt Lewin, a world-renowned psychologist seen as one of the 'fathers of social psychology' described three kinds of conflicts that relate to change: approach-approach, approach-avoidance, and avoidance-avoidance. I will use food examples to make this as relatable as possible. The approach-approach conflict refers to the need to choose between two great alternatives; for instance, if you had to choose between eating authentic Jamaican or Trinidadian food, both freshly prepared with island spices, herbs, and flavors. Approach-avoidance relates to making a decision that has both positives and negatives, like wanting to eat hot and spicy Korean food but fearing it may further exacerbate a worsening stomach ulcer. Avoidance-avoidance conflicts are some of the most difficult to resolve. This is when we have to choose between two undesirable alternatives like eating an unseasoned, rubber-tasting bologna sandwich or an undercooked potato salad prepared with expired mayonnaise.

There is also a fourth category of particular interest here. This is the *double* approach-avoidance conflict. It occurs when:

a person is torn between two alternatives (lovers, lifestyles, etc.), each of which has enticing positive and powerful negative aspects. As the person moves closer to option A, the disadvantages of A become more salient and the advantages of B seem brighter. When the person then turns and starts moving toward B, the downsides of B become clearer and A starts looking more attractive. (Miller & Rollnick, 2012, p. 15)

Many clients face such a scenario in their everyday lives. When faced with maintaining or changing the status quo, the disadvantages of each option are not always clear-cut, and the advantages often are also not obvious. As a result, it can be very difficult to break the state of ambivalence, and we may become stuck in limbo and prevented from fully committing to change. To clarify such dilemmas, we can create what Miller and Rollnick term a *decisional balance* in order to get an accurate representation of the costs and benefits of going with either option.

Whenever people need to make a major life decision, they must weigh the pros (advantages) and cons (disadvantages) of either decision. These decisions are impacted by their sense of identity, which in turn is related to social context. As Miller and Sollnick (2012) put it, "social and cultural factors affect people's perceptions of their behavior, as well as their evaluation of its costs and benefits . . . [and] a person's motivational balance and ambivalence cannot be understood outside the social context of family, friends and community" (pp. 16–17).Both the client and therapist walk into the therapy session at a disadvantage if they are not conscious of both who benefits from therapeutic progress and who benefits from its absence.

Implementation of the PROS/CONS Balance Sheet

The PROS/CONS balance sheet is used strategically in Rhythm and Processing to illustrate the balance of decisional factors and, more importantly, to make the preconscious motivations conscious and the secondary gain elements available for discussion with the therapist. More effective plans for change can then take place. Using any spreadsheet software, a balance sheet like the following can be created with the client to illustrate the PROS and CONS of the status quo vs change. The top left quadrant lists the PROS of the status quo and the top right quadrant the CONS. The bottom left quadrant then represents the PROS of change and the bottom right the CONS. Different colors are used to distinguish the PROS and CONS as clearly as possible.

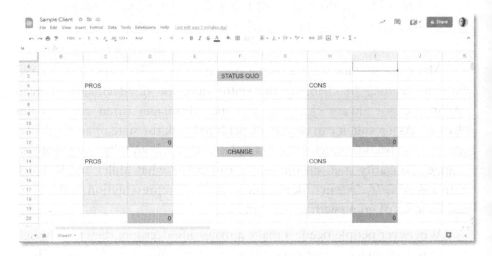

The therapist creates the spreadsheet while following the above template, and the client and therapist complete it together. In the following example, the client is a young Black woman we will call Elena. Although she at first described the problem as having to do with dating, the intake process revealed that early and continued experiences of anti-Black racism, as well as being raised in a largely white environment, have caused her to internalize racist and sexist beliefs about Black women, leading to a self-fulfilling prophecy of self-sabotage and shame in her relationships. It therefore became necessary to clarify the goals of treatment in the second session. Our collaboration to accomplish this went as follows:

> **Therapist:** So, I would now like us to try an exercise that can help us develop our treatment plan. I would like for us to start by explaining where we're at and where you want to go. We'll start with explaining the status quo and then the change. The status quo represents everything we were talking about in our first session. All the reasons you have come to

> therapy. The change represents the person you want to become after you have healed from all the trauma and recovered from all of the difficulty. It's who you become after therapy is done. Does that make sense?

Client:	OK, sure.
Therapist:	If you could describe it in one word or phrase, what would you say is the name of the problem? What is the name that we can give to the status quo in order to distinguish it from the goal of therapy.
Client:	Hmm...how about "sick of feeling alone"?
Therapist:	OK great, we can name it that. Now let me ask, what is the name that you would like to give to the state of mind you want to achieve after completing all of the trauma targets, after all of our sessions have been completed.
Client:	[Hesitates] . . . Oh, I know. "Queen!"
Therapist:	That's a good one. OK, now let me type those names into our balance sheet.

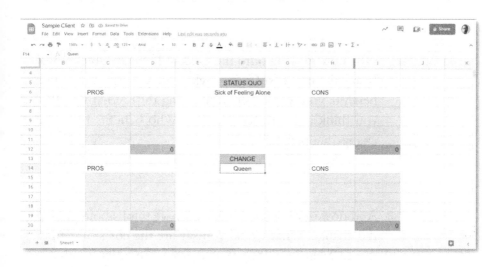

Therapist:	So now we have identified where we're at and where we want to go. The next step I would like us to make is to think, what are some of the things we get from keeping the status quo. Let's start first with being "sick of feeling alone." I know this may seem counterintuitive, but I would like to start by validating the problem. There have to be reasons why the problem exists, right? So what would you say are some of the advantages of holding on to the problem? Is there anything that this status quo protects you from or keeps from happening to you? Let's see if we can list five.

[Five PROS for status quo are listed]

Therapist:	Now let's think of the CONS. I would like to ask, kind of like what we were talking about last session, what are the downsides to the status quo? What would you say are the costs to you of keeping this problem going? Remember, you were talking about having trouble sleeping and some physical health complaints during the intake?

[Five CONS for status quo are listed]

Therapist:	OK, now moving onto the Queen! If we are able to heal from all of the suffering, what do you think are five benefits you would get from doing this? What is it that you think is worth fighting for? Who benefits from the change happening?

[Five PROS for change are listed]

Therapist:	And now our last category, where we think about getting the change. What would you say are the costs of getting there? What would we have to give up in order to achieve this? What are the downsides to getting rid of the status quo?

[Five CONS for change are listed]

| Therapist: | OK, great. Let's take a look at it now. |

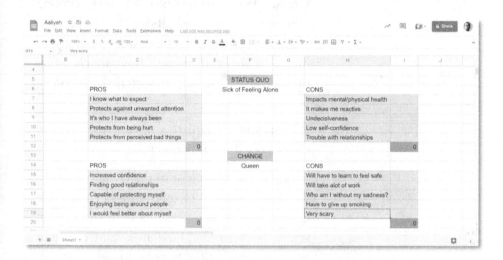

Therapist:	Great, so now we have been able to identify the advantages and disadvantages of both the status quo and of changing it. But because all of these are built differently and some cause more harm than others, I would like for us to think about the level of importance that each of these have. How much of a benefit do each of these give you on a scale of one to five? Just know you can have multiple fives, multiple fours, that's no problem. So, starting with the PROS for the status quo, even though we might not like the status quo, how much of an advantage is it that it helps you say "I know what to expect"?
Client:	Maybe . . . four.
Therapist:	OK next.

	[Elena and therapist complete the list for PROS of the status quo, listing a level of importance for each item.]
Therapist:	Great. OK, moving onto the next section, now we want to think about the CONS for the status quo. On a scale of one to five, how much of a disadvantage, how much of a problem, is "Impacts my mental/ physical health"?
	[Client and therapist complete the list of CONS for the status quo.]
Therapist:	All right, so moving onto the change now. If we are going to change and become the Queen, let's look at the PROS of that. On a scale of one to five, how important would it be, how much of a benefit would it be, to have "increased confidence?"
	[Elena and therapist complete the list of PROS for change.]
Therapist:	OK, so now we are at our last category. When we think about the change, what is the level of the downsides of getting this change? How much of a challenge would it be if we were to address each of these problems? How hard would they be to overcome?
	[Elena and therapist complete the list of CONS for change.]
Therapist:	OK great, now, let's calculate all these numbers on our Excel spreadsheet. As you can tell, I love Excel spreadsheets! Now, I would like for us to take a look at these results and for you to tell me what you think. Just to know, though, that this is a matter of

ambivalence, meaning that if I would have asked you these questions yesterday or if I ask them again tomorrow, the level of importance will change. A three might be a two or a four depending on how you feel that day, though most times a five is going to be five and usually never lower than a four. In any case, the numbers are a reflection of the things that you value in this present moment. So when we look at these calculations, what are your thoughts?

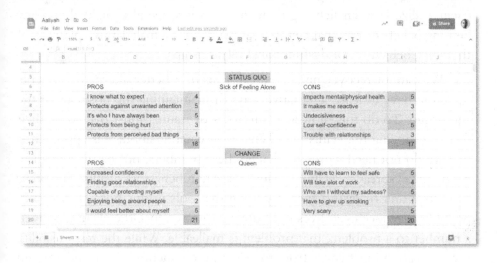

Once the therapist inserts the numbers into a spreadsheet, it becomes clear that there are advantages for the client to making sure the status quo does not change. Note too that some of the information in the first and fourth quadrants may have been preconscious. The client may never have previously verbalized the advantages of maintaining the problem or the problems they will need to overcome if they want to maintain the desired changes.

The information in the second and third quadrants may have already been discussed. Clients know what the problem is and are usually aware of why the problem is undesirable. They may also know *some* of why it is advantageous to change, so asking about the information in either of these quadrants is usually not as challenging as eliciting the information for the first and fourth quadrants.

In the example above, there is practically no statistical difference between the PROS and CONS of the status quo and change categories. Many clients have these double-approach avoidance difficulties. This is what makes some of their problems so resistant to change. The first quadrant often contains information related to feeling-states or to dysfunctional positive affect. The fourth quadrant contains information related to limiting beliefs or possible obstacles that can drive any attempt at reprocessing trauma straight into the mud. We cannot heal if our identity is dependent on maintaining our suffering. A result like the one shown above can help the client realize how challenging their dilemma is while also highlighting any limiting beliefs or external factors that maintain the maladaptive patterns of thoughts, behaviors, or dysfunctional relationships.

We cannot recover unless we can discern a better alternative. Clients therefore have to learn alternative ways of maintaining the positives of the status quo. To do this, however, survivors of trauma must overcome their fear of changing the status quo. What is fascinating about this approach is that we do not need words to change these numbers, not because this is a handy Excel spreadsheet, but because these numbers work just like any other subjective unit of disturbance. By using the tools in this book, it becomes possible to reduce even fives right down to ones. Once the client has given a number to a problem, that problem is malleable. While the responsibility for motivation must come from the client, the structure of our therapy can reduce the scale of the obstacles and create handy little resources that the client can use to manage future problems. I have used this strategy to motivate clients with mental health concerns and with the complications of everyday life. I hope this helps you the next time you catch yourself in the realms of ambivalence too.

Summary

Ambivalence is not a problem unique to substance abusers. Racial trauma survivors often internalize the oppression from their oppressors and blame themselves for violence while getting lost in a limbo that requires their inaction and their lack of justice. The concept of feeling-states is helpful for explaining why certain patterns of behavior are more treatment-resistant than others. When we yearn for positive experiences and we find vices that fit the description, the brain can make intractable associations to stimuli, leading to deeply seated limiting beliefs and contributing to high levels of intrapsychic resistance to change. Though we may not be able to access our *deepest* unconscious reasons for maintaining self-destructive behaviors, through the PROS/CONS balance sheet, we can gain awareness and insights into the values and beliefs of the client. By knowing what they want to approach and what they want to avoid, we can affirm their strengths and reinforce their resources to overcome challenges.

CHAPTER 7

STRUCTURAL DISSOCIATION AND RESOURCE INTEGRATION

Putting the Pieces Together

Before starting any task, there are things to be considered. If you want to put together even the simplest piece of furniture, for example, there are requirements to take into account beyond just the wood and nails you'll need. Do you have sufficient time, energy, and skills? Do you have the patience to wrap your brain around the confusing instructions? How large is the item? Does it need more than one person to build? These are questions about resources. The more challenging and complex your task is, the more extensive are the resources you will need.

In discussing resources and their integration through therapy, this chapter will often refer to what are commonly known as "parts." Not all clients have an intrapsychic experience of separate or dissociative emotional parts, but providing the reader with an introduction to the concept of structural dissociation using the concept of parts will nevertheless be helpful in understanding resource integration. At the same time, we must always be guided by the client's internal felt experience rather than imposing our own theories on them.

Structural Dissociation: The Effects of Severe and Chronic Traumatization

The resources of a trauma survivor are often depleted, and the more severe the trauma, the more depleted their available resources are likely to be. We have spoken about the costs to the nervous system, but there are other costs too. Racial trauma leaves its mark on the nervous system, but it can also rupture the structure of the survivor's personality. To return to our furniture analogy for a moment, imagine thinking about putting a table together while having an inner voice that says "people like you are worthless," "you always fail," "nothing you do will ever work," and so on. Or being inundated with visual thought intrusions that predict failure or replay past failures. When the mind makes an enemy of itself, even if you have all the other resources that you need for the task, it becomes easy to doubt yourself. This explains why those who suffer from psychopathology have difficulties even with daily living tasks, not to mention social interactions and expectations from others. These are issues related to *structural dissociation*. Having explained in the previous chapter the obstacle to change posed by the client's ambivalence toward their trauma, we turn our attention now to issues of structural dissociation.

Van der Hart, Nijenhuis and Steele (2006) explain that chronic traumatization, as well as extreme threats to the safety of the trauma survivor, can cause a structural dissociation of the personality. This causes the survivor to alternate between reexperiencing their trauma and being detached from it. Structural dissociation of the personality can coincide with many mental health disorders on the spectrum of PTSD, disorders of extreme stress, and other trauma-related dissociative disorders.

The divisions of the personality create more than just intrapsychic consequences. Nijenhuis and colleagues (2010) explain that reexperiencing trauma is associated with innate evolutionary systems of defense that respond to severe threats (real or perceived). These are connected to our basic fight, flight, or freeze survival responses. Detachment from trauma is also related to Panksepp's (1998) concept of action systems, which enable people to focus on the continued survival of the species based on attachment needs and caring for offspring. These psychobiological systems are needed to help us engage in action tendencies that are advantageous for our continued participation in everyday life.

After a highly distressing traumatic experience, a split can take place that results in a conflict between the part of the individual that is "stuck" reexperiencing the traumatic material and the part that seeks to avoid it in order to get on with daily life. The former is termed the "emotional part" of the personality (EP); the latter is known as the "apparently normal" part of the personality (ANP). The EP experience is characterized by vivid sensorimotor experiences and highly charged emotions; the ANP achieves its detached state by creating amnestic barriers that block traumatic material from interfering with everyday life. Van der Hart and colleagues (2006, pp. 6–8) conclude that trauma-related structural dissociation relates to a lack of unison and cooperation between the different systems that make up who the individual is. They outline three types of structural dissociation:

➤ Primary structural dissociation.

- Consists of a singular ANP and a singular EP.
- The ANP is the primary driver of the personality while the EP is unelaborated and limited.
- Associated with acute stress disorder and simpler forms of PTSD.

➤ Secondary Structural Dissociation

- Consists of a singular ANP, but lack of integration leads to more than one EP.
- EPs can act with more independence than in primary structural dissociation. Multiple defensive action systems can lead to different combinations of fight, flight, freeze, and total submission responses.
- Associated with complex PTSD, Disorders of Extreme Stress Not Otherwise Specified (DESNOS), and trauma-related borderline personality disorder.

➤ Tertiary Structural Dissociation

- Consists of multiple ANPs and multiple EPs.
- Occurs when triggers in daily life consistently reactivate trauma from the past through repetition and conditioning. The functioning of ANP is insufficient to manage the stresses and leads to the development of additional ANPs. In severe cases of secondary and all cases of tertiary dissociation, more than a single part may have a strong degree of elaboration (e.g., names, ages, genders, all kinds of preferences [the authors use this term to represent significant avoidances or avoidances], and *emancipation*.[27] In this case, there are multiple ANPs and multiple EPs.
- Associated with Dissociative Identity Disorder (DID).

---

[27] Janet's (1907) term that denotes "actual or perceived separation and autonomy from the influence of other dissociative parts" (p. 6).

Robin Shapiro's excellent Easy Ego-State Interventions: Strategies for Working with Parts (2016) makes a distinction between non-dissociated ego-states and dissociative parts that is very important to keep in mind when assessing the needs of trauma survivors. In this book, Shaipro discusses a conversation she had with Kathy Steele, one of the authors I have made reference to in this book for information about structural dissociation, in which they note that dissociative parts are more complex than ego-states in that dissociative parts will likely have their own sense of self, amnesiac barriers between parts, and even Schneiderian symptoms of schizophrenia. This is because, while ego-states "arise from job descriptions: the part of me that knows how to do therapy; the part of me that knows how to relate to cats; my nurturer; my aggressive competitor" (p. 35) and so forth. Dissociation arises from a person's reflexive attempt to deal with attachment ruptures or trauma by shifting into a separate neural gear disconnected from the core self. Dissociative "parts" are thus more strongly delineated because "survival was at stake when they arose" (p. 35).

Once again, it is up to the therapist to complete a proper assessment to determine which category, if either, the client falls into. There is no substitute for doing a thorough case history. If we fail to understand the client's unique configuration, we can cause serious harm. We will not be adequately prepared to help in case the client "switches."

Tread carefully. Seek additional training, consultation, or supervision from experienced clinicians when in doubt.

Understand that in the realm of trauma, clients can present anywhere on the spectrum described above.

Mental Levels, Substitute Actions, and Integration

The concept of *mental level* introduced in the late nineteenth century by one of the "fathers" of psychology, Pierre Janet, is still relevant to all three types of structural dissociation. Van der halt and colleagues (2006, p. 9) succinctly define this concept as "the ability to efficiently focus and use whatever mental energy is available in the moment" and point out that "being able to reach a high mental level is fundamental to one's capacity to integrate experiences."

When life is more challenging than a person can tolerate, their mental level suffers. We all have the need to connect with others and to self-soothe when difficulties happen. When we are at a low mental level, however, we lack adequate mental energy to restore balance and self-regulate. Self-harming, self-starving, or alternately binging and purging are ineffective and counterproductive ways of addressing our emotional needs when our mental level is under too much stress. They end up worsening the problem rather than resolving it. While intended to satisfy the needs of attachment or emotion regulation, they are maladaptive coping mechanisms that exacerbate distress and self-destructiveness as the survivor develops a greater reliance on them. They are *substitute actions*: "People not only fall back on substitute actions when they are unable to engage in higher order adaptive actions, but also when integration is not yet attainable" (Van der Halt et al., 2006, p. 10).

When we can't get our needs met, we may drink to excess, binge on food, or even self-mutilate as substitutes. These actions do not satisfy the need, of course, but they may be connected to feeling-states and prior mental associations that relate to feeling special or safe. Such actions can become compulsive behaviours associated to cues or obsessions in the external environment. They can also be internal thoughts or "vehement emotions" that keep us company when we are alone but then provoke negative self-attributions and may progress to suicidal ideation. In the moment, these actions can bring temporary relief, but if we continue to resort to them, we harm our health and overall well-being while further reducing the likelihood of getting our needs met in the future.

Finally, part of the goal of trauma treatment is to promote actions that lead to proper integration of the personality structure. In Van der Halt and colleagues' theory, integration relates to the assimilation of dissociative parts of the personality and the ability to reprocess traumatic memories in a way that allows the person to function at a higher level. Integration involves two elements:

- *synthesis,* through which we associate and distinguish between different interoceptive and exteroceptive events across time periods.
- *realization,* when we use mental actions that enable the ANP and EP to experience the present moment fully.

In trauma survivors, the ANP is phobic of EP because of the possibility of vehement, overwhelming emotions and other substitute actions that threaten the system's overall well-being. The EP also suffers intrinsically due to the experience of being stuck in the past moment of traumatization. Emotion regulation strategies that orient the system to the present moment and create distance from the past are essential to resolve and adaptively integrate the survivor's personality system.

Van der Hart and colleagues outline three treatment phases in the proper resolution of trauma. The first phase involves the stabilization and reduction of symptoms. Here the focus is on improving the client's mental level and promoting actions that enable participation in daily life activities. The second phase involves trauma treatment, with a focus on reducing the phobic response that the ANP and/or the different EPs hold toward traumatic memories. The third phase shifts to the integration of the personality and the promotion of realization. These goals involve ridding the client of the substitute actions that complicate their daily life and practicing coping mechanisms that require higher mental levels and greater mental efficiency.

The Skill of Resource Integration

It is likely that trauma survivors have not been able to properly assimilate traumatic material on their own. As the wheel metaphor (see Chapter 4) for the cycle of consolidation shows, negative beliefs about ourselves are linked to negative feelings in the body. This linkage forms the hub of the wheel. An endless array of possible triggers are linked to the hub through the spokes, connecting to our stored memories and our internal stressors (the tire). The external environment is the endless road that contacts the wheel and feeds into further consolidation of a distressful experience. In many cases, the cycle of consolidation propels us toward substitute actions that may provide temporary relief but at the cost of deepening the rupture of our self and continuing the re-enactment of trauma, thus preventing integration of our personality.

Actions that serve to improve our mental level are capable of changing the pattern of suffering. They can be actual activities, but they can also be imagined ones; the brain does not clearly distinguish between real or perceived events. This is our opportunity to generate "overturning information" that can function as sufficient disconfirming evidence to displace the pattern at the hub of the wheel. A major contributor to that goal is by developing and installing resources that enable integration. The use of our imagination is not to be downplayed. As Dana (2018) notes,

> remembering and imagining moments of reciprocity inhibits autonomic defense systems and activates the ventral vagal system [the part of the nervous system that promotes calmness and stability] and its move toward safety and connections . . . For clients who don't have a reliable social support network, [imagining moments of reciprocity] offer[s] a way to have an experience of connection when it is needed and when safe people are not available. (p. 48)

Our nervous systems can respond to our imagination, so there are ways of improving our mental level through visualization and experiential activities. Once adequate resources have been developed and installed, they can be further developed, cultivated, and summoned by the client at will to address the challenges of their everyday experience.

Careful preparation is essential before addressing traumatic material (Shapiro, 2018). In EMDR therapy, a number of different approaches ranging from listening to audio recordings, learning guided relaxation techniques such as visualizing calm or safe places, and healing light visualizations can be employed. Shapiro (2018) also emphasizes the use of resource development and installation (RDI) for clients who may have survived more complex forms of trauma. Andrew Leeds pioneered the protocol for RDI by combining previously established ego-strengthening approaches, especially hypnotherapy-related interventions, into his treatment model, which is also distinctive in its inclusion of bilateral stimulation; "the inclusion of the bilateral stimulation in the protocol appears to lead to spontaneous, rapid increases in affective intensity within an initially selected memory network and to rich, emotionally vivid associations to other functional (positive) memory networks" (Korn & Leeds, 2002, p. 1469). Within this protocol, bilateral stimulation is used to *deepen* the experiences that the client conjures up. In this way, it provides sufficient amplification of certain emotional states to satisfy the conditions for overturning information and thus to override the psychosomatic experience of the negative cognition. The resources that are recommended to be installed relate to positive affects, adaptive responses in others, experiences of mastery, and relational figures or figures that carry symbolic or metaphorical significance (Shapiro, 2018).

Although Shapiro (2018) describes the implementation of RDI, and Leeds (2016) explains its implementation quite thoroughly, the approach that I am proposing is different, although it plays a similar role. Resource integration can be used for an expanded range of issues. In keeping with the idea that how one feels about a problem links with the negative cognition that surrounds it, if a person nullifies the negative aspects and therefore feels differently about a problem, they gain access to adaptive beliefs about themselves. Using the cycle of consolidation metaphor, rather than trying to coax the client into steering out of the way of every possible pothole in a road filled with triggers and obstacles, the focus of my method is to change the relationship between the forces in the center of the hub. The solutions do not need to come from the therapist. Clients have unlimited stores of knowledge that they do not know about or believe they have access to until they try something different that leads them to take a new road altogether.

The Process of Installing the Resource

Resource Integration is meant to help clients rapidly change how they feel by tuning into their brain's adaptive memory and their own creative imagination. It is primarily used to challenge limiting beliefs as well as to solidify learnings after successful integration and overturning of the negative cognition formed from a prior traumatic event. In Rhythm and Processing Strategies, resource integration is used not only to reduce the value ascribed to the limiting belief or secondary gain issues (see Chapter 6) but also to install and consolidate learnings from the installation of positive beliefs after traumatic targets have been sufficiently desensitized. The three stages of resource integration proceed as follows.

Resource Setup

1. Identify the current life stressor.

2. Elicit three negative self-critical thoughts that the stressor engenders. Record them.

3. After these self-critical thoughts have been recorded, the therapist reads them aloud and asks, "What happens in the body when you say these words?"

4. Client describes the sensations.

5. Therapist asks where in the body or mind they experience the sensations

6. Client describes the physical location of the somatic experience.

7. Therapist then requests a subjective unit of disturbance (SUD) from the client based on the sensation.

8. Therapist asks, while putting up one hand, "If the experience of disturbance is represented by [physical description] in the [physical location] . . . then [therapist holds up other hand] . . . what would be the word, characteristic of yourself, symbol, or ancestor, that could help us to cope [therapist places one hand into the other] with this feeling?"

9. Client responds with an answer. The answer is recorded. This answer is the resource.

10. Therapist requests the client to think of a visual image that represents, for the client, the essence of this resource.

11. Client describes the image.

12. Therapist asks about the dominant color that represents the resource.

13. Therapist then asks for additional sensory information represented by the image.

14. The emotion experienced in that moment is then elicited.

15. The body location of the emotion is elicited.

This procedure allows the client to experience an inhibitory response to the initial complaint. In much the same way that mindful color breathing elicits the opposite experience, resource integration is meant to trigger a process of mutual exclusion such that the negative cognition or somatic complaint cannot be activated at the same time as the positive experience.

Resource Installation

1. The therapist instructs the client to hold in mind the positive image and feeling and to alternately tap using the butterfly hug (right hand taps the left shoulder while left hand taps the right shoulder).
2. Therapist models the action, setting the rhythm of tapping (approximately one second between each tap) while the client follows along.
3. Therapist and client complete seven pairs of alternating hand taps together.
4. Therapist instructs the client to take a deep breath. They breathe in and exhale together.
5. Therapist then asks, "What do you notice now?"
6. Client reports.
7. Therapist says, "notice that" or "go with that."

If the client has any negative experience during the installation, this will be due to using an inappropriate visual image or one that is weak. Clients should therefore be encouraged to make sure they select options that satisfy the conditions of being COM. Difficulty finding a proper focus image may require reinitiating steps 8 to 10 of the setup (identifying the overturning information, naming the applicable resource, conjuring up an appropriate visual image). It is not recommended to install imagery that could reinforce negative cognitions or is not capable of producing overturning information.

Integrating with the Resource

After several rounds in which the client reports positive affect, that is, feelings that contradict their previous experience, the therapist, after ascertaining that the client's body and mind are clear of any disturbance, asks, "What are the words of wisdom that come to your awareness?" The client then proceeds to give themselves verbal advice that contradicts their previous state of mind. The therapist responds with "Notice that." Additional rounds of bilateral tapping are then used to deepen the experience of the clients own capacities for self-regulation.

At this point, the client may exhibit signs of pleasure, yawning, or other indicators of parasympathetic nervous system-based relaxation. If the client continues to report positive experiences after another round, the therapist provides additional guidance by raising their right hand while saying, "If before, you were looking at the image as being separate from yourself. . ." and then raises the left hand while adding, "I would like for you now to become one with the image." The therapist now brings both hands together and says, "I would like for you to integrate with this resource in a way that is comfortable for you."

The therapist's input is intentionally vague here. This allows the client to discover for themselves the meaning of becoming "one" with a resource. If the therapist is too descriptive, they may inadvertently limit the client's own expectation of what is possible. The therapist then asks, "What was your experience that time?" If the integration has been successful, the client will often report feeling "empowered," "light," or "calm." In some cases, clients may need an extra attempt. In other cases, the integration is successful with only an additional repetition emphasizing the integrative power of their "infinite creativity." With sufficient encouragement, clients can find ways of experiencing their resource in this new way. The therapist should now inform the client that they have succeeded in integrating and installing the resource but must practice experiencing it. This will ensure that the client continues to challenge the pattern of the status quo. Responding to negative beliefs with a positive visual and kinesthetic prompting creates a pattern interrupt.

Fine Tuning the Resource

The therapist now proceeds to demonstrate a pattern interrupt by recalling the client's previous negative, self-critical thoughts and gauging the SUD (0-10 rating of discomfort) and the body location that is activated. In subsequent rounds, the client is asked to notice the negative feeling while "overlaying" it with the integrated imagery and experience. When both competing experiences are held in mind simultaneously, the positive affect and adaptive information tend to dominate, although this can take several rounds of the therapist tapping along with the client and inhaling and exhaling with them. The activity must be shared. The therapist is both a witness and participant in the client's healing process.

Once the SUD is reduced to a zero, the therapist activates the third phase of therapeutic reconsolidation by restating the self-critical thoughts (first recorded in step 2 of resource setup) and checking to see if these thoughts prompt any further disturbance. This process is repeated until a zero is achieved, at which point a prompt is made for the client once again to "overlay" the image while expressing gratitude to themselves. The process is continued until the negative self-critical statements (of the second step of resource setup) no longer bring about any somatic experience or measurement of disturbance. When there is no further negative report, it is likely that the client's perspective on the difficulty will also prove to have changed. For example, they may state that the negative critical thoughts are no longer "true," or that they are laughable or may have been "melodramatic." It will be helpful for the therapist to comment with "I know my handwriting is bad, but you did make these statements while we were setting this all up a few minutes ago, right?" This often elicits a laugh from the client.

Because the client feels different now, they behave differently when presented with their earlier negative cognitions. As stated earlier, what is most amazing is the evidence this provides that people's beliefs are intricately linked with how they feel about them. This is why it is possible—when we develop sufficient resources to support the client—not only to tip the scales of ambivalence but to address compulsive urges, paranoid delusions, eating disorders, and other concerns that are normally treatment-resistant. All substitute actions have a motivation, but they cannot be changed without a sufficient mental level. Resource integration takes just about 20 minutes or so. The client's experience in session that they have been able to change their mind within one clinical hour generates hope for the future. And the fact that they achieved this change by themselves, without the therapist dictating what they should see or what words of wisdom they should use, contributes powerfully to a greater level of self-efficacy and an increased level of trust in the relationship between all parts of the client's internal system.

Summary

Structural dissociation is an important concept to consider because it appears to explain the spectrum of responses to trauma. The impact of trauma leads to injuries not just at the level of the nervous system but also at the level of the individual's personality structure. The apparently normal part of the personality (ANP) is driven toward survival and perpetual avoidance of the traumatic reminders while the emotional part (EP) is frozen in time at the age of the original incident and susceptible to triggers and vehement, overwhelming emotions. Low mental levels lead to substitute actions meant to reduce pain but that often exacerbate it. For those with complex trauma, RDI is recommended before addressing traumatic memories. For all clients who fall on any part of the spectrum, resource integration not only increases mental level but can also resolve issues of ambivalence and address limiting beliefs in the possibility of change. The rhythm is set by the therapist as an active participant in the session, but the real expertise lies within the infinite creativity of the client. They may have the problem, but they also have the solution. Our job is just to elicit it.

CHAPTER 8

THE RHYTHM AND PROCESSING TECHNIQUE

Check the Technique

This chapter explains how to effectively and efficiently reprocess traumatic events using the insights and practices discussed in previous chapters, my own training, and my experience of a variety of approaches with the clinical populations I am most in contact with. My clinical experience is especially important. My work as an anti-racist psychotherapist in the multicultural environment of Montreal has enabled me to get feedback from people of all races and many different backgrounds, while my own identity and background as a Black Jamaican African Canadian has given me a unique interpretive perspective on their issues and problems. Over the years, I have further refined my approach by collaborating in person and online with American therapists on the other side of the border. This chapter outlines the techniques of the Rhythm and Processing approach I have developed from this combination of perspectives and experience.

Precursors to the RAP Technique

I start with a brief account of some of the interventions that may have informed the Rhythm and Processing approach. While EMDR therapy can be effective for treating PTSD, not all patients respond well, and some can be overwhelmed by the effects of confronting their traumatic past or integrating the dissociated emotional parts of the personality. Treatments need to take into account the risk of emotional flooding or dissociation that can occur with complex PTSD and extreme features of dissociative symptoms (Shapiro, 2018). Numerous interventions and alternative approaches have been used to address the challenges of dissociative parts and the overwhelming abreactive tendency to be caught in a cycle of reexperiencing past difficulties. An approach that has been especially helpful in my own practice is Flash Technique (FT).

The Flash Technique

Originally seen as an adjunct to EMDR therapy's preparation phase (before addressing traumatic memories), FT is now a standalone, evidenced-based approach used to quickly and safely reduce intense SUD levels. Its ability to address overwhelming traumatic experiences is theorized to come from taxing working memory, pendulation, and maintaining an orientation to the present moment. Hypothesized mechanisms of action for FT also appear to be related to memory reconsolidation, prediction errors, and updating memory at the source (Manfield et al., 2017).

Researchers have found that FT is at least as effective as EMDR therapy in its capacity to reduce the emotional intensity and vividness of aversive autobiographical memories (Brouwers et al., 2021). There are also some case reports indicating its suitability for working with highly dissociative clients, although more research is needed (Wong, 2019). Even with single instances of treatment, statistically significant gains appear possible with this approach. In one study of a single instance of FT with a group of 17 residents in psychiatry and psychology, the students demonstrated statistically significant differences—which held up after one week and at a follow-up a month later—in treating psychological trauma using FT (Yasar et al., 2019). During the COVID-19 pandemic, a study was conducted using a group protocol for FT with a large group of 175 healthcare providers. After only two short interventions, reductions in disturbance were noted immediately afterwards and a week later (Manfield et al., 2021).

Although Flash Technique is still under development, Manfield and colleagues list the following steps.

- ➤ Choose a disturbing memory
  - Selecting the target for the intervention.

- ➤ Selecting a positive and engaging focus (PEF)
  - Selecting a visualization that leads to a positive feeling.

- ➤ Initiating a distracting action
  - Alternately tapping on thighs while thinking and focus are kept on the PEF.

- ➤ Flash
  - Therapist prompts client to rapidly blink eyes three to five times.

➤ Check-in
- Verification to determine reduction of SUDs.

➤ Instructions during check-ins
- Clients are provided feedback and additional explanation to make adjustments if they have seen no reduction in SUDs.

➤ Feeder memories
- Determine if a more disturbing, earlier memory contributes to present distress.

➤ If using FT within standard EMDR
- Depending on the phase of EMDR treatment, return to the appropriate phase.

Although this version of FT has been very helpful in my work with eating-disordered clients as well as clients across the dissociative spectrum, there have been some obstacles. Some clients are unable to think of a positive engaging focus. This can happen when a client is too overwhelmed to be able to return to a baseline where they can access adaptive information. There are work-arounds in development for this problem, but there have been instances in my practice where FT was unable to address the needs of clients suffering mainly from secondary and tertiary levels of structural dissociation.

Zimmerman's Four Blinks Approach

The next advance in trauma treatment, the Four Blinks version of FT, is based on Thomas Zimmerman's method. It is an "open-source" approach unlike anything I have previously seen in our field. Zimmerman's website[28] explains why it was created as an alternative to standard FT. Because Manfield's version of FT is still in development, there are different hypotheses for why it is effective. Zimmerman's approach avoids these

---

[28] https://fourblinks.com/2022/05/21/what-is-different-about-the-four-blinks-version-of-flash/

uncertainties by focusing on an approach that augments the use of memory reconsolidation. In his Four Blinks method, bilateral stimulation, deep breathing, and client self-distractions are no longer needed.

Zimmerman stipulates six steps.[29]

> ➢ Step 1: Develop a "container"
>
>   - The client uses a visualized imaginary container capable of holding intense traumatic material or dysfunctional affect. This step is helpful for sequestering high levels of disturbance.
>
> ➢ Step 2: Develop a calm scene
>
>   - The client is asked to imagine a scene that allows them to feel calmness or other positive states of mind (happiness, pride, joy, etc.). This can be a visualization by the client or anything else in their immediate vicinity (including music, videos, scenes of nature, pets, etc.).
>
> ➢ Step 3: Identify the memory that holds a disturbance
>
>   - Place this memory in the container.
>
> ➢ Step 4: Activate the calm scene while guiding the client to blink
>
>   - By looking at the calm scene while blinking, the client registers a multitude of disconfirming experiences.
>
> ➢ Step 5: Gently activate the memory and use the container once more
>
>   - Return to step 4 and repeat using specific methods to manage resistant disturbance ratings (including use of "vacuum cleaner" visualization) and managing flashbacks.
>
> ➢ Step 6: "Walk through the memory" and manage any residual disturbances.

---

[29] https://www.youtube.com/watch?v=CaKzTbU3h2U

On his website, Zimmerman provides links to all of the information needed for the Four Blinks version of FT. Everything on the site is "public domain," and Zimmerman has been training people for several months without asking for any remuneration. As he explains:

> We have remarkably few ways for people to reliably, safely, and rapidly heal. We don't have time to ration healing pathways that have been with us for as long as we have been human. This pathway exists. It is in your genes. It is redundantly twisted into every cell. The fact that it has taken us this long to discover it has more to say about our cultural blindness to trauma than the simplicity of this approach. If you are already a trauma focused therapist, I don't have to explain this to you. If this is a way that humans can heal from the longest and most pervasive public health crisis in the history of humanity, nobody owns that. We should be teaching this to our parents and we should be teaching this to our children.[30]

Part of the reason that further refinements of Flash Technique became necessary was the inability of some clients to self-soothe effectively or attain levels of zero disturbance. Perhaps because Four Blinks is designed to be as efficient as possible and relies on memory reconsolidation in its purest form, these problems no longer occur either when using Zimmerman's original method or my derived approach of Rhythm and Processing. The Rhythm and Processing technique makes extensive use of technology because it is intended to be used as a virtual form of therapy in conjunction with any other approach. As I am primarily an EMDR therapist, I have found that it lends itself most easily to that modality, but any other approach that uses therapeutic reconsolidation or experiential interventions in session can be adapted to work well with it.

The Setup: RAP Initialization

The therapist first asks the client to explain the target (their specific point of concern or general life stressor) if they feel that they can. Some

---

[30] https://fourblinks.com/2022/05/21/what-is-different-about-the-four-blinks-version-of-flash/

clients may be reluctant to share this information (due to client transference, shame, fear of being "judged," or perceived lack of understanding from the therapist). However, it is not necessary to elicit the details of the problem. It is sufficient at this stage simply to identify the problem so as to establish a "pointer" to its location (its memory address). After establishing the memory address, the therapist elicits an SUD (subjective unit of disturbance) from the client. The client is then instructed to rate the severity of the SUD on a scale of zero to ten. This provides a baseline measurement while also allowing the intensity of the problem to become malleable. Some clients have difficulty coming up with a number. The therapist should encourage them by explaining that the number should be thought of as a metaphor and does not need to be carved in stone. One person's three is another's six. Still, knowing that the problem is rated as a five as a specific number enable both client and therapist to gauge whether subsequent interventions yield an increase or decrease, an alleviation of suffering or an increase in distress, or if they change nothing at all.

After this subjective measurement has been elicited, the therapist shares on their screen (using video conferencing software, or if in person, a laptop or PC monitor) a script that explains the RAP procedure and an explanation of the concept of SUD along the following lines:

> **Therapist:** So you are at a six. We know that when people are feeling a zero this is usually when they feel completely calm. As the number goes up, some people might feel higher levels of disturbance, so at one or two the stress is not as much as when you're at a seven, eight, nine, or a ten. As the number increases, we also experience stronger somatic sensations, feelings in the body, like a tightness in the chest or stomach as well as a whole bunch of thoughts and negative thought loops, right? For these reasons, the first part of this technique involves *containing* all of that.

The first page on the screen shows an image that explains the concept of the container. The client is instructed to visualize a container that is robust, large, and strong enough to contain and seal any traumatic material.

The therapist verifies with the client that the container is good enough and notes that it can be placed as far away as the client would like it to be—down the street, at the bottom of the ocean, or even on another planet. The client is encouraged to keep things simple though. Clients are advised to streamline the process so it feels like simply inserting an object into a box and sealing it rather than needing a complex padlock system with digital combinations and secure security access levels.

Before scrolling to the next page, the therapist introduces the client to the concept of "vacuuming." The interaction at this point might typically go like this:

Therapist:	So we know that sometimes when we put things away there can be remnants of it, like a remaining somatic experience or an echo of the thoughts or stress. That's why in addition to the container, we want to make sure we can also visualize an industrial strength vacuum cleaner.

[Therapist scrolls to the following page, which shows a large commercial vacuum cleaner.]

Client:	[laughs]
Therapist:	Yeah, we want to make sure we vacuum up every last bit of the problem. From the floors to the drapes to the ceiling. Then we put all of that into the container. And look, I'm not talking about no Walmart vacuum cleaner, I want you to upgrade that. At least get a Dyson brand. You can feel free to upgrade your vacuum and container anytime you feel like it. But first, wanna try it?
Client:	Yeah.

With their eyes open or closed, the client attempts to vacuum up the problem and place it into the container of their choice. The process may take only ten seconds for some or up to 45 seconds or a minute for others. What is important is to verify that they are able to achieve the feat successfully. When they have finished, the therapist asks, "How did that go?" Some clients may be surprised that they have been able to do it. This may be partly because they have been asked to do an unusual procedure that was unexpected. Some clients may have difficulty. The therapist gauges this and addresses specific concerns to troubleshoot the difficulty and help the client achieve this small victory.

Once the client is satisfied that the vacuuming is complete, the therapist moves on to the next page. This shows an image of a beach and a campsite.

Therapist:	The next step will help us to heal whatever you just put in that container. We need a COM image. COM stands for "calm or motivating." But it can also be soothing, exciting, or awesome. One important thing though. If the trauma happened at a beach, we are not going to use a beach. If the trauma happened at a campsite, we're not going to a campsite. We have many other options for things that provide disconfirming knowledge and overturning information. It could be an image of you chilling with friends, a piece of furniture in your home that looks comfortable, or even you looking outside at the clouds or the stars . . . anything in nature.
Client:	[Looking to their upper right and then upper left, accessing an imagined state or attempting memory retrieval].
Therapist:	Yes, but hold on one sec, we will get to that. The important thing is that when you are looking at the COM scene, you need to inform me if there is ever any negative feeling whatsoever. Interrupt me if you don't feel good. I want to make sure you can fully associate good feelings with this good image.
Client:	Oh, OK.

With that proviso, the therapist moves onto the next page. This shows a meme of a person blinking their eyes. The therapist provides context for the image.

Therapist:	So next is how we activate the COM image. When I say the word RAP you will blink quickly three to five times. The word doesn't really matter though. I can say FLASH or BLINK or anything else. Is there a specific word that would work best for you?
Client:	[laughs] No, any word is OK, I think.
Therapist:	OK, great, so we will go with RAP as the word. When I say this word, you will blink about four times. Also, if you were to be focusing on a COM image which would help you to focus better, if I were to count like 1 . . . 2 . . . 3 . . . .4 . . . RAP, or if I were to wait about four to five seconds in silence and then say RAP. Which would you prefer?
Client:	Any is fine.
Therapist:	OK so we will go with counting out loud.

The final part of this setup involves choosing the image. The next page is now pulled up showing an image of a beach with several URLs listed below it.

Therapist:	So, because this is the future and we have the power of the internet on our side, you will not need to imagine the image only in your mind. We can share it together. With your headphones and screen, even if we can't go to nature, we can bring nature to us. Here you will see a list of different videos that others have used. We've got beaches, forests, waterfalls, we even have Japanese *onsen* (hot spring baths), and cat videos. Let me know if you would like to choose any of these client favorites or if there is any other awesome video on YouTube you would like to use.

When the client chooses a video, the setup phase is complete. The target has been identified, the vacuum/container combination established, and the positive focus selected. All the necessary conditions are now in place to process the difficult experience.

The Process: Using the RAP Technique

After the setup has been completed, all of the necessary variables are now initialized, and it becomes possible to commence the RAP procedure itself. With practice and guidance, the client's identified problems can achieve an SUD rating of zero in anywhere from 20 to 40 minutes. To clarify the underlying logical structure of the process, I will list the steps like a coding sequence starting with what I call the GeneralScan (see Appendix II, page 229).

Initiate GeneralScan

> Step 0: Therapist shares screen showing video or music streaming site (YouTube, Vimeo, Spotify, etc.) and invites client to choose a video or song that that will allow them to feel COM (Calm or Motivated). Therapist can give suggestions, but the client must choose.

> Step 1: Therapist asks client to select a problem to address.

> Step 2: Therapist elicits an SUD from client.

> Step 3: Client utilizes vacuum/container to remove the disturbance

> Step 4: Initiation of **RAP technique**: Therapist instructs client to attend to the positive focus (plays selected content on shared screen) and repeats the following pattern:

1...2...3...4...RAP [client blinks rapidly]

1...2...3...4...5...RAP [client blinks rapidly]

1...2...3...4...RAP [client blinks rapidly]

1...2...3...4...5...RAP [client blinks rapidly].

> Step 5: Therapist asks if client was able to remain calm or feel centered in the present moment (or within window of affect tolerance) while watching and listening to the online content.

If yes: Proceed to step 6

Otherwise: Assure client that there are other options, for example, "upgrading" their vacuum, improving the container, or selecting another video. Present the options until the client reports satisfaction with their choices. Then repeat from step 2.

➤ Step 6: Therapist asks client to "lightly check in" with the target to determine if there is any remaining disturbance (without actively eliciting an SUD, just getting a general sense of whether the target has been completed or not).

If there is any remaining disturbance then

Return to step 3

If there is no longer any detectable disturbance then

Initiate DeepScan

Initiate DeepScan

This is a deeper form of treatment than the GeneralScan. The GeneralScan is intended to take the edge off of the stress at the surface level, but a DeepScan targets the dysfunctional memory information that prevents proper integration and that fuels much of the negative cognition and somatic discomfort (see Appendix II, page 230).

➤ Step 7: Therapist asks client to imagine that the problem has a beginning and an end like a movie, then asks them to scan through every unique scene in the imagined movie to check whether there is any remaining disturbance when they imagine the target.

➤ Step 8: Client scans memory for any remaining disturbance.

If there is any remaining disturbance then

Begin the following loop:

- Therapist elicits SUD for this specific part of the target
- Client vacuums any residual disturbance and reinitiates **RAP technique**

- Therapist verifies the client is calm, present, and within window of affect tolerance
- Reevaluate SUD (on scale of 0 to 10)

If SUD is greater than 0 (meaning there is still some remaining distress for this specific scene)

Reinitiate loop starting at vacuuming the residual disturbance and continuing from there

Otherwise, if SUD=0 (meaning there is no longer any remaining distress for this specific scene)

Exit loop and return to the beginning of Step 8 (to verify if there are any other remaining scenes that cause discomfort)

If there is no longer any remaining disturbance in any specific scene then:

Verify it. Scan through the whole target and re-evaluate the SUD once more when client revisits the whole target.

If SUD is greater than 0

There is still a remaining scene or disturbing aspect concerning the target; scan for it once more.

Reinitiate Step 8

Otherwise, if SUD =0

There is no remaining disturbance in any part of the target; exit the program.

Exit DeepScan program

➤ RAP technique has been completed.

Deepening the Experience

Butterfly hugs are used at different points in the intervention because bilateral stimulation has a way of linking to adaptive memory networks

(Shapiro, 2018). Moreover, it can also assist clients in linking to multiple interrelated targets and reprocessing them simultaneously.

People are capable of focusing on multiple things at the same time. For example, when a client walks into the office and rates an SUD at eight, this is likely because they are overwhelmed by the body sensation of stress, the negative cognition, problems in their relationships, their body image issues, and so on. The subjective unit of disturbance represents an accumulation of parallel processes that the individual is focusing on at a given moment. The utility of RAP (and related approaches that utilize memory reconsolidation) is that we will not always need to pull apart and distill every unique element of distress through endless questions and discussions.

The brain is complex enough to hold multiple streams of data in working memory. RAP makes use of this multitasking capacity more than other techniques, and therefore, it can achieve a zero in a much shorter time. All people can recover using this modality that, to the surprise of many, results in fewer experiences of abreaction, less ambivalence about trauma reprocessing, and more joy. Who would have thought that people could recover from racial trauma while looking at videos of underwater sea turtles? The brain is capable of marvelous things, but we have to be willing to think outside the box.

Summary

This chapter has explained the working mechanisms of Rhythm and Processing Strategies. While EMDR therapy and other modalities can be highly effective for resolving stresses linked to PTSD and other mental health concerns, they require adaptations to address the difficulties of clients who struggle with higher levels of structural dissociation and more complex sequalae. Flash Technique was meant to address this gap and has been fairly successful at doing so. Four Blinks builds upon Flash while placing a greater emphasis on memory reconsolidation. Rhythm and Processing is a derivative of the Four Blinks technique that emphasizes the use of technology while incorporating bilateral stimulation at key moments. By moving from a general scan to a deeper scan, and then incorporating bilateral stimulation into this rapid and effective process, we increase the chance of generalizing the positive gains from reprocessing trauma to more than just the target memory. The benefit of reconsolidating memories with this method is then hypothesized to a greater number of other related memories and events. By using the RAP technique and its associated strategies, we safely and efficiently reduce the experience of distress in people and provide hope and confidence in ways that feel natural, joyful, and empowering.

CHAPTER 9

POLYVAGAL THEORY AND LEGACIES THROUGH GENOGRAMS

Our Interdependent Existence

Peaple are wired for connection. As children, we cannot survive without the care of others, and to develop into functional adults, the kind of caregiving we receive matters deeply. Our caregivers and home environment don't need to be perfect, but they must provide sufficient emotional support to enable us to cope with life outside the home. When we are sufficiently resourced, external stresses are less likely to exceed what we can manage or jeopardize our survival. When people talk about trauma, they often focus on a person's individual circumstances rather than their environment and their collective social identity. In this chapter, I emphasize what is around the client more than just what is in them. This reflects both the social context and family systems core of anti-racist psychotherapy (ARP).

The Social Context's Harm to Indigenous People

Let us first consider our precious Indigenous brothers and sisters who have been impacted by the insecurity of whiteness. The peoples who have been attacked in the past by the scourge of colonization continue to bear the scars in the present. As just one example, in Australia, New Zealand, Canada, and the United States, the members of Indigenous communities have a disproportionate involvement with child-protective services compared to other races or ethnicities. These settler countries have both higher rates of investigation of child mistreatment and higher rates of Indigenous children being placed in out-of-home care (McKenzie et al., 2016).

The oppression did not begin just in this past decade. The original treaties between the Indigenous peoples and the colonizers in my own country, Canada, were not intended to make peace, as until recently our children were taught at school, but to justify seizing the lands of Indigenous people. At the same time, the Indigenous nations were subjected to systematic cultural genocide through the now notorious residential schools system; a collaboration between church and state, two of the largest and most powerful institutions in the country, with the official goal to "kill the Indian in the child."31 The plan was announced in the House of Commons in 1883 by then Public Works Minister Hector Langevin, who said: "In order to educate the children properly we must separate them from their families. Some may say that this is hard, but if we want to civilize them we must do that."32

The racist myth of the "white man's burden," nowadays more accurately known as the white saviour complex, lies behind residential schools and uncountable other atrocities throughout the Western world as well as in Africa and Asia. It has come to light only recently that not only did the authorities who monitored and administered the schools participate in rampant physical, emotional, and sexual abuse of minors, they also killed many hundreds of Indigenous children. A national shame has been placed upon Canada due to the discovery of thousands of unmarked graves of Indigenous children sent to these schools. In May 2021, the hashtag #215children went viral. By August of 2021, more than 5,000 children had been found in these graves. This number will most likely rise, as we have only started to be aware that similar atrocities have been taking place in the United States, which for some reason has not been getting as much attention.

Indigenous communities throughout the world continue to contend with government policies that practically mandate poverty and isolation and prevent participation in the rest of society. Some of them are more subtle than others. My province, for example, regulates who can practice certain professions, including psychotherapy. The intention is good—to protect the public—but the policy is in force for professions that require graduation from programmes that Black and Indigenous students already face numerous barriers entering or succeeding in. This reduces the number of eligible graduates from these groups being empowered to serve their respective communities in many vitally important professions. The impact of this places too much reliance on Quebec's white health professionals and psychotherapists rather than on our own professionals. To make matters worse, our universities are almost all located in the southernmost part of the province, neglecting the higher-education needs of people in the North,

---

31 https://ottawacitizen.com/news/politics/simply-a-savage-how-the-residential-schools-came-to-be
32 Ibid.

where most of Quebec's Indigenous people live. These are subtle yet effective ways in which structural racism prevents access and maintains the status quo.

When we discuss substance abuse, suicide, and lack of access to clean water in Indigenous communities, the social structure benefits from victim blaming rather than addressing the structural problems fuel these crises. Much as we should focus not only on the symptoms but address the cause, in my time as an addictions counsellor, I found that my clients usually grew up in an environment of systemic discrimination, whether based on ethnicity, income, "race," or some combination of these factors. As I learned more about their forebears, I met individuals whose parents had survived the horrible conditions of residential schools or who were survivors of these schools themselves, whose ancestors had been sexually molested, viciously beaten, and hesitant even to teach their children their Indigenous language due to fears that speaking it would result in beatings or other abuse by nuns and priests.

Trapped in patterns of institutionalized violence and betrayal, and prevented from constructively channelling or recovering from suffering, they developed maladaptive behaviours that were passed down from generation to generation. A combination of nature and nurture, vulnerabilities to mental health stressors, and witnessing or experiencing violence in close-knit communities, together with parental role models who struggled with emotion regulation (because they were in the same situation) has been the perfect recipe for hopelessness and social defeat. All of this occurs while the insecure power structure of whiteness, with its goal of Indigenous eradication, avoided scrutiny. The government and the churches buried any link to their atrocities underneath these schools—which in reality operated more as death camps—and behind the treaties they imposed to steal the lands of the original peoples. The binary complex trauma cycle of dissociation from blame while directing shame and hardship toward the oppressed returns once again. All of this suffering lives on unconsciously in the mind of the substance abuser, initiated by the multigenerational transmission of victimization due to colonization and state-sanctioned violence.

A Brief Summary of Polyvagal Theory

Polyvagal theory, pioneered by Stephen Porges at the University of Illinois Brain-Body Center in the 1990s, explains many of the intergenerational effects of the kinds of trauma we have been discussing. Although it was not originally designed to be used as a psychotherapeutic resource, it contains some essential learnings relevant to Rhythm and Processing Strategies and addressing racial trauma events. The complex-trauma consultant, Deb Dana, at the Kinsey Institute provides a helpful, simplified explanation of polyvagal theory and the ways in which its concepts can be incorporated into clinical practice in her most recent book on the subject (Dana, 2018). Her account of what she terms the three organizing principals of polyvagal theory can be summarized as follows.

Hierarchy

The autonomic nervous system reacts to the environment through three different pathways: the sympathetic branch of the nervous system (responsible for fight-or-flight responses); the dorsal vagus (part of the parasympathetic branch of the nervous system responsible for immobilization responses); and the ventral vagus pathway (also initiated by the parasympathetic nervous system, responsible for safety and social engagement). In our evolutionary timeline, they are, from oldest to newest: the dorsal vagal pathway (immobilization in response to mortal threats to existence); the sympathetic nervous system (mobilization to respond to acute threats to safety); and the ventral vagal pathway (social engagement to respond and engage with safety and security). The first responds to threats to existence, the second to danger through mobilization, and the third to seeking safety through engagement with social systems.

Neuroception

Porges defines *neuroception* (a term he coined) as the ways through which the nervous system identifies stimuli as either safe or threatening. This occurs at a threshold below our conscious awareness.

Coregulation

This final key concept in polyvagal theory refers to our capacity to alleviate and manage troubling or painful feelings. As Dana (p. 4) explains, it is "a need that must be met to sustain life. It is through reciprocal regulation of our autonomic states that we feel safe to move into connection and create trusting relationships." The capacity for coregulation should be developed in childhood through positive bonding with parents and other caregivers.

The Ladder Metaphor of Polyvagal Theory

Dana uses the metaphor of a ladder to illustrate how the autonomic nervous system responds to external stimuli (2018, pp. 10–12). When we are in the present moment, we are the top of the ladder and feel connected to our environment and the people in it. Physiologically, we experience the feeling of safety that this gives us a well-regulated heart rate, normal blood pressure, and a relaxed, comfortable breathing rhythm. In this state, our immune system functions properly and our health is optimal. This is when the ventral vagal part of the parasympathetic nervous system is most active.

The halfway point on the ladder represents our state when we detect threats, sense that the environment is dangerous or unsafe, and prepare to either flee (if the threat can be escaped) or fight (if it cannot). We will feel adrenaline rushing through our bodies as our heart pounds and our breath becomes shallow. In this state, we will have difficulty focusing and may experience cardiovascular problems, chronic pain, panic attacks, or a weakened immune system. These responses occur because of the sympathetic branch of the nervous system.

The lowest step on the ladder represents a situation in which the threat exceeds our capacity to fight or flee. The system now responds with an "emergency brake" reaction, shutting down and dissociating from the present moment. In our bodies, we experience feelings of derealization, depersonalization, and a deep sense of emptiness. A lack of energy, problems with memory recall, and a mental "fog" seem to envelop our daily life. This state can lead to fibromyalgia, increased weight, a high risk of diabetes, and low blood pressure. In this state, we experience the dorsal vagal part of the parasympathetic nervous system.

The Need to Connect

When we engage the ventral vagal part of our nervous system (the top rungs of the ladder), we are engaging the part of us that can soothe and be soothed by others. In this state, we feel connection to our environment and to others. As Dana (2018, p. 27) explains,

> when clients are in a ventral vagal state of regulation, there is a feeling of connection in the room. The session has a rhythm. Even though the work may be difficult, there is a sense of groundedness. Ventral vagal energy brings curiosity and a willingness to experiment.

When clients feel safe in the session, they are more willing to explore their feelings, thoughts, beliefs, and experiences. The session has a flow, a rhythm, a balance. Many of us will have experienced this level of comfort in our close and loving relationships.

The ventral vagus also has pathways that connect to the face and head. When the client is engaged at this level, not only do they search for cues that are safe for connection, they also express warmth outwards. The client's vocal tone and facial expressions convey an openness to friendship. We see a relaxation in the face and may hear laughter. The client welcomes novel experiences. In this state, there is an opportunity to mobilize one very important way of regulating the nervous system: reciprocity. When the ventral vagal pathway is active, people will non-verbally broadcast safety and become more open to welcoming others as well. These connections evolved to help us recognize when people should be trusted and when we can feel safe to connect with others. The use of visualizing resources is important (see chapter 7 for a detailed discussion of resources). Imagining and visualizing safety also creates physiological changes in the body and nervous system.

All people come pre-equipped with the ability for individual emotion regulation and mutual, interpersonal coregulation. Reciprocity is hardwired into our nervous system as a fail-safe that allows us to experience safety. Interestingly, as clients gain trust in the process and complete their trauma targets, they may demonstrate a greater tendency to laugh, develop more spontaneous or improvised self-regulation strategies, and report a deeper experience of emotional intimacy and trust. Based on the types of questions we ask—and our position and frame as a therapist—we can then help clients to experience trust and reciprocity despite a hostile social and political environment or a difficult family background.

Tracing Our Roots: Using the Genogram

Some of the most stable patterns in our experience are triangular. The triangle we are concerned with in this chapter is the basic family unit of parents and child. The survivor of trauma often experiences a feeling of separateness. While it is important to restore integration both in their personality and their connection to others, the therapist who seeks insight into racial trauma must also accompany the client in reconstructing the building blocks of their past. In many instances, their family system was one of the primary places of injury. In others, key family members may be absent. Constructing a genogram allows for a subjective understanding of one's origin. From the perspective of the client, the presence and absence of family members helps reveal which resources may be lacking and also which ones need reinforcement.

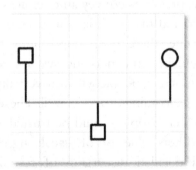

Genogram: The father is located at the top left, the mother at the top right, and the son at the center below. The lines show the biological connections. In this case, the son has two biological parents.[33]

---

[33] If some of your clients, like many of mine, have diverse gender identities, be sure whatever software you use allows for more than just the gender binary of square and circle shown in this chapter.

Although the use of genograms was first popularized by systems theorists such as the family therapists Monica McGoldrick and Randy Gerson in the 1980s, the creator of the device was the psychiatrist Murray Bowen in the 1950s (Stagoll & Lang, 1980). Bowen was one of the first to develop a systems theory of the family. In the process, he brought several major theoretical concepts to the practice of family therapy, including triangles, differentiation of self, emotional cut-off, and the multigenerational transmission process, to name a few. However, because my main focus here is not an in-depth analysis of what the client presents with (as the construction and completion of a genogram can easily take several sessions), the rest of this section will only provide a rudimentary account of the basic requirements to create a genogram.

The genogram is more than just a family tree. It enables the client and therapist to see the dynamics of interactions in the client's primary family system and, in particular, to gain an idea of "what happened" to the client. This reduces the chance of conveying a pathologizing perspective and creates a systems-based focus rather than cultivating individual blame. In short, the genogram helps to clarify *why* the client presents in therapy. A genogram will often require different labels and legends to assist both the client and therapist to keep track of the various relational dynamics, as it can get very busy very fast when we are listing all the family members that have impacted the client in some way. The genogram shown below illustrates some of the concepts that inform its use in therapy.

Genogram Considerations and Suggestions

To create genograms, I primarily use the program GenoPro, and I screen share the process using video conferencing software like Google Meet. I share with the client because they appreciate the visual representation and the co-construction of the process. It also permits the client to be the expert. The therapist follows directions, building the sequence as determined by the client's retelling of their story. I start with creating the client first, then get names, genders, and ages of all other immediate members of the family. I ask the client whether they have any siblings, whether they are currently in a relationship, and whether there have been any early pregnancy losses or abortions that they experienced or that preceded or followed their own births. Then I move to the level of the parents, starting with the paternal grandparental system, then the maternal grandparental system.[34]

Next, I ask about the culture or racial background of the grandparents, and elicit three details about each member of the family. The question is intentionally vague, but if the client requires additional instruction, I add that we are looking for any details that seem most salient to the client about that person, or even three random things that come to the client's mind in relation the person. Finally I ask, how the client would describe the relationship between the various members of a given subsystem. This leads us to generate lines connecting each individual.

Interpreting the Genogram

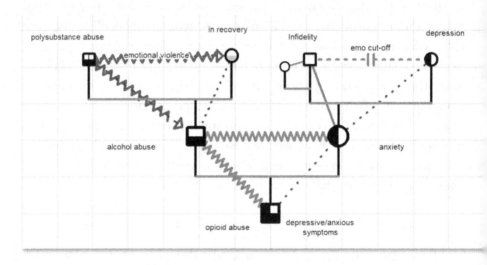

Sample of genogram with relational lines. Typically, there will be much more text and many more relational lines to represent the complex interactions between siblings, cousins, or other family members of interest.

---

[34] Here, I use the terms systems in a general way. The maternal grandparental system may be composed of the mother's biological parents, but it could also include people who stepped in to fill absences. Some people were raised by aunties, uncles, or caregivers who were unrelated, such as fictive kin or adoptive parents. Every family is unique and as complex as the individuals who come from them.

Let's start interpreting the shapes of the genogram. In this figure, the client is the square at the bottom. The shading on the client's square represents the presence of substance abuse (opioid abuse in this case) and the mental health issues (depressive/anxious symptoms.). As we move upward, we see that the square on the left above (the client's father) is half shaded in (horizontally). This represents the father's present experience with substance abuse (in his case, alcohol abuse). To the right, the client's mother is represented by a circle that is half shaded in (vertically). Vertical shading represents a mental health concern (in this case, anxiety). At the level of grandparents at the top of the illustration (from left to right), we see similar patterns relating to either polysubstance abuse, being in recovery from substance abuse, (perceived) absence of either substance abuse or mental health issues, and the presence of a mental health concern on its own.

Just this information on its own can help reveal why the client may have experienced some form of multigenerational transmission of mental health concerns. But names and disorders alone are insufficient. Often, what tells an even fuller story are the connections between individuals. Starting from the paternal grandfather (top left), the blue lines that point to the paternal grandmother and the client's father represent emotional violence. The paternal grandmother's dotted line connecting to the client's father represents the poor or distant relationship established between that parent and child. Some of these connections may help to explain the rigid conflictual lines that run between the client's father and mother as well as between the father and the client.

In the maternal grandparents' system, there was infidelity and emotional cut-off (a complete lack of communication) between the grandparents. Lines representing a distant relationship connect through to the maternal grandmother, the client's mother, and the client himself. The only positive (green) lines appear to be between the maternal grandfather and his new partner and between the client's mother and her father. A therapist can draw numerous inferences and clinical case theories from seeing this unconventional setup. However, it is what the client believes about a connection that is more important.

Typically, the information I ask a client about on a genogram concerns the relationships between grandparents and between grandparents and parents. These relationships offer an understanding of gender roles in some cases as well as power dynamics, boundaries (whether respected or not), and the role that violence has played in the family. In some cases, asking about topics such as these concerning people who are "around" the therapy session but not "in" it can produce insights into the client's understanding of their own family and their beliefs about their own relationships. Sometimes, clients will completely reject what came before them. At other times, they may be surprised to see that they have been unconsciously repeating the past.

The therapist should feel free to ask more questions about cultural formation, migration routes, traditions, myths, or rules of communication in addition to the relational lines. The caveat is that we only need to know a certain amount of information (but not everything) about the family's unique configuration before moving on to the immediate family of origin. Being concise is key here because most clients who have identity-based trauma may have very complex and extended family systems. What I am most concerned with is the client's relationship (or lack of relationship) with their immediate caregivers (whether biological parents, parental substitutes, or non-biological caregivers who helped to raise the client, etc.) as well as how and to what extent these relationships have changed over time. Only when we have finished building the shapes (client, parents, and grandparents), family characteristics (three things about each person), and relationship lines (conflictual, distant, emotionally cut-off, etc.) will I then ask whether there were ever any mental health disorders (professionally diagnosed or in the client's own estimation), substance abuse issues, or cases of physical, emotional, or sexual abuse between members of the overall family system. Talking about such issues can distress the client but can also help to explain what may have affected the formation of the client's schema on a multitude of different concerns.

Because these questions can elicit intense feelings, it is the responsibility of the therapist to practice emotion regulation strategies with the client *before* attempting to construct a genogram. Even in the absence of such questions, we are likely to stir up preconscious or unconscious traumatic experiences that some clients have gone to considerable lengths to forget. Even asking about early pregnancy losses or abortions runs the risk of the client reexperiencing the trauma of the medical procedure or the shame from her family. The therapist must be ready to stop sharing their screen and utilize the full range of skills discussed in this book, especially those of RAP, in order to reduce the discomfort as rapidly as possible. As a bonus, when the client finds that they can use RAP (or another resource) to reduce their discomfort surprisingly quickly, we are building confidence that our therapy really can help to manage difficult emotions, thoughts, or beliefs. This discovery provides more overturning information in the form of physical and emotional reassurance that contrasts with the expectation of discomfort. This creates hope for change.

Anti-Racist Psychotherapy Recommendations

My anti-racist psychotherapy-based recommendations for the use of the genogram definitely include questions about culture and race, especially if the client does not explicitly state where their grandparents came from. In some family systems, unions between French and German families, for example, or between East Indian and West Indian families, can be controversial. The therapist understands that even in the context of same-race relationships, every relationship is intercultural whether by virtue of one member being socialized as a male and the other as female or even by a family of origin's opinions about sexuality, gender, or relationship roles. Because every upbringing is different, every identity is different. Hence, culture is an inherently dynamic concept.

There are three further recommendations that I consider very important to follow when using the genogram.

Help the client to know they are not their problem.

The genogram is a visual representation of the client's family system, but it is also a glimpse into a history of family events and interactions. The multigenerational transmission of trauma suggests that certain patterns can return through generations, perhaps not as explicit duplicates but certainly as echoes; a pattern may not reproduce itself identically but in another form. Thus, parents of alcoholics are not always alcoholics themselves, but they may have had difficulties with emotion regulation or engaged in other substitute actions to cope with undesirable emotional parts (see Chapter 7). In West Indian families, we sometimes see the absence of father figures or even multiple female partners for some men. Reasons for paternal absences may vary though; in some cases, the absent father also cannot manage the financial responsibilities due to the crushing blows of widespread poverty or systemic barriers to wealth. In any case, the family system suffers, and members of the community (grandparents, aunties, uncles) mobilize to fill in the gaps caused by the insecure power structures.

Additionally, because issues of racism and patriarchy are linked, by returning far enough into the past, we will see that white enslavers often stole family members, creating voids in family systems, and viciously raped vulnerable Black women and girls to terrorize our enslaved ancestors and produce more victims for selfish gain. Some people identify with the oppressor due to their own trauma histories and continue harming their own people through time. Once again, the traumatic patterns that exist today are not always replications, but they follow a similar rhythm to what our ancestors experienced.

We are all a series of things we have survived.

Even if the client already knows this, it can be helpful to explain that the violence their parents expressed toward them was a consequence of the violence the parents themselves experienced. This is not to excuse bad behaviour but to underscore that trauma impacts beliefs about the self that then impact people's behaviours. Even in the context of the genogram, we help the client to know that any fight/flight/freeze symptoms they experience are a consequence of their emotional parts doing everything they could have done to survive. We explain how automatic processes and substitute actions may replicate themselves in the unconscious, but that by bringing them into consciousness, we have the ability to alter the pattern so that it does not replicate itself in the next generation.

Negative and positive legacies are inherited.

Even in the most difficult situations, lessons can be learned. While the genogram may typically show rigid red and blue lines that can startle a person at first glance, we have to see if there are any lessons the client has internalized. After explaining to the client how multigenerational transmission occurs—and stressing that different people do different things, whether maladaptive or adaptive, in order to survive—we ask them to list a minimum of three negative and three positive legacies they have inherited. They may be aware already that their mental health issues come from elsewhere (whether from their trauma history or otherwise) but rarely do people take the time to think of what positive legacies they have inherited. The answers are likely to surprise both client and therapist. If we give the client the opportunity to think about the adaptive nature of their mental health stresses, once again we contradict an old story. We provide disconfirming knowledge.

At the end of the session, regardless of how the client experienced the exercise, we ask if any insights or reflections came from the exercise. I have had some clients who were frustrated by not being able to provide the dates of births or names for the members of their grandparental systems but who then come to the next session stating that they had reconnected with their parents in order to ask certain questions to clarify and complete the genogram. Although this is not the purpose of the genogram, we want to be aware of how they have experienced the session, whether for better or worse.

Before ending the session, we use a grounding technique to reinforce in the client's mind the association between talking about these challenging topics and leaving the session without severe disorientation or discomfort. Doing this ends the session on a good note and challenges any doubts the client may have about whether healing is possible for them.

Summary

When we are looking at an individual, we are looking at more than the sum of their experiences. An understanding of polyvagal theory can help us know whether the client is in a dorsolateral, sympathetic, or ventral vagal response. We must always be aware of what place we are at on the ladder in order to assist the client appropriately. The use of resources in sessions and the facilitation by the therapist are meant to be a reciprocal event in which the client can experience a state of safety that they can learn to recreate at will. The trauma-inducing events may not have happened strictly in their family of origin, but we need to see both the client and their ancestors. Asking the right questions provides the client with insight into the fact that they are not their problem and that there is always an opportunity to break the cycles of racial trauma when we become conscious of them and when the motivation for change is present. Clients must understand that they have inherited positive legacies as well as negative ones. Once they become conscious of both types of inheritance, they can change them not only in the present but forever more. This potential for change is what we will address in the next chapter as we begin to look at how we use the client's trauma history in our therapy sessions.

CHAPTER 10

THE RACIAL TRAUMA TARGET HISTORY

Planning the Path Toward Recovery

This chapter explains how to create a list of trauma targets using the trauma history of the racial trauma survivor. Many of the trauma targets that fuel present-day distress occur within the family systems context of anti-racist psychotherapy. The family systems context is not limited to family members. Many of our difficulties are interpersonal: conflict with relational/ attachment figures, emotional betrayals, rejection, or other events that could lead to shame or isolation. In evolutionary terms, many of these types of difficulties can be conceptualized as threats to our ancestors' existence. Because we inherited these nervous systems through the generations to ensure our continued survival, we inadvertently replicate these associations in the present. Our associations to these negative events fuel our negative cognitions, and the somatic experiences of discomfort unconsciously fuel our present-day decisions of approach or avoidance.

Polyvagal theory (see Chapter 9) informs the trauma history process in that we are addressing traumatic experiences that have left a mark on sympathetic responses (fight/flight) or dorsal vagal responses (freeze, immobilization, play dead). Once we resolve the traumatic experiences, the reconsolidation of these memories leads to improvements in the activation and efficacy of ventral vagal systems (increasing experiences of safety and connection in the client) as well as promoting integration of the personality, thus reducing the experience of pathological dissociation for ANP and EP (see Chapter 7). The resolution of traumatic material is an essential part of treating the underlying negative cognitions that fuel distress in the client, so it is highly recommended that any ambivalence toward the process be managed beforehand (as outline in Chapter 6). Otherwise, processing memories will inevitably become obstructed by limiting beliefs or secondary gain issues.

By creating a trauma history, the client is able to determine the process and progress of sessions. Some trauma therapists enter each session with a complex-trauma survivor by engaging with what some call the client's COW (Crisis of the Week), but such knee-jerk approaches to treatment are inefficient in the long run. There is no overall plan, the client is under-resourced, the therapist is reactive, and the purpose of the sessions is strictly damage control. Some therapists new to EMDR therapy and trained by other trainers have told me that their primary way of working with clients was based only on session-to-session plans, using only the floatback technique or affect bridges[35] put in place with no overall framework. While using the floatback does serve a purpose, relying on one approach alone will not permit the therapist and client to plan effective strategies for target completion. To achieve target completion, therapy needs to be proactive rather than reactive. Clients and therapists will therefore benefit from first creating a list of trauma targets to generate items to work on organized by themes and updatable from session to session. A treatment plan is set, and the client is motivated in the process.

Creating the Racial Trauma Target History

I recommend listing the targets on a spreadsheet that you can screenshare with the client. This allows for ease of future reference and has other advantages that will be discussed in later sections. First, however, it is important to remember that before starting to list the trauma history, the therapist must ensure that the client has acquired sufficient resources (e.g., mindful color breathing, resource integration, etc.). The process of listing trauma targets can be destabilizing for those who are ill-prepared.

The template below illustrates the layout and categories of a trauma history spreadsheet: Age, Trauma, Intensity/SUDs, Theme, Date Started, Date Completed, and Target #. The columns can then be filled in with the various traumatogenic events and themes (and other relevant data as indicated) of the client's history. It is important at this point to explain to the client that there may have been experiences in the past that contribute to their present distress.

---

[35] Related to hypnotherapeutic interventions, this is a process that enables the client to draw a connection from present-day distress to the memory of the first or etiological event that may be the initial precipitant of the present complaint.

Trauma history columns in a spreadsheet.

In your own words, you should also explain the difference between "small t" and "large T" traumas and how both can impact our negative cognitions about ourselves. Explain that there may have been earlier events that could have set the stage for later ones and that this is why we list them in chronological order (e.g., conflict with or separation from our attachment figures can impact how we see toxic relationships or breakups in our adolescent relationships). We also list items chronologically because this will assist us with target selection later on.

It is important to keep in mind that talking about trauma targets can cause distress. Be sure, therefore, to inform the client that, if bringing up any specific event is too disturbing, we can stop at any time. You may need to check in with the client to assess their SUD level after listing certain events. If it reaches a three or four, that may be time to reactivate their resources and reestablish safety before continuing. A three or four can quickly grow into a ten depending on what the process brings up. Erring on the side of caution will save time and solidify the alliance between client and therapist in the long run. Let the client know that it is OK if listing their trauma history takes a full session, or even two. We want to take the time to honor their story.

Special Considerations

Clients will be tempted to tell you all the details of their history and turn the session into talk therapy. Do not allow this to happen. The purpose of this session is not to process but simply to list our targets. We do not require the whole story when using an approach based on memory reconsolidation. Let the client know that you will need to interrupt them in case they veer off course. In order to initiate the process, we only need the bare minimum, so

I tell them we do not need to know the whole "newspaper article." All we need are:

- ➤ The client's age when it happened. (Enter "0" if it happened before they were born.)
- ➤ The "headline" of the story (e.g., "When my father beat me," "The accident," "Rage").
- ➤ The SUD (i.e., how much the trauma bothers them in this present moment).
- ➤ The general theme that the trauma falls under (e.g., "Family," "Relationships," "Sexual violence," etc.)

The basis of trauma history creation can be summed up as: **if we don't ask, they won't tell**. We must be comfortable asking about uncomfortable topics, but we do not need every last detail about every traumatic event. A balance should be maintained. Talking about problems is not the same as resolving them and we can risk retraumatizing the client if they share needless details. This is done to protect the client, structure the process, and generate a list of targets that the client will be motivated to recover from.

Race and Socially Constructed Identities

I call this part of the therapeutic process "racial trauma target selection" to emphasize that race is a fake concept with real consequences. It is not a biological reality; the impact of the label is highly situational, and the client's "race" is influenced by their social context. In these ways, race is like gender. Gender is a completely fabricated social construction, but a client's assigned gender nevertheless impacts the list of traumatogenic events they will tell you. For example, people who are socialized as women are more likely to report certain forms of gendered violence. However, we still ask heterosexual cisgendered men about whether they have experienced sexual violence events because they can often underreport these. This tendency may not be fully their fault; therapists likely avoid asking men questions of this nature due to their own social programming and expectations.

In general, I assume that everyone "has" a race just as most people can be placed somewhere on the gender spectrum. In therapy, race is a placeholder concept for social identities of significance to the client, regardless of whether the therapist is conscious of them or not. However, race and gender are by no means the only identity categories that may be relevant. If during your initial assessment, you feel there are cultural or identity-based themes that are necessary to include for a particular client (e.g., military/first-responder trauma categories), feel free to include them. I created this document because I have noticed that most trauma-informed therapists (EMDR trained and otherwise) do not ask these questions, and many trainings do not include such themes. Feel free to include any other relevant categories that I have not included but are relevant to your client's identity and circumstances. We are looking for any touchstone events that maintain negative cognitions. Touchstone target memories can sometimes be completely unexpected and impossible to know in advance. But having a list that exhausts multiple categories—and even asks about the top ten worst experiences—will likely reveal useful targets for resolving the client's cycles of consolidation and deep-rooted issues of concern.

Age

When creating the trauma history, we proceed chronologically. Sometimes we will be asking about childhood, but the client wants to list something from infancy or adolescence. If any traumas are mentioned that happened outside of the identified age range, you should still list them, but remember to return to where you left off. Structuring the questionnaire by age helps the client remember and keeps the session on track. The categories are purposeful; we use specific age ranges to jog the memory. Between sessions (if the trauma history listing continues into the next session), be sure to take note of which developmental category you left off at. Do not restart from the beginning.

Shame

There are endless possible issues or events that the client may unconsciously suppress or even hesitate consciously to report because of shame. The client may fear the consequences of admitting to certain things due to either the transference or countertransference dynamic. It is expected that clients will have varying degrees of reluctance before listing trauma targets. Assure them that it is OK to have these kinds of feelings and doubts and invite them to assign a name to the trauma that will enable it to be listed without revealing its content. The point of naming the trauma is not to enable the therapist to understand what happened but only to make it easier for the client to "tune into" it at a later date. Any name—"Purple," "Shadow," "Darkness,"—is OK provided the client will be able to remember what it refers to next week or the week after. They should feel free to share details or not, but usually it is unnecessary for the therapist to know the exact circumstances at this stage, or at all.

It is possible to use the Blind2therapist approach[36] for events that are not to be spoken about or shared due to fear, shame, or risk of retribution. This approach was recently used successfully with Yezidi survivors of terrorist attacks in northern Iraq who suffered from implicit trauma (Farrell et al., 2020). Unlike EMDR therapy's standard protocol for phase 3, the only information necessary for reprocessing is the target memory or cue word, the emotions brought up by the target, the SUD, and the location of the body sensation. The findings of the Yezidi study support this modality. A further study also supports the use of the Blind2Therapist approach with video conferencing software (Farrell et al., 2021). This is important here because Rhythm and Processing also works in both in-person and virtual settings.

First, Worst, Most Recent

The client may say there are "hundreds" of instances of "X" trauma event or "too many to count," but all that we need are the first, the worst, and the most recent. We only need three targets (and sometimes fewer even than that) because the general human ability to generalize enables some targets that resemble others to be indirectly processed either during or at the end of another target's completion.

Representative and Composite Targets

In cases where the details were too uncertain or unclear at the time of the event, or if clients have trouble identifying a specific memory or image

---

[36] An EMDR therapy-based approach to reprocessing in which details of the trauma target are limited to the point where the therapist could not possibly deduce what the target is. This protects the client from feeling unnecessary shame about the traumatic event. Reprocessing of traumatic material is still very much possible with this method..

before they imitate therapeutic reconsolidation, it can sometimes be helpful to instead use a *representative* target. This does not need to be something that actually happened or happened in a particular way. For example, it can be a (representative) composite image of several events. During the accessing sequence of the therapeutic reconsolidation process (see Chapter 4), the goal is to activate the corresponding neural network that relates to the target memory.[37] We do not need much extraneous or even verifiable material before we can target traumatic events. The brain is highly capable and sophisticated; it knows how best to target the underlying disturbance. Do not get lost in semantics. Our brains are efficient, and memory reconsolidation-based approaches are highly robust when used strategically.

White Therapists with Equity-denied Racialized Groups and First Peoples

The other day a trainee asked me a question about white therapists working with clients from diverse racial communities. I responded like this:

> I let all of my clients know that they can talk freely about race, gender, and sexuality. However, as a white therapist, you need to work on any unconscious or socially accepted racial animosity that you may have accumulated toward people who have been denied racial equity. Do this *before* you consider whether to open up the gates about race in a session.

Our society is based on the binary complex trauma cycle of white insecurity and Black suffering and all of the assumptions that go with that. It does not matter which celebrities you follow on social media or who your favorite presidents are, we all have internalized assumptions—especially about Black people.

So do not give Black clients the option to talk about race and then have a strong negative counter-transference reaction when they tell you about their family and personal history. Avoid gaslighting or whitesplaining. Above

---

[37] In EMDR therapy, this corresponds to eliciting the TICES (trigger, image, cognition, emotions, sensations) during the assessment phase (phase 3).

all, commit to educating yourself on these topics and issues to bring your assumptions and limitations to light *outside* of your role as a therapist.

I have met clients who have been harmed by therapists who wanted to work on others before working on themselves. Years ago, while searching for an EMDR therapist myself, I (as a client) encountered white therapists who denied access to the topic of racism. In one case, an older female therapist told me about their "Black friend" who had said there was "no such thing as racism" right after I described my presenting problem, which was clearly related to my experience of systemic racism. Her message was clear, and so was my reaction— that was the last I needed to see of that therapist.

This white resistance to discussing race causes many racially diverse clients to drop out of therapy prematurely or avoid therapy in the first place. Racial microaggressions are well documented in the research. Let's not contribute to it. Let the client have a space where they can speak freely about racial trauma. Be a great therapist instead. Be present, acknowledge there is a problem, and care about making a difference. Find a therapist for yourself who specializes in managing internalized racism or biases. Getting good consultation and supervision will also help. Let's work on ourselves *because* we work with others.

Trauma History Questions:

After explaining the procedure and setting the stage for discussing the trauma history items, we are now ready to ask questions to fill our trauma history list with the client. The following section outlines this process in the order of topics that I recommend, starting with racial trauma.

Racial Trauma Questions

I begin by explaining, "Now first, we are going to start from way back. Before you were even born." I then ask, "Were there ever any events that happened before you were born that still to this day affect you? Any events relating to racial trauma, gender, culture, or any other identity-based traumas?"

If they say "no," I move on to the next set of questions. If they say "yes," I elicit the following information and enter it in the spreadsheet:

> ➢ The client's age at the time of the event (in this example, "0" to indicate it was before they were born).

> ➢ The trauma (I ask, "What would you say the name of this trauma is?")

> ➢ The SUDS ("On a scale of zero to ten what's the intensity that you feel now?)

> ➢ The *general* theme ("What's the general theme or category we should list this trauma under?").

I then say:

> Good job. This is the minimum information we need in order to initiate the reconsolidation process in a later session. We do not need anything else to reprocess the targets. This initial information is sufficient to enable you to activate the relevant memory networks and fill in the blanks. However, we don't stop here. We need to complete our list by moving on chronologically.

Pre-birth Trauma Questions

I now ask about any traumatic events they know of that happened in the period shortly before they were born. I ask, "Were there any traumas that your mother went through while you were in the womb? . . . Any difficulties during labor? . . . Anything happening to or happening between your parents around the time of your birth?"

Once again for each event they mention, I enter the following in the list:

- Their age at the time.

- The name of the trauma or "title of the story."

- The SUDs or "intensity" of their feelings about the event.

- The general theme.

Infancy to Preschool

For the first few years of life (ages one to four), we do a simple chronological scan and enter the relevant data as above. I ask, "Any events at the age of one? . . . Any traumas at the age of two?" and so on through their preschool years. They may not have anything to report from these years. That is OK, and this should be made clear to them. They may say they can't remember those years. That too is fine. Not every question will get an answer, but there are some who may mention significant preverbal or early childhood trauma. For those clients, it is important to elicit, as above, the bare-bones information about such events and enter this data in the list. We can then proceed to the client's school years, but now we ask about age ranges rather than individual years.

Early Childhood

Starting with ages five to ten, we begin to ask more specific questions.

➤ **Have you ever experienced any traumas relating to:**
- Transitioning into elementary school?
- Difficulties with separation anxiety?
- Problems at school from teachers or other students in class?
- Being bullied? Or you bullying someone else?
- Anything relating to your identity (racial, gender, culture, sexuality, etc.)?
- Anything concerning your accent, your dialect, or where you came from?
- Problems relating to siblings, cousins, or other family members?
- Issues with financial hardship, poverty, or any other money problems?
- Physical, emotional, or sexual violence that you experienced or witnessed?
- Any loss of life (loved ones, friends, or pets)?
- Any emergency situations (accidents, hospitalizations, experience of terror?)

Pre-puberty (ages 10 to 13)

➤ **Have you ever experienced any traumas relating to:**
- Sexual or gender identity?
- Physical appearance or puberty experience?
- Body image issues?
- Problems at school from teachers or other students?
- Bullying, loss of friendships, betrayals, or relationships?
- Discipline or neglect by caregivers at home?
- Physical, emotional, or sexual violence?
- Any loss of life (loved ones, friends, or pets)?
- Any emergency situations (accidents, hospitalization, experience of terror?)

Adolescence and Young Adulthood (ages 14 to 18)

➤ **Have you ever experienced any traumas relating to:**
- Transitioning into high school?
- Loss of identity or rejection because of identity?
- Bullying, loss of friendships, betrayals, or relationships?
- Problems at school from teachers or other students in class?
- Early sexual experiences?
- Physical, emotional, or sexual violence?
- Body-image issues or lack of confidence issues?
- Rejections in social situations or intimate relationships?
- Any experiences of shame or guilt?
- Any suicidal or self-harm thoughts or acts?
- Substance abuse: blackouts, bad trips, or addiction?

Young Adulthood and Later Life

After the formative years, we no longer need to proceed chronologically. We move instead into more general experiential categories. Any that do not apply to the particular client (e.g., parenting, if they have no children) should of course be skipped.

➢ Have you ever experienced any traumas relating to:

- Post-secondary education (university, college, technical or vocational training, etc.), whether attended or not?
- Social identity or culture-based stresses?
- Rejection, bad breakups, or toxic relationships?
- Physical, emotional, or sexual violence?
- Experiences of failure or missing out?
- Any abortions or early pregnancy losses?
- Medical issues, hospitalizations, severe accidents?
- Any regrets about something you did, got involved in, or witnessed?

➢ Traumas relating to employment:

- Looking for work, starting out and first jobs, being fired, or toxic work environments?
- Disappointments, regrets, conflicts with co-workers or betrayals at work?
- Work-stress management, loss of opportunities, or burnouts?

➢ Traumas relating to family relationships/parenting:

- In a marriage (past or present)?
- In a past or present courtship/dating relationship?
- From interference by external family members?
- Physical, emotional, or sexual violence?
- Difficulties with child-bearing, early pregnancy loss, raising children, or coping with an "empty nest"?

➤ Miscellaneous trauma:

- Any other phobic responses?
- Any existential issues relating to life or reality?
- Any spiritual or moral injuries, or issues with religion?
- Any socio-political stresses?
- Any limiting beliefs, such as beliefs about being "broken"?

To complete the task of filling the trauma history list, we need to ask one further question to help us prioritize our trauma targets. We close the process by asking, "*Are there any traumas we did not cover that you would rank in the top ten worst experiences of your life?*" and insert any that are mentioned into the trauma list.

Completing the Trauma History

The spreadsheet below is an example of what we would typically expect by the end of these questions. I have streamlined it for ease of reference, however; the example shown is much shorter than I would create with my clients. I like to use the "Google Sheets" app to create my spreadsheets, but you can use any spreadsheet app you are comfortable with. Using the autofilter option, I sort the items by age (but again you should feel free to sort by other fields if they seem better suited to the needs of your client.

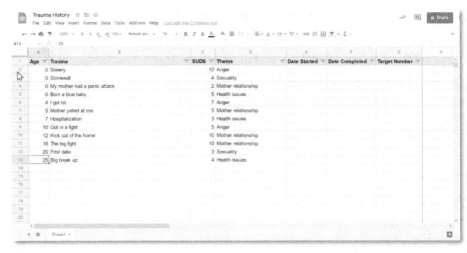

Example of completed trauma history list

Once the trauma list is complete, it's a good idea to take a moment to distinguish between the targets that the therapist recommends addressing from a trauma-informed perspective and those the client would like to address from a **client-directed perspective**. A trauma-informed perspective takes into account "touchstone" memories, which can be identified on the basis of high SUD ratings, related themes, and earlier formative experiences that may have laid the foundation for later traumatic experiences and events. Drawing on Emotional Freedom Technique (EFT), I use the metaphor of a table top to clarify this strategy. Let's say the "table top" the client seeks to knock down is an anger management problem. It is more efficient to knock out the table legs that hold up this negative behaviour than to bang on the top of the table.

For the same reason, it is more effective and strategic to target themes that relate to the anger chronologically rather than addressing the present manifestations of anger directly. Thus, for the trauma history illustrated above, our agenda would address the traumatic triggers beginning with "slavery" at age zero and then "I got hit" at age four and "Got in a fight" at age ten. It is better to target them in that order; the third target problem is likely to be easier to resolve after the first two have been resolved. This is because the lingering effects of the earlier targets are likely to make the later one difficult to resolve without first addressing the earlier ones. Additionally, because of the mind's ability to generalize across different contexts, it is also likely that reprocessing some strategic, earlier "table legs" can bring the whole table down without even needing to address the third target. It is not unusual to find, after completing three to five earlier targets, that some later events are no longer problematic.

There are connections outside conscious awareness. For this reason, I recommend selecting thematically related targets chronologically in order to deal with the fact that blocked processing is usually based on unconscious limiting beliefs installed at earlier ages.

Clients are also instructed to highlight the targets that they would need to reprocess to consider the therapy successful. This has two advantages. First, it makes the client part of the decision-making process rather than a passive "patient" or a crisis-of-the-week responder. By selecting for themselves what they want to work on, they effectively commit to resolving those targets. When the client is empowered to plan their therapy with the therapist, they feel more of a sense of agency. They gain confidence when they can choose a target and complete it, and each successful round increases their confidence—and the likelihood of success—in the next.

At a workshop, a white therapist once asked me, "Why doesn't my client admit to having racial trauma? They keep denying that it's a problem." I explained that, "what we don't want to do is say, hey, you're Black, you *should* work on this as a racial trauma problem." I added that, when we let the client take turns selecting the target, we find that they are often the best decider of what should be addressed, so we end up working *with* rather than *against* them. Another example comes from my work with polysubstance abusers. When I was a budding young therapist, I would sometimes get concerned about a client's marijuana use and frustrated that they were not always ready to give it up in the first session. I didn't realize at the time that marijuana helped them to cope with the effects of withdrawal from more serious addictions. Learning to follow their lead, built trust and taught me that the client is the expert on their own life; the therapist does not always know best. The same principle applies to racial trauma. When the client is given power and control, and we work *with* them instead of against them, we build trust with each completed target. Take the time to collaborate. Slow is fast and fast is slow.

Color Coding the Trauma History

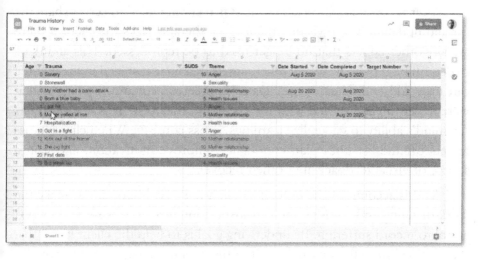

After we have filled in the trauma history list, we can use green to highlight the events with the highest SUDs as well as the earliest or first/most significant experiences of the theme (for example, the first self-harm or first sexual violence event). I then invite the client to select a different color and highlight the targets they believe they need to complete in order to consider the therapy a success. In the case illustrated above, they used magenta to color in the events at ages 12 and 16. The client will not always select maximum-SUD events, and they need not do so, but choosing them indicates that they still hold great meaning even if this was not revealed to the therapist beforehand. And again, enabling the client to choose motivates and creates engagement in the change being sought.

The decision about which event to target is always made in collaboration with the client. Anti-racist therapists always provide choices for their recommendations rather than binding the client to hidden agendas. This approach is intentional; it demonstrates "working with" the client rather than "doing therapy on" them. After initiating a trauma target, we list the date we did ("date started") and the target number (indicating the order in which each one was dealt with). After completing each target, we enter that date ("date completed") and highlight the event in a different color. In this case, the client selected orange. This gives the client confidence that we are making progress.

After reconsolidating each event, it is recommended to screenshare the list and update it. On revisiting the list, the therapist asks the client if there are any other targets that no longer need to be reprocessed. This allows us to determine if there were any other targets that were resolved indirectly. We can then add end dates to the "Date Completed" column for targets that were never directly started with the client and therapist. This demonstrates the mind's ability to generalize learnings across contexts. When clients cross targets off the list, they gain confidence, improve motivation, and gain a source of visual feedback about their recovery.

As this account of the process implies, it is very important to make the work of filling and coloring the spreadsheet interactive. It is more than just a tool to record suffering. Its underlying goal is to help the client know that they *can* heal from their past. As part of the interactive nature of the process, we can use any colors of the client's choosing to highlight events in the list. And to further build confidence, the client should be reassured that sometimes reprocessing one target reprocesses others indirectly. For example, reprocessing an event relating to early racial injustice at age five may make later identity-based workplace stressors at age 25 no longer relevant.

Final Notes on Racial Trauma Target Selection

The order of trauma target selection is directed by the client and informed by the recommendations of the therapist. Therapists are advised to use clinical judgment and avoid placing the client at undue risk, for example attempting trauma reprocessing before sufficient resources are installed or targeting a highly distressing target at the end of a session (or before going on a vacation, etc.) without the possibility for follow-up. For those who wish to address negative cognitions that underlie current distress, it may not be possible to predict the best order of target selection/completion because some negative cognitions connect to multiple events.

Going even further, some traumatic memories are more resistant to immediate therapeutic reconsolidation (requiring more than one session), as they may make a larger contribution to the entrenchment of a deeply consolidated negative cognition. Knowing which events hold this greater share cannot be known in advance due to the incalculable and unpredictable complexity of the associations that lie dormant in the unconscious mind. In practice, it appears that reconsolidation of the more challenging targets yields the most significant shifts in mental level, relationship and self-esteem. Even so, the reconsolidation of several lower-SUD targets can also possibly cast a wider benefit across different themes and can still be advantageous.

Typically, it is recommended that our first target will be the pre-birth racial trauma target (at age zero). Why? Because I want to start with something that both happened earlier and will not feel as intense or jarring to the client. I want them to understand that we can address *anything* that bothers them, but that it will be better to start with something they may have some distance from. It is preferable to talk about "slavery" or "Black women couldn't vote" as a general concept before talking about "the breakup that ruined my life." I want to lay the foundation for a "winning streak" while also giving the client an introduction to what RAP is all about with easier targets before we take on the bigger ones.

There is, of course, no guarantee that starting with a pre-birth racial trauma target will be easy for a client. Indeed, it may well be linked to complex present struggles with their identity. Still, for our first RAP target, we want to go with something early that may not necessarily relate to later complex trauma instigators or severe attachment disruptions. Starting with these may confuse and intimidate the client.

Every client is different, but I have had great success starting with an initial racial trauma event (even with white clients). It creates a momentum for change, and it was the client's first "lesson" on the planet. If the client's first trauma holds a negative cognition about who they are as a person, replacing this with a positive cognition may create confidence about who they are.

Once again, nothing is set in stone. Tread carefully, be compassionate, and seek clinical consultation from experienced colleagues when in doubt.

Summary

The racial trauma target selection process allows the therapy to adopt a strategic approach. Using this approach helps to conceptualize treatment plans with clients and create a map to navigate the terrain of trauma reprocessing. It may not always be necessary, and in some cases it may be preferable, to deal with crises as they come up, but who doesn't like a proper plan? When we ask the right questions, the client is likely to answer them. If we never ask about race, gender, sexuality, or identity-based issues, there is a chance that the client will not admit them either. Be sure to use the Blind2Therapist approach and have clients list the trauma targets in whatever way they feel most comfortable and that represents them best. Empower them to set the priorities for what should change. Lists also streamline the process. Clients will feel better when they see a list of targets rather than worrying that therapy may last forever. If you target events strategically and show clients their progress, there is a good chance that you and they together can make the journey of healing from suffering both encouraging and satisfying.

CHAPTER 11

A SESSION IN RHYTHM AND PROCESSING

Rhythm and Processing in Action

Having listed the client's trauma events chronologically, named them, and prioritized our targets for therapy, we can now turn our attention to the work of reconsolidation. In this chapter, I will explain how to use Rhythm and Processing Strategies alongside an EMDR therapy-informed approach. Because Rhythm and Processing is largely inspired by EMDR therapy, it can be used either as an adjunctive or independent approach. I begin with a case overview that illustrates the use of the Rhythm and Processing Strategies described in this book. I end the chapter with the completion of the first trauma target (in the example case, racial trauma before the client's birth). The precise nature of the first trauma target depends on the client's priorities, but as previously noted, I usually start with something before the client's birth or even the birth itself (marked as age 0).

The Rhythm and Processing Technique can be used on any trauma target generated in the racial trauma target selection process (bad breakups, racial microaggressions, accidents, betrayal trauma, etc.). Keep in mind that the targeted "events" do not need to correspond to actual events that took place because trauma is based on the subjective meaning the client ascribes to it rather than the factual events that have generated it.

Setting the Stage for Recovery

For this case the client, Nia, presented for therapy. The first session was based on the session setup described in Chapter 5, which included an evaluation of the presenting issues. Information gathering from the Four Cores revealed that there were interpersonal difficulties, lack of recognition at work, intrusive thoughts, and difficulty sleeping. During the initial session, the client was taught mindful color breathing (MCB) and instructed to practice it using the gratitude journal. Nia reported a benefit from these tools.

At the beginning of the second session, the progress made using these two tools was discussed. Nia stated that she had been able to get mild relief from their use and that this had come as a pleasant surprise. However, she still had some difficulties with overthinking and with her emotional parts intruding into consciousness before going to bed. The PROS/CONS balance sheet was used to address her ambivalence and reveal the advantages of the disadvantages. Secondary gain issues were also identified. At this point, she was introduced to the Rhythm and Processing approach, which was used to reduce the salience of her negative limiting beliefs about her ability to change the status quo. The setup for RAP took place as described in Chapter 8, and after experiencing a reduction in the strength of these beliefs, Nia gained more motivation to practice the resources she had learned thus far.

In the third session, Nia reported some further improvements, revealing that she had practiced Rhythm and Processing Strategies differently from how the therapist suggested (for example, streaming clips of nature scenes while working) and that this had helped to manage some of her symptoms. She explained that she was still having some difficulty sleeping, however. The negative beliefs that disturbed her before going to bed provided an opportunity to install a resource, and resource integration was then used to cultivate "self-love." A future integration was also used to help Nia imagine being able to act with self-love confidently over the next few days and weeks. Nia received these interventions well.

In the fourth session, Nia reported that using the resources she had learned had increased her feelings of stability as well as her confidence and ability to self-regulate. She stated that she was ready to proceed without the use of any additional resources. Because there was no evidence of unsustainable life stressors or emotion regulation difficulties, the therapist proceeded to the next step. The genogram was initiated and completed in this session. It revealed that she was actually a white- passing individual and that her maternal grandparents had been "pure laine" (literally, pure wool), that is, white Quebecers who never intermixed with other races. Her paternal grandparents had been immigrants who were denied racial equity and forced to assimilate and hide their ancestry.

We discussed the anxieties about lack of acceptance that the genogram revealed, as well as patterns of gendered violence in both her paternal and maternal upbringing. She described a history of being mistreated due to needing to conceal her identity and distance herself from her father at family events. Tears came up while discussing this and related topics. The use of the RAP technique was helpful in containing her feelings of being overwhelmed while recounting events from the genogram. This helped her restore balance, gain awareness of her inherited legacies, and end the session without losing confidence in the process.

In the fifth session, Nia expressed a feeling of relief that she had been able to gain a better sense of who she was and also said she now felt ready to complete the trauma history list. She also explained that she had combined the resources from previous sessions and was using them to good effect in ways not described by the therapist. For example, she sometimes combined mindful color breathing with resource integration, envisioning herself flowing down a river, in order to manage feelings of self-doubt. This had given her the confidence to now work on trauma targets.

Trauma targets that corresponded to what she wanted to work on were highlighted in yellow, and those the therapist believed would generate the greatest degree of the generalization effect were highlighted in green. The first target addressed was "My grandparents called me the n-word before I was even born."38 The intensity rating was five. The therapist explained that this would be the perfect starting point because it would introduce Nia to using RAP therapy and show her what to expect before taking on more challenging targets.

Reconsolidating the Traumatic Memory

We begin the reprocessing in the sixth session. As Nia comes into the session, the therapist first verifies that she has a reliable internet connection and a backup phone number in case of connection drops. She is then asked if she has any questions or concerns up to this point in the therapy and advised that a follow-up session can be booked in case of any discomfort or

---

38 For those who may be unclear about how a trauma target with such a title could occur at age 0, a reminder: clients give only the "headline" of the story, not the full "newspaper article" that would describe what actually transpired. It does not need to be logical to the therapist. The trauma title captures words of significance for the client. They are meant to enable the client to bring their mind's attention to the memory address that stores the dysfunctional material (negative cognition, somatic experience, etc.). The therapist should not to question the trauma event's title just because it challenges their own perspective on "reality." For example, I have worked with Wiccan clients who had a form of "racial" trauma target that resembled a past-life regression. The content of the memory was reported as being killed at the stake after accusations of witchcraft. A negative cognition, physical discomfort, and high SUD were attached to an event that did not happen in their lifetime and may not have happened to "them" at all, but a significant benefit was gained through the "memory's" reconsolidation. Remember, the definition of racial trauma encompasses "real or perceived" experiences of harm. It is about the significance that clients assign the target, and the impact it makes on them, not about whether the therapist sees it as valid/"true" or not.

overwhelming emotions between future sessions. The therapist assures her that, while such reactions are rare, sometimes clients can reexperience traumatic reminders or make attempts to distance themselves from the dysfunctional material in ways that can cause distress before the targets are fully completed.

The resources developed and practiced over the past few weeks provide all that is needed to manage the vast majority of any possible negative reactions. Nevertheless, between sessions the client is welcome to schedule a 15-to-20-minute crisis phone call with the therapist if these resources prove inadequate. In my practice, crisis phone calls are factored into the cost of therapy, and no additional charge is made for them.

Nia expresses relief and motivation to continue. After this, a brief reminder of the setup phase for RAP (see Chapter 8) needs to take place. It is important to make sure that the client consents fully to the procedure before moving on. In particular, the therapist should reiterate that the client can use a vacuum/container combo as well as selecting a COM video. As this is a virtual session, the therapist then shares their screen with the client. The following is a typical example of the ensuing dialogue.

Therapist:	OK what would you like for me to search for?
Nia:	Hmm . . . I don't know, how about this time we can try a river or a stream?
Therapist:	Sure, OK now help me find the best stream on YouTube.
Nia:	[laughs] OK
Therapist:	Let's just make sure, though, that it's not a documentary on streams, we don't want any annoying people interrupting our healing with all their talking . . . So sure, let me know if you want me to scroll down through the list . . . How about some of these?
Nia:	[Selects their preferred video]

Accessing the Target

The setup is now complete. The next steps resemble standard EMDR protocol's assessment phase 3. RAP can be used independently too, but what is important is that the client is tuned into the target memory and identifies a negative and a positive belief as well as an SUD and its body location.

Therapist:	OK so if you're ready for RAP let's go. [Therapist stops sharing his screen of the video]
Nia:	OK.
Therapist:	So when we think about this specific target at age zero—"My grandparents called me the n-word before I was even born"—what is the image that comes up that represents the *worst* part about this trauma for you?

When Nia gives their visual description of the worst part of the event, the therapist should not challenge any aspect of what is "remembered" even if the client was not there to "see" what happened. It is how the event appears to the client and the effect of holding the pathological associations in their memory that are important. In addition to visual information, clients may also sometimes list words, emotions, epithets, feelings, or metaphors. This should not be discouraged either.

Therapist:	OK, so when we look at this target, what's the negative belief about *yourself* that comes up? We are looking for a statement that starts with the word "I".
Nia:	I am not liked by them.

In this situation, Nia has provided a negative belief that may be factually correct. This is not the negative cognition to change; we are not seeking to distort reality. It goes without saying that her grandparents probably were not going to win any popularity contests anytime soon. Instead, what we want is the client's dysfunctional self- attribution because of the event. So in this case, the therapist may need to rephrase the question.

> **Therapist:** Let's see if we can find a core belief behind this that can extend or *generalize* beyond just your grandparents. If it is true that "you are not liked by them," what would that mean about you as a person?
>
> **Nia:** Hmm... OK... "I am unlovable"

In this case, Nia has chosen a belief about herself that may have a greater chance of being generalized to other targets or that is likely also to be tied into other events. It can be hypothesized, therefore, that after completing this initial target, future targets that relate to not being lovable will be completed more easily and possibly present with lower SUD ratings due to the groundwork accomplished in this session. The therapist now asks:

> **Therapist:** While looking at this picture, instead of the negative belief of 'I am unlovable,' what would be the *positive* belief that you don't yet believe but would *like* to believe about yourself today?

This question conveys to the client the implication that the positive belief is currently not held or not fully held. The intention is to prompt an even greater perspective shift after completing the target. At this point, the client may take time to contemplate and consider the new, positive belief. It is fine if they do not conceptualize the positive belief right away. A key part of their problem is that they do not believe that a positive belief can be associated with such a terrible memory. It is this conceptual barrier that sustains the dysfunctional memory network and the negative somatic experiences in the first place. They can therefore be given a minute or two to provide an answer.

> **Nia:** Hmm... Good question... Maybe, "I am loveable?"
>
> **Therapist:** OK, great.

The following section is optional but to demonstrate RAP's ability to be used as an adjunct to the standard EMDR protocol, therapists might include something similar to the following:

Therapist:	And on a scale of one to seven, with one meaning completely false and seven completely true, when you think about the original target and think of the words "I am loveable," how true is this belief to you on a gut level. Remember, one means it's completely false, seven means it's completely true.
Nia:	Zero, or I mean one.
Therapist:	And when you think about the fact that it doesn't feel true, when you think about the negative belief and the target, what are the emotions that come to your awareness?
Nia:	[Eyes well up in tears] Sadness, rejection, not being worth it.

Resuming the RAP protocol, the therapist now asks,

Therapist:	And when we think about this sadness, this rejection, the image of how they looked, the negative belief of I am unlovable... on a scale of zero to 10, what's the level of disturbance right now?
Nia:	Eight.

We take the initial ratings clients give us during the trauma history with a grain of salt. In this case, they initially recorded a six, but now it's an eight. However, what they record on the trauma list is just an initial estimate of how much distress the target will cause before it has been fully activated. Now we are loading the dysfunctional memory network, and it is being brought to awareness, so it is predictably more intense than the first time they mentioned it.

The therapist then asks the client where they feel that SUD in their body and mind. Not all clients feel trauma-related bodily sensations in the same way. Therefore, we say body *and* mind because, in some experiences of depersonalization or derealization, the body is completely "off limits," and we do not question the client's way of representing their distress. In this case, Nia responded, "In my heart."

Initiating the Transformation

Therapist:	OK, let's see if we can *RAP* this up. Use your vacuum [inhales and raises hand] and put that over into the container [exhales and moves hand over to the right]. Let me know when you're ready.
Nia:	[Closes eyes and remains silent for a few moments.]

By this time the therapist and client will already have practiced RAP several times. The client is unlikely to be overwhelmed or confused about the process. This is why it is important to start with lower SUD targets on the trauma history before targeting the major ones.

Nia:	OK, ready.
Therapist:	Alright, let's do this.
	[The therapist shares the screen, starts the video.]
Therapist:	1...2...3...4...RAP. [client blinks rapidly]
	1...2...3...4...5...RAP. [client blinks rapidly]
	1...2...3...4...RAP. [client blinks rapidly]
	1...2...3...4...5...RAP. [client blinks rapidly]

The word *RAP* is used as the cue to have the client blink rapidly four to five times. Once again, blinking serves to interrupt the experience of the COM video. Four interruptions of a positive stimulus lead to five sequential presentations of a positive stimulus. As stated in earlier chapters, this is an unusual experience. Previous exposures to negative cognitions or trauma reminders would usually not follow such a sequence or have a resultant positive feeling. In this case, it leads to overturning information. Counting to four and then switching back to five generates a unique rhythm to the presentation of the COM material. It serves an additional role of challenging the attentional load on the client's working memory, which keeps clients slightly more engaged than if they were to count to the same number each time; it makes them less likely to zone out or participate from a rote, repetitive standpoint.[39]

After each round, we check in with the client to ensure they were able to stay within their threshold of affect tolerance and that the video was suitably engaging.

[The therapist stops the video from playing.]	
Therapist:	Feeling calm?
Nia:	[takes a sigh of relief] Yes. I can breathe a little easier now.
Therapist:	It's a nice video, isn't it?
Nia:	[laughs] Yeah!

In the initial phase, especially when starting on a new target, two rounds are advisable before assessing if there has been any reduction. Sometimes, clients need to get used to watching the new video and being guided to blink to reprocess trauma. Sometimes, they need to upgrade their vacuum or container. Doing two initial rounds back-to-back ensures that Nia has a good chance of achieving a reduction.

Therapist:	Ready for another round?
Nia:	Yes.
Therapist:	Let's go. [starts the video]
	1...2...3...4...RAP. [client blinks rapidly]
	1...2...3...4...5...RAP. [client blinks rapidly]
	1...2...3...4...RAP. [client blinks rapidly]
	1...2...3...4...5...RAP. [client blinks rapidly]

---

[39] Also, because it follows a predictable yet dynamic rhythm. The ABAB rhyme scheme is a classic and common form of rhyming in popular and lyrical forms of music like reggae, dancehall, hip-hop or rap music. Heavily inspired by music and art, this was also a personal touch added by the author to distinguish it from other therapies.

Therapist:	[Stops video] Able to feel calm through all that?
Nia:	Yes!
Therapist:	Good. Now I would like for you to just lightly check in… Any remaining intensity?
Nia:	Yeah, but it went down a lot…
Therapist:	No problem, let's vacuum *all* of it up now, put it all in that container . . . Let me know when you're ready.
Nia:	[Closes eyes, staying silent for a moment, then nods her head] OK.
Therapist:	Alright, let's go.

[Process continues until the step 6 condition is met, i.e., the disturbance is equal to "False"]

Therapist:	Feeling calm?
Nia:	Definitely!
Therapist:	OK, *any* remaining disturbance.
Nia:	Nah, I'm good.
Therapist:	All right. [spreading hands from one side of the screen to the other] So I would like for us now to do a deep scan. Scan through the target and check to see if are there any remaining parts of this target that still cause any suffering for you. Scan from beginning to end.
Nia:	[Closes their eyes, visualizing for several moments] Yes, I think I got something.
Therapist:	OK, scale of zero to ten?
Nia:	Not much, like a four.
Therapist:	Alright let's scoop that up. Put it into the container and let me know when you're ready.
Nia:	OK.

[Process continues, but something is wrong when the therapist checks again]

Therapist: Feeling calm?

Nia: Uhh, for some reason I don't think that did much.

Therapist: OK, no problem, zero to ten?

Nia: Still a four, I think.

Therapist: OK, so what I would like for you to do now is use a new metaphor. Sometimes, when the disturbance doesn't go down, we need to do something a little differently. [Opens palms in the shape of a box] Sometimes we need to vacuum maybe a little bit off the top or a little bit off the bottom. Sometimes we might need to vacuum a little bit off the sides. Try it again, and this time, see if it's possible to vacuum it up a little differently.

The abstract and unusual nature of this suggestion frees the client to use their creativity. It empowers the client to be more flexible and autonomous in addressing the problem.

Nia: OK. Ready.

Therapist: Let's go.

Using their own modified way of vacuuming, Nia is now able to reduce the intensity and has less difficulty containing the emotional difficulty. This helps the client gain more flexibility in solving problems and adds a satisfying element to the practice. RAP is continued until the difficulty subsides to a zero.

Therapist: How much are we at now?

Nia: Zero.

Therapist: Let's scan through and check if there's anything else.

Nia: [Closes eyes for a few moments] Nope, we're all clear.

> **Therapist:** That's great. I would like for you to use butterfly tapping now while acknowledging that you have been able to reduce all this to a zero.

At this point, we want to be sure that the SUD really is at zero, while providing a light transition before returning to more disturbing scenes. This will also let us see if there is any remaining discomfort relating to the SUD being reduced and maintained at a zero.[40] BLS is meant to stimulate memory networks and deepen the experience of calm but can also link to more disturbing memory items. The resolution of any directly connected traumatic material is often necessary before resolving the initial complaint. This would be a manual form of the generalization effect where we would need to specifically target the associated material, although in many cases it happens incidentally. In any event, at this stage, after getting a zero through RAP, we can predict an additional zero through this round of tapping.

> **Therapist:** What was your experience?
>
> **Nia:** I just felt the same. Still feel calm.
>
> **Therapist:** Great. So now let's reevaluate. I would like for you to think back to the original target and tell me, what do you notice now?

When returning to the target, the therapist must be careful not to refer back to any of the material described during the initial assessment. This is to encourage the client to take a fresh look at the material and promote a new understanding of it. The therapist only says, "Let's return to the original target to verify whether the material has changed." After taking a moment to do so, if the session has enabled a new perspective, the client may reply,

---

[40] There are some people who express disbelief or even discomfort in relation to getting a SUD of zero. In cases where it cannot be reduced to a zero, there are often limiting beliefs that are responsible (If I forgive them who will I become? There is something wrong with me if I'm not sad). Targeting the origin of the limiting belief usually leads to a resolution of a different (but related) target, allowing a much smoother resolution of the initial issue.

| Nia: | Well . . . it seems very distant now. I am also feeling more compassion toward myself. |

This kind of result is not unusual. After reprocessing trauma targets, whether they occurred directly or indirectly (as in this example), the client often no longer reexperiences the traumatic event in the same way. The memory is now experienced as something distant rather than present, and a greater awareness of the present moment is also common. The polyvagal response of the ventral vagal system now activates, the faces of clients relax, their breathing achieves a steadier rhythm, and they report feelings of openness and safety. Additionally, in cases where violence or severe forms of oppression have occurred, clients will often report feelings of compassion, self-acceptance, or empowerment. These have not come from suggestions by the therapist. The natural progression of releasing negative thoughts and conditions in itself leads many clients to conclusions that allow them to see a bigger picture. It is not unlikely for clients even to espouse profound and wise insights after reducing the salience of negative emotions while releasing their attachments to the suffering encased in the traumatic event.

In the case I am using as an example here, when the therapist asked about the remaining level of disturbance in the target, Nia suggested it had now reduced to a one but wasn't sure. This too was not unexpected. In a few cases, there may be some remaining intensity. If so, this just means there is something that was not specifically targeted during the original scan. In other cases, the client may express disbelief or confusion about the speed and extent of change. The therapist does not probe into reactions like these but merely asks if the client would prefer to address the remaining intensity with tapping or return to the video.

The therapist always provides options when using RAP. There is more than one way to reprocess material, and giving options is likely to increase the client's motivation, often resulting in a choice that produces an experience that overturns the harmful information. Most clients have never been given the option to look at their trauma differently. The trauma survivor rarely had a choice in the matter. But through tapping, they often come up with creative interpretations that spontaneously resolve the trauma. They are likely to do the same through the video technique, but with an added quieting of the mind.

After three or four rounds of tapping or a single round of RAP, the target is once again reevaluated.

Verification of Target Completion

Therapist:	When you think back to the original target now, what's your experience of it?
Nia:	OK, now I feel it has been put up on the shelf. I'm having trouble even bringing it up.
Therapist:	Zero to ten?
Nia:	We are good. Zero.
Therapist:	And before the negative cognition you said was "I am unlovable." When you think about the original target and you say those words, what happens now?

Bringing the original negative cognition into the new context (a desensitized memory) like this is not part of EMDR therapy but is designed to provide additional overturning information and verify that there are no remaining negative feelings or associations to the hub of the cycle of consolidation.

Nia:	Nah, that does not sound true anymore. It's not my problem it has always been *their* problem.
Therapist:	That's right! I want you to notice that. [Therapist and client use butterfly tapping to reinforce the experience.]
Therapist:	What do you notice now?
Nia:	That felt good to say. It feels good. I see an image of my younger self. She looks so innocent. Like I don't want anything bad to happen to her.
Therapist:	[Takes note that an image of Nia's younger self appeared] And I just want to double-check, what's the intensity at now?
Nia:	It's not bad or anything, still zero.

> **Therapist:** That's great! One last thing now. Because we are using Rhythm and Processing and there are resources you have now that you might never have had in the past, are there any resources that we need to give to your younger self? Whether it is a round of RAP, words of wisdom, or any physical gestures? Check to see which one would be best. What do you think would be best to help to support this young one?

This is the "rescuing ourselves" intervention. When phrased in this way, it frees and empowers the client to choose something to leave with the ego-state or dissociated emotional part most impacted by the trauma.

Some cautions, however: not all clients will need this for a proper resolution, and it can be counterproductive to throw this in if it is outside the client's world view or phenomenological experience. For those that do bring up their "younger" self, attempting this before achieving an SUD of zero is usually very problematic. Some parts of the client's emotional system that feel justified in their pain and suffering can get very resentful and angry. But rather than trying to change our emotional parts, we are assisting them to heal and recover. When in doubt, validation is usually one of the most important strategies when using interventions that correspond to aspects of one's internal system (Schwartz & Sweezy, 2019). Some parts of the system want to be left alone; some appreciate participating in RAP alongside the client's ANP. However, all clients benefit from interacting with a visualization of their younger self in a context that enables positive visualization.

It can be a very moving scene when a client is helped to visualize giving a hug to a younger version of themselves or even a few words of encouragement or explanation that no adult at the time gave them. Clients are asked to do this visualization while using bilateral tapping.

> **Nia:** I just want to give her a hug, and tell her everything will be OK.

Therapist:	OK. If she accepts and if that works for you, go ahead. And notice what happens [Therapist and client do a round of tapping while client visualizes the hug].
Therapist:	OK, now let's take a deep breath [both inhale] . . . and let it go [both exhale] . . . What do you notice now?
Nia:	My younger self is protected.
Therapist:	And how does that feel?
Nia:	It feels right.
Therapist:	Is there anything else that your younger self needs or is she all right now?
Nia:	Umm . . . Yes. But I would like to give her the resource I made a few sessions back. I would like for her to have a panther too. [Client gives younger self a protective resource we developed in an earlier session to help her in present-day activities].
Therapist:	OK great, notice that. [Both start tapping] All right, now let's take in a deep breath [both inhale] . . . and let it go [both exhale] . . . And what's goin' on now.
Nia:	[tears]I feel emotional.
Therapist:	Everything OK? Zero to ten?
Nia:	No these are good tears...She feels empowered now!
Therapist:	There we go. Is there anything else to do now with this young one?
Nia:	No she is good now.
Therapist:	OK, cool. When you think back to the original target now, what happens?
Nia:	Nothing. I feel at peace with it.
Therapist:	Zero to ten?
Nia:	Zero.

> **Therapist:** OK, good. Now that we have reduced the strength of the negative belief, I would like us to focus on installing the *positive* belief. The positive belief you mentioned earlier was "I am loveable." When you think back to the original memory, are these still the words you would like to believe about yourself, or is there something different now?

In some cases, what has been processed so far, the act of going back and "rescuing" oneself, or even just the passage of time allows a different positive cognition to emerge. The role of the therapist is to provide the client with an opportunity to find the words that resonate most with them. It does not matter whether the words are new ones or not.

> **Nia:** No, I think I will keep this one.
>
> **Therapist:** OK, so now when we think about the original target and say the words, "I am loveable," how true is this belief on a scale from zero percent to 100 percent?

At this point, I use a zero-to-100 scale with RAP because saying that something is 100 percent true demonstrates much more conviction than any other alternative, and perhaps surprisingly, using bilateral stimulation and RAP make this level of client confidence possible. When a client cannot see the positive cognition as 100 percent true, this is likely due to the continued presence of limiting beliefs or other, earlier feeder memories or touchstone targets that prevent full certainty.

> **Nia:** It feels about 80% true.
>
> **Therapist:** OK notice that [both begin tapping].

It is important to note at this point that the validity of the positive cognition can be increased by using *either* bilateral tapping or the RAP approach, perhaps because what prevents a person from being able to see a belief as true can be represented as a *somatic* experience (whether of skepticism or fear). Hence, using any proven tools for reprocessing dysfunctional information can reduce emotional blockages and promote the integration of adaptive material.

Therapist:	Take in a deep breath [both inhale], and let it go [both exhale]. What do you notice now?
Nia:	That felt good. I felt a little more lightness.
Therapist:	Great and how true would you say it is now?
Nia:	It feels like it's at 90% and I don't know if it can move any higher. Can I really see this as being true?
Therapist:	OK, well, this time I would like for us to try something different. While thinking about the positive belief and tapping from left to right, I would like you to imagine that it is completely true. [Both start tapping.] See yourself in the future, having internalized this belief about yourself. How would it feel in the body if this belief were 100 percent true? How would your posture be? How would your tone of voice be? How would you move through the world? Take a moment to notice what it feels like when this belief is completely true.

Because Nia still has some difficulty seeing the belief as completely true, the next logical step is to imagine if it were true. Because the brain cannot distinguish between real and perceived events, doing this intervention appears to guarantee an increase in confidence about the positive belief. It will also cause the client to experience more positive feelings in general. However, if any negative feelings whatsoever arise during the installation of the positive belief, the therapist should switch to RAP to ensure that all negative associations really are cleared. Installing the positive belief must occur without tensions or difficulty. This is very important.

The conscientious therapist will make an effort to check in with the client at each step when installing a belief that has never been installed before. Watch the nonverbal cues, and whenever there are any indications of discomfort, check in with the client to see if an SUD rating has re-emerged.

Clearing that remaining SUD with RAP often helps strengthen the validity of the positive cognition.

Therapist:	Take in a deep breath [both inhale], and let it go [both exhale]. What do you notice now?
Nia:	That felt good.
Therapist:	And how true does it feel now?
Nia:	100 percent!
Therapist:	Let's go with that. [Both begin tapping] … Take in a deep breath [both inhale], and let it go [both exhale]. What do you notice now?
Nia:	Everything is still good. I feel more solid in my core.
Therapist:	Good work. And just to double-check, how true is the positive belief now when you think about the original target?

It is essential to verify that the belief is still true for the client. The benefit to them of experiencing and verbalizing the positive sensations from the installation of the belief can never be understated.

Nia:	It's still true, 100 percent. Now I feel a sense of peace.
Therapist:	Very good. Let's now do the body scan. When we think back to the original target and we say the words "I am loveable," we want to check to see that all parts of the body, all aspects of the self, are on board. [both start tapping] Let's scan through from the top of the head down to the end of the toes to make sure that all parts of the body are in agreement with this new belief "I am loveable."

A certain vagueness is used here to suggest that different ego states or dissociated EPs (emotional parts) can also have a say in whether the belief is successfully installed. Most often, if there is any remaining discomfort, it may present as a slight tension, a tingle, or another bodily sensation. Regardless of how it represents itself, the therapist should give the client the option of using additional rounds of butterfly tapping or using RAP.

Therapist:	Let's take another deep breath [both inhale] . . . and let it go [both exhale] . . . So how did that go, any discomfort of any kind?
Nia:	No, I feel really relaxed. Thanks.
Therapist:	Very good. Well, in that case congratulations you have reconsolidated your first target.
Nia:	[Laughs] thank you!

Closing the Program

Whenever the body scan is completed without any sign of discomfort, there is a high chance that the target will have been fully reconsolidated without the need for further follow-up. Without this final step, there is a greater chance that the body and mind will continue working on the difficulty between sessions. In between sessions, this client's mind can produce a range of experiences that range from positive insights gained from the material to offenders from the trauma target reappearing in dream material. Although not every client will reexperience difficulties in between sessions, we have to be mindful of closing what we open and refrain from starting to address trauma targets if there is insufficient time to complete them. If there is only one minute left in the session before the installation or body scan, it is sometimes prudent to close by using RAP to completely contain any remaining distress rather than improperly proceeding with a rushed version of the procedure. But if there is sufficient time after the body scan, it is advisable to proceed with future integration. We want to give the client opportunities to envision how they will navigate through the world with the new perspective. In the client's mind, envisioning such a future will be an equivalent of "practicing" a means of coping with difficulty. If they can successfully imagine coping well, they are more likely to cope well in actual difficult situations. Regardless of what the available time makes possible, the therapist can finish the session by asking,

| Therapist: | Are there any insights or reflections from our session that can help to guide you until the next time we meet? |

In this way, we leave it up to the client to provide wisdom. Of course, we are free to summarize and provide our own reflections at the end, but it is especially important to let the client, in effect, create their own homework assignment. What they say at the end of the session will most likely impact both the client and therapist. However, even if they have nothing profound to say, a summary from the therapist reflecting on the client's growth and the significance of completing these targets will be welcome.

Summary

This chapter summarized the RAP protocol and demonstrated how it can be used in a therapy session. What is especially notable about RAP is its flexibility, which is a key aspect of its unique anti-racist approach to therapy. In RAP, responsibility for bringing about change is no longer restricted to just the therapist. Each of the sessions before the initial reprocessing session is a step in setting the stage for the reconsolidation of traumatic material. The example used in this chapter focused on a racial trauma event from the client's past, but all events that leave a mark on a client function in a similar way, and can be cleared in the same way. What is important is that, after reprocessing the target, the client no longer reexperiences the difficulty in the same way. This is due to the transformational sequence of therapeutic reconsolidation, with repeated verifications, together with giving the client choices throughout the process. The dysfunctionally stored information relating to the past traumatic material can be reprocessed through the same methods we use for entertainment. Who would have thought that YouTube could be used to reprocess trauma? Who would have thought that healing could be fun?

CHAPTER 12

WRAPPING IT UP: ANTI-RACIST REFLECTIONS

Final Thoughts Relating to the Protocol

Using RAP demonstrably brings about healing and recovery, but certain features of the method have led some to wonder about its high rate of success. First, although the client and therapist can look forward to stable, positive results by adopting RAP, there is always an element of surprise in the process. The therapist can never know in advance what video a client will choose, and the client could never have predicted that successfully completing their targets could have been so effective. Moreover, as Zimmerman once explained to me, the field of psychotherapy has popularized two myths about itself: that catharsis is necessary for change and that change requires a significant amount of time (Personal communication, 2022). The rapid change that RAP facilitates therefore causes some clients to question whether their trauma has truly been resolved and others to wonder whether it will last.

When I sense these kinds of doubts, I ask the client to think back to the original target and notice what happens. Therapeutic reconsolidation predicts that the memory address storing the information will have been resolved. The AIP model predicts that the dysfunctional stored material cannot maintain its state-specific form after using bilateral stimulation and a standardized protocol. RAP theory explains that, once we change the negative belief, it can never feed back into the somatic experience that fuelled it. The cycle is broken. While there may still be additional memories that need to be treated to ensure that the problem is completely resolved, this is how we repair symptoms—by targeting them at the source.

Insights and Challenges Between Sessions

Clients are also reminded that there may be dream material or processing that occurs between sessions. These may take place in the form of insights in which adaptive information becomes salient or may come in the form of challenges to the integrity of the positive cognition. Insights can manifest in numerous ways. At one extreme, they may occur in our waking lives and be fully present to awareness. At the other extreme, they may be unconscious and outside our awareness or may even arise in disguised forms through dream material. It is not unusual for clients to experience spontaneous feelings of gratitude between sessions, or have dreams with unexpectedly happy endings such as the final instance of a recurring nightmare concluding with a completely different, positive ending. Clients may experience validation from external sources, or catch themselves being surprised by their own internal validation. For this reason, at the beginning of a new session, we ask clients if they have had any insights or other positive experiences relating to either the negative cognition or the positive cognition from the previous session between then and now. The insights may be either concrete ones or metaphoric interpretations. After successfully completing the reconsolidation process, clients regularly report a reduction in their susceptibility to negative aspects of the reprocessed target or an increase in their ability to reject dysfunctional material about the target either by verbalizations ("No, that's not who I am anymore") or visual imagery (e.g., a door being swiftly closed on the intruding belief).

Still, challenges are expected. Due to insufficient preparation or incomplete sessions, clients may experience a reminder of some of the material that has been worked on. For example, a client who worked on an insect phobia was unable to complete the installation of the positive belief before closing a session. At the next sessions' reevaluation, she recounted the following experience.

Client:	The other day I was showering and the lights went out. It was so dark and I thought... "but... what if... bugs? And I FREAKED OUT! [laughing]
Therapist:	[laughing] Wow now that's funny!
Client:	I know, right? But it was only for a minute. Usually, I would get really worked up after something like that, but this time I was able to remember the forest and calm myself down. I didn't need my boyfriend's help. I realized that I felt calmer quicker than I ever did before. So, I thought to myself, this RAP is NO JOKE!

What is fascinating about such reports is to find that even the initiation of memory reconsolidation can have significant changes on the target material. Thus, doing even a little bit is still doing a lot. During the remainder of the session with this client, we completed the target, and at our next session she reported that the phobic response was completely resolved without any further inter-session triggers or bug scares.

Sharing Our Screen to Address Phobias

With another client who had a phobia about snakes, we used the RAP procedure to reduce the intensity of the fear. Before the phobia developed, she used to go on daily runs, but after she started worrying about snakes, her health suffered because she could no longer practice her fitness routine. Some years previously, she had come upon a snake in the grass. This created a dysfunctional association in her mind. After that pathological association was installed, even mistaking a branch for a snake or seeing a snake on television would cause her to panic and trigger an urge to flee. This had led to increasing social isolation.

We treated the problem by using RAP to zero in on the root of problem. After using an affect bridge, we connected to the touchstone event that housed the negative belief "I can't handle the pain." We discovered that this was linked not only to a fear of snakes but also to the crushing weight of violence she had suffered during childhood. Her parents, faced with unbelievable poverty and social challenges related to racial inequity and systemic barriers, had taken out their frustrations on her, beating her with long brown belts when they would take her outside in the backyard to "discipline" her. An association was made in her mind between the belts they used and snakes, which caused her sympathetic nervous system to become activated when she saw or thought about a snake.

Reprocessing the target delinked the negative belief from the image of snakes (or any animal) and led to an immediate reduction in the phobic response. How was this verified? Because since I was already sharing my screen with a positive video, there was nothing to stop us from sharing the screen while doing a YouTube video search for "scary snake." She and I both laughed about the fact that I was more uncomfortable with the video than she now was. Of course, reaching this point did take work, including treating additional memories relating to parental violence, working through inter-session ambivalence to recovery, and integrating essential resources for her overwhelmed emotional parts, but it is often surprising even to the therapist how effective using our technology can be for enacting rapid change.

Negative associations are stored in our mind in a similar way. For this reason, treating racial trauma is similar to the treatment of phobic responses and other severe mental health concerns. Even the treatment of some psychoses can be supported using EMDR therapy, as some symptoms are based on traumatic experiences as well (Miller, 2015). All of these issues, and more, are characterized by etiological events from the past and limiting beliefs in the present, leading to expectations of a future haunted by the phantoms of suffering and adversity. The prudent therapist must therefore attend to the past, present, and future of the client, but when using RAP we go a step further; we even leave a reminder of the resource with an aspect of our past self and encourage the client to predict a positive future with 100 percent certainty. We use our technology, together with the alliance between therapist and client, to ensure this.

Working with Instead of Against our Client

Additionally, from the transcripts of parts of sessions included in Chapters 4 through 11, the reader may also have noticed that the therapist does not need to say much for the change to happen. Rhythm and Processing shares many similarities with EMDR therapy and this is one of them. For example, part of what makes EMDR therapy in general so helpful is what Leeds (2016) refers to as "contingent responses." Much like a child attending to a parent with complete attention on facial expression, tone of voice, and subtle movements, the client on the verge of encountering what they have thus far perceived to be insurmountable difficulties relies on the presence of the therapist for safety. Nonspecific comments such as "notice that" or "go with that" and attention-guiding questions like "what do you notice now?" or "what's going on now?" provide room for the client to weave their own story. After the client responds, as long as they are within their window of tolerance of the disturbing material, the therapist follows up with "go with that" and "let's go with that." Through this process, the client feels "followed" and "seen" by these subtly encouraging comments. The client is then able to venture into the great unknown knowing that the therapist is holding space for the process of therapeutic reconsolidation.

As the transcriptions from sessions show, the therapist taps and breathes along with the client. This makes the client feel that they are participating in a healing partnership with the therapist rather than being a "patient" who is the "object" of a treatment. During the process of recovery, the therapist and client are in a community with one another. Further research may find that there is a stimulation of mirror neurons or even a polyvagal process of reciprocity in the process that contributes to the enhanced results. Even the shared viewing of the video may be discovered to have verifiable neurological or polyvagal effects. In practical terms, however, the important thing is that the therapy makes clients feel that we are collaborating *with* them rather than performing a procedure *on* them. RAP in particular is designed to be an approach that promotes a sense of play that contrasts positively with the difficulties and challenges of living in our present society. It shows that healing, even from severe trauma, can be enjoyable and does not need to focus solely on suffering in order to be successful. At the time of this writing, I have not used the RAP technique with couples, families, and groups in clinical settings, but there is no doubt that healing in community with others would be the next frontier.

Racial trauma recovery is not possible only though the individualized approach of RAP. If we use the right technology in a collaborative spirit, all of our psychotherapies can be congenial and community-building. Let us work towards a future where racial trauma recovery becomes accessible and applicable for all people—literally in the blink of an eye.

Summarizing our Work Together

Before summing up the key ideas of this book, I want to take a moment to thank the reader for accompanying me on this journey toward the transmutation of suffering into wisdom. For me, it has been fun as well as professionally satisfying to help people to heal and recover using this enhanced integrative approach to memory reconsolidation. I hope you have enjoyed the journey too, and more importantly, that you will benefit from its insights and suggestions. To sum up my approach, I will summarize the main ideas of racial trauma recovery from each of the preceding chapters.

1. We recognize that anti-Black racism and the negative social appraisal of individuals who do not fit a white, heterosexual, male, able-bodied label feed into cycles of harm in a social structure that privileges certain members over others.

2. Knowledge of the fundamental Africentric dimensions is the necessary basis for a healthy working alliance between client and therapist, while the Adaptive Information Processing model assists in showing us both how problems are stored in memory and how to resolve them.

3. Discussions of racial trauma must consider the neurobiological impacts of trauma in addition to the effects of social, economic, and political factors. An understanding of Massey's model of structural racism is essential.

4. The symptom cycle helps to explain how RAP strategies target the source of mental health problems in conjunction with the sequence of therapeutic reconsolidation.

5. The therapeutic alliance and information gathering are informed by the Four Cores of anti-racist psychotherapy as well as by factoring in the power dynamic between therapist and client.

6. Ambivalence should be treated as a natural part of psychotherapy that can contribute to treatment plan development using the PROS/CONS balance sheet.

7. A basic knowledge of structural dissociation helps to explain why certain emotional parts can feel reluctant about change. It also helps tell us which resources must be integrated before progress can be made.

8. The Rhythm and Processing technique is derived from the Four Blinks method, which is a derivative, in turn, of Flash Technique. Used properly, all these approaches (and others related to them) can bring about safe, rapid, and effective change for those suffering from complex trauma.

9. Polyvagal theory helps us to see how the approach/avoidance behaviors of ANP and EP are linked to basic evolutionary survival instincts. Genograms allow us to see how these behaviors may have emerged.

10.   Using a racial trauma target history that lists and prioritizes potential targets for intervention enables a strategic, collaborative approach to treatment planning and enhances clients' confidence and motivation for change.

11.   Finally, by using Rhythm and Processing Strategies, we can quickly and effectively target racial trauma targets from the past, change limiting beliefs in the present, and reduce emotional drivers that threaten the possibilities of the future.

Final Reflections on Racial Trauma

I would like to end this book by talking at more length about the idea of racial trauma. This topic is both very important to me personally and in my clinical practice but also the main theme of this book as a whole.

Comas-Díaz and colleagues (2019) explain that racial trauma and race-based stress refer to real or perceived experiences that compromise one's sense of safety from racial discrimination. Anti-racist psychotherapy expands this definition. It incorporates multigenerational transmission from forebears and ancestors with present-day experiences of retraumatization from ongoing structures and practices of oppression and emphasizes the need to confront a social structure that reinforces racial trauma by means of denial, complacent neutrality, or complicit acceptance. When I talk about racial trauma, I intentionally center my focus on the experience of Black people. This is not because I seek to exclude others, however. The problem of anti-Black racism affects people of all races. Recently, many white people have become more comfortable with interrogating their own whiteness in public. All people are racialized, but some of us are racialized to a disadvantage; many white people are racialized to an advantage. I believe the absence of discussions of race leads to the continuation of injustice. Resolving the issue of race can only take place when we acknowledge we all have it. Race is not just about Blackness but about the social construction of an identities and all that goes with them.

So while my focus is on racial trauma recovery, many of the conclusions can apply to several other socially constructed identities. The hypervigilance of the Black person is similar to the extra concern younger women of all races face when going out late at night by themselves, wary of male predators obsessed with asserting their precarious masculinity. The allophone immigrant must be wary when going into environments where their language may be unwelcome. The transwoman will likely be hesitant when meeting a new therapist because there is the chance she may encounter one who hates her simply because of her identity. I recently met a client who identified as queer and confided in me that their previous therapist told them that they could not identify that way and would "have to choose" if they wanted that therapist's help. Both the client and therapist were white, but heterosexism also operates within the realms of the binary complex trauma cycle.

Therapists grow up and are trained in the same racist, heterosexist, imperialist, patriarchal society as everyone else. We are not immune to perpetuating its effects, but for the sake of our clients, we must do better. An individual's identity—or more accurately, how society characterizes the individual's identity—creates a propensity for certain types of adverse experiences. I wish to emphasize this point: racial trauma and other identity-based stresses are not just located in the Black body or consciousness. The problem originates in the offender, not the victim. Rather than putting the responsibility on the oppressed to render themselves less vulnerable, those who have the most power must do their part to reduce harm.

Nevertheless, Black people can internalize the effects of anti-Black racism. When this happens, they view themselves through the lens of a social structure that privileges white bodies. The Black person who internalizes the microaggressions and negative cognitions of the Eurocentric social structure inadvertently sees herself as lesser-than due to her Blackness. Because she is part of a social structure where she is forced to internalize shame due to her appearance, she will also, predictably, view other Black people as deficient. The association lies deep in the nervous system, and when the sympathetic nervous system activates it at the sight of a brother, the capacity for ventral vagal reciprocity is completely prevented.

However, non-Black people are also impacted by the effects of anti-Black racism. Frequently, white people, too, internalize the effects of anti-Black racism, in part because they are supposed to be seen as the standard for an unattainable perfection. As they have created this social structure to benefit themselves, they participate by pathologically viewing the Black body from both a distorted and a mythical perspective. But internalization of this racist discourse is not without adverse consequences for themselves. For one thing, white people necessarily also view themselves through a distorted and dysfunctional lens. The white person who internalizes anti-Black racism believes whiteness makes them superior to all things in nature. In seeing other white people as worth more than those who are not white, they place a heavy psychic burden on themselves. Their whiteness must be kept to a certain standard . . . or else.

The White Person's Internalization of Anti-Black Racism

Deep down, the white person who internalizes racism fears that one day they will be rejected, dethroned, or rendered irrelevant (see Appendix II, page 225). Otherwise there would be no need to cultivate a belief in white supremacy. White supremacy is the ultimate oppressor of our time, culminating in the destructive nature of capitalism, genocide, and orientalism (Smith, 2012, p. 66), but not without a cost; I have never met a bully that came from a well-adjusted, loving family. Beliefs in supremacy or the maintenance of privilege are inextricably linked with insecurity. The white racist fears that whiteness will one day vanish forever. Resmaa Menakem (2021) speaks eloquently about this trauma response of whiteness, noting that present-day white people's colonial ancestors were in a fight/flight response when they arrived on this content. The settler-colonialist was either running away from something to get here or fighting against someone in order to stay. Frequently, it was both. There is an ever present fear of not satisfying the exclusive standard of whiteness, and participation in a field of violence is required to set foot in the category in the first place.

The split in races between white and Black, meant to represent perfect and imperfect, creates a conceptual separation, but also a perpetual comparison. A pathological relationship exists between white and Black because whiteness needs Blackness in order to exist. Franz Fanon was one of the first to show how deeply related negrophilia and negrophobia are. The white interest in Black culture is linked to the fear of it. The fetishization and hypersexualization of the Black body is linked to the violence toward it. The primary consumers of rap music are white people. There are many theories and explanations for this, but they are not primarily anti-racist in origin. Bill

Yousman (2003) discusses "blackophilia" and "blackophobia" in a similar way, demonstrating that the interest in Black media serves a political function: "mediated images of violence and chaos perpetrated by Blacks may attract White consumers while reinforcing the fear and anxieties that these young people subconsciously (or not) harbor toward Blacks. . . . These are the same images that both mainstream conservative politicians and far-right White supremacists invoke to justify regressive social policies or violent 'reprisals' (p. 379). While rappers usually get blamed for this, the record executives who cut their checks don't seem to mind as long as the violence is not toward white people and the racial slurs are only toward one group.

In this way, rap becomes a safe haven for white people, while the content reinforces the Black experience as dangerous, and all for the sake of profit. Many lynch mobs in the United States were formed when white women accused Black men of sexual advances. In 1955, not coincidentally at the beginning of the civil rights campaign, Carolyn Bryant, a 21-year-old white woman, accused Emmet Till, a 14-year-old African-American, of whistling at her, effectively sentencing him to a gruesome death by two white male acquaintances. It was documented that her accusations were embellishments and partially false. The murderers were never charged even though they admitted to lynching him.

In August 2022, a grand jury declined to indict Bryant for manslaughter and kidnapping charges.[41] There was an unserved arrest warrant dated August 29, 1955 that was only discovered recently, but white people are not to be punished for crimes against Black people, so at the time of this writing, no one has been held accountable for Emmet Till's murder. We could discuss uncountable other examples of white women inciting lynch mobs, but what is important for my argument here is that these stories live on in the white collective unconscious. Bill Cosby and R. Kelly, while by no means innocent or flawless, have become the most high-profile faces of male sexual violence, while the most powerful white men seemingly avoid being held accountable. We live in a system that colludes with white supremacy by

---

[41] https://www.cnn.com/2022/08/09/us/emmett-till-carolyn-bryant-no-indictment-reaj/index.html

allotting harsher penalties on the basis of melanin and filling prisons with Black men for the sake of profit.

The Social Construction of Suffering

Yokum (2022), reviewing Fanon's foundational argument, suggests that, in order to address what we term throughout this book as the social construction of racial trauma, we need to engage with "sociodiagnostics," by which she means making the client aware of the social causes of their suffering.

Fanon relates, for example, that to treat a patient suffering due to culturally implanted fantasies about evil Black men, he encourages them to "choose action. . . with respect to . . . the social structure" (1958; 2008, p. 80). As Yokum (2022, p. 4) points out,

> It would not be adequate, in this kind of situation, to help the individual to cleanse themselves of their pernicious negative ideas about Blackness; when those associations are rampant in the culture, they will continue to be a source of affliction for oneself and others. Thus, to address the actual source of the problem, one must take social and political action aimed at changing the culture and the social structure—a tall order, perhaps, but a more honest approach to alleviating psychic illness than an individually-based, Freudian-style "talking cure" (and one that avoids the charge . . . against the normalizing tendencies of psychoanalysis).

The solution for racial trauma can never be psychotherapy alone. In fact, many therapies inadvertently help clients to feel "neutral" about racism and related social injustices. The problem of anti-Black racism can only be resolved when white people recognize there is no long-term benefit to having a system that prioritizes their survival over the survival of everyone and everything else on the planet.

But I wonder how likely this will ever be. I think of how many white male mass shooters are even now being radicalized or emboldened by the American attack on its own country on January 6, 2021. What kinds of distortions have to be held in a person's mind to prompt such self-destruction even in a context where they have the power, the laws, and the courts on their side? But while the threat of neo-fascist white nationalism rears its ugly head in everyday political discourse, I will never reserve my condemnation for right-wing extremism alone, because so-called moderates and liberals are equally culpable. Where they are elected—in large part through the votes of those who have been historically marginalized—they still behave as "nice" non-racists (as opposed to anti-racists) and always say "not now" when they have an opportunity to make a radical change. They also take oppressed racial groups for granted. Before being elected, President Biden had the temerity to tell Black people "you ain't Black" unless they voted for him. [42] More recently, First Lady Jill Biden drew swift condemnation after comparing Latino supporters to tacos. [43] If it is not fetishization, the oppressed experience an endless objectification. In this political system, we can be taken for granted and conned into helping maintain a wretched status quo. We are cursed with a vanilla "neutrality" whose poles swing between accidental racism and outright fascism. We live in an age where we see the social structure cannibalizing itself.

The psychological impacts of racism, whether resulting from internalized oppression or fear of white inferiority, are natural targets for RAP. The internalization of anti-Black racism creates negative cognitions and somatic experiences that drive all racial groups to fight, flee, or freeze. But while RAP (and other memory reconsolidation-based approaches) can successfully target the client's negative associations as well as make the client more aware of the broader systemic nature of racism, changing this larger system will not happen overnight. This saddens me, because I know that therapy is reactive in nature. It can only target trauma that has been consolidated in the individual's memory network. Ultimately, we require an approach that makes therapy no longer necessary. This must be a comprehensive, proactive, political approach. We need policies that *prevent* trauma. We need measures that address both racism and poverty. We need to make health care a human right. We need action.

---

[42] https://www.politico.com/news/2020/05/22/joe-biden-breakfast-club-interview-274490

[43] https://www.usatoday.com/story/entertainment/celebrities/2022/07/12/jill-biden-breakfast-tacos-speech-backlash/10035923002/

Be About It

At a recent workshop, a white woman asked me what she can do to be a better anti-racist psychotherapist. I explained that she has to *be* about it rather than just *talk* about it. Then I gave her an example. I said:

> The other day I went to the hospital with my partner to open a file. We were attended by a receptionist who appeared to be a dark-skinned South Asian man. His confidence was shot. From working among a group of white and white-passing colleagues, he had clearly internalized the negative belief "I am not good enough." He spoke to us through stutters, and his fingers jittered as he typed; he looked like he was on the verge of burnout. A white supervisor approached him from behind and chastised him because he made a mistake on our   hospital card. "What's wrong with you, what are you doing?" she asked. She used her big, burly presence to tower over the man and demonstrate dominance while reducing her cowed colleague into rubble. I leapt to his defense, "Hey," I told her, "don't talk down to him like that!" She replied, "I wasn't talking down to him!" and then directed her frustration at me. "Why do YOU want a card?" she demanded. She was clearly upset that I had had the "nerve" to call her out for her arrogance.
>
> By this point, my adrenaline was pumping, and my cortisol-infused response to a perceived threat had been activated. Noticing this, my partner intervened to calm the situation by directing attention toward herself. The bully could see she was outnumbered and switched back to her "regularly scheduled program." She calmed her tone and explained that she only wanted to prevent errors so she would not be yelled at by her own supervisor. We continued with opening the file, and at the end of the process, the supervisor said "Thank you" as we got ready to leave. As we stood up, I exclaimed, "You see, this is how

calm you can be. Next time don't bring that kind of energy around here," and we started walking out. But before I turned around, I could see that the young receptionist had a smile on his face. That smile whispered,

"Finally! No one ever talked to her like that."

Although I was not as professional-sounding during this encounter as I need to be in the edited pages of a book or workshop, and while it is not possible to know if that situation actually improved anything, at least I stepped in. I was willing to make myself vulnerable to defend the interests of some guy I will likely never see again in my life. This is what anti-racism is. Don't just stand there, *do* something in the face of injustice. When in doubt about what to do, protect others.

Fight against oppression.

In this world based on capital and power, people either create, consume, or are consumed by things. You can consume the endless highlights of social media and remain complacent or be consumed by your own privilege and look the other way. Our society is traumatized by its own substitute actions and self-defeating responses. Idleness and "neutrality" do nothing to stop the warmongers, greedy businessmen and the drivers of climate change that threaten our collective existence. Genuine anti-racism operates very differently. Don't do it for a thank you note or a white savior gift card. Being an anti-racist psychotherapist means you create change in your own community. Be an experiential therapist and strive to be a courageous person. Don't just talk about it, *be* about it.

Summary

Because in RAP we are using unconventional ways of helping people, the results can exceed what they thought was possible. Through the reconsolidation of traumatic memories, clients can spontaneously gain insights. Because RAP can be facilitated by sharing the therapist's screen, we can also use exposure-based approaches to create healing in unique ways. Throughout this book, my intention has been to teach unique strategies based on the rhythm of the client-therapist interaction and the untapped processing power of our complex neurobiology.

Because of our infinite creativity as human beings, it may very well be possible to help people recover from the experience of racial trauma. But RAP also has another broader goal. It seeks to prevent the trauma from happening in the first place. It is my hope that in reading this book you have been able to comprehend that racial trauma is more than just a Black problem. It is everyone's problem, and the apolitical therapist is a therapist who sides with the oppressor. When witnessing violence and victimization, there is no such thing as "neutrality." Sure, we can't all be activists who fight for justice out on the streets, but by using our know-how and the available technology to help clients to recover their dignity, we can encourage others to stand up and confront oppression in all of its manifestations. Let us do what we can to help the world to heal, but let's start with ourselves. Heal yourself, *then* heal your community. Let's change the world one racial trauma target at a time.

Blessings and Strength,

-David Archer

APPENDIX I

---❧---

BLACK MEDITATION SCRIPTS

The following lists scripts that come from this author's previous title: Black Meditation: Ten Practices for Self-Care, Mindfulness, and Self-Determination

Skill #3: Guided Earth Meditation

Take some time to sit or rest in a comfortable position. Be aware that if at any time you need to shift to adjust your position during the meditation, that is perfectly fine. If you are sitting upright, see if it is possible to assume a posture of dignity, an awareness and acknowledgement of your purpose as you prepare to start.

I would like for you to breathe in a comfortable way... and take in some deep breaths. Continue to breathe in . . . and breathe out. You will notice that as you continue to breathe in . . . and breathe out, you will develop your own rhythm. And as you continue to breathe in . . . and breathe out, carry no expectation. Breathe in . . . and breathe out without judgment of whether it is being done right or wrong. As you breathe, there may be thoughts that come to your awareness. The idea is not to pull any thoughts toward you or to push any thoughts aside. You are simply to return to the breath.

As you continue to breathe in and breathe out, I would like for you now to bring your attention to the feeling of your feet, or any part of your body that supports your movement. I would like for you to breathe in . . . and breathe out. Take some time to acknowledge that your feet have been around for many, many years, that your body has allowed for you to move from one destination to another, either with the assistance of others or even on your own. And still, to this day, your feet—the lower part of your body—continues to support you, allowing you to move to the places where you need to go. Express gratitude for the parts of the body that allow you to travel the world.

Return to the breath. Breathing in . . . and breathing out. Notice the feeling of air entering the body and leaving the body. Return to the breath if there are distractions; notice the rising and falling of the breath instead.

As you continue to breathe in and breathe out, I would like for you to bring your attention to your back, now. I would like for you to acknowledge that your back, too, has been with you for many, many years. As the core of your body, your back has done everything that it can to support you. Acknowledge that still to this day, your back continues to allow you to align yourself to your path, to face forward and see the world as it is. Express gratitude to the parts of your body that allow you to face the world.

Return to the breath, breathing in . . . and breathing out. On your inhalation, nourish yourself with the breath. On exhalation, release what is unnecessary.

As you continue to breathe in and breathe out—acknowledging the body that sustains you, acknowledging the parts of your body that allow you to move through the world—I would like for you to bring your visualization deeper, to look deep down, below the dirt and into the earth. I would like for you to notice the planet itself and acknowledge that the planet, too, has been around for many, many years. Our Earth too, has been through many challenges and many changes, but still to this very day continues to provide the very sustenance that maintains life on the planet. The Earth provides an atmosphere that protects us, allowing for oxygen to proliferate the planet. We notice its ability to create life and to allow for us to take in the very breath that we are now breathing in . . . and breathing out. We express gratitude to the planet, as we breathe in . . . and breathe out. Breathing in . . . and breathing out.

Understand that as the body supports you, as you have the ability to breathe and move, even the planet can support you whenever you bring your mind to it.

Breathing in . . . and breathing out . . . now take in a deeper breath . . . and let it go . . .

Take some time to reflect. How do you feel in the body? How do you feel in the mind? How do you feel in your spirit?

Skill #4: Mindful Color Breathing

In the previous chapters, you have practiced noticing the breath and the energy associated with it. In this chapter, we will attempt a skill that involves a combination of breathing, awareness of the body, and visualization. The mindful color breathing technique is very helpful for people who need mild relief from stress. It involves the acknowledgement of suffering and its corresponding opposite. I would like for you to follow along. It would be best if you record this meditation in advance so you can close your eyes during the process. But even if you keep them open you can still enjoy the benefit.

I would like for you to assume a stance and posture where you can rest for 10 to 15 minutes. We carve out this space to allow for dignity and respect toward ourselves, where you can be free of distraction. Put your cellphone on silent; turn off your notifications and cultivate your awareness.

Once again, I would like for you to first acknowledge the body. Notice the placement of your feet; notice the posture of your back. Be aware of the feeling of different body parts. Notice the temperature of the air in the room. Acknowledge any sounds in the environment, placing no judgment, but just acknowledging.

Now I would like for you to start breathing in a way that is comfortable for you. Breathe in . . . and breathe out. Breathing in . . . and breathing out. Noticing the rhythm that is helpful for you. Acknowledging what happens when you breathe into the belly rather than the chest. Seeing what happens when you breathe into different body parts by bringing your awareness to them. Breathing in . . . and breathing out. Breathing in . . . and breathing out.

If there are any thoughts that distract your attention, that is perfectly fine. Compassionately, without judgement, return to the breath. Notice the parts of the body that rise and fall when you breathe. The body is the anchor that brings you back from the sea of thoughts.

I would now like for you to bring your awareness to different parts of the body. Notice, is there a part of the body that holds some form of stress at this time? Where is it located? How does it feel? Is it a tension;

is it a pressure? Without judgment, notice it. And next, I would like to ask you a strange question because it is our job to ask these strange questions… What is the color of the stress? See if you can come up with an answer of your own. No answer is strange to this question; we are just learning the language of the body. Let us consider this as color "**A**."

If on one hand the color of stress or suffering is color "**A**," then let me ask, what is the color of healing? Think about it, and then you will visualize the color of healing. Let us call this color "**B**."

Now, as you are breathing in and breathing out, I would like for you to visualize that you can breathe color "**B**" into the body. Breathe the color of healing into the body. Breathe in the feeling of healing into the body. And on the exhalation, release a different color. Breathe in the color that represents healing for you, and on the exhalation, release a different color. Notice the experience of breathing in and breathing out.

Experiment with your visualization. What form of nature does healing look like? Is it a landscape? Does it look like water or air? What is the visualization that corresponds to your process? Be curious with your infinite creativity. Take some time once more to breathe in the color of healing, but this time add a little special something to it. Some people can choose a visual, auditory, or even a felt sense of nature to the breath. Use your creativity, breathe in the color of healing with that extra special something to it. Breathing in . . . and letting it go. Breathing in . . . and breathing out. And one more time, take in a deep breath of that healing, with that extra something special to it . . . and let it go.

When you are ready you can open your eyes, return fully revitalized and ready to continue the rest of your day. If you have used this to relax before bed, you can rest if you need to, acknowledging that you have calmed the body. Have a nice rest.

Skill #6: Five Grateful Things Exercise

For this exercise you will need a pen and notebook. If you don't have a notebook, just write in the margins of this book, type in an electronic device, or record yourself on your cellphone. Use whatever you've got. The key is to record your experience and to read what you have written in your own handwriting (if it's recorded, listen to it in your own voice).

On the first blank page, I would like for you to write the following words: "Gratitude Journal." Feel free to customize anything else about the title. Designs, decals . . . all of this is to be customized to your look and feel.

On the next page—and the pages that follow—you can structure it however you would like, but I recommend that you start each entry with a date. You can title each entry if you would like, as well.

In each entry, you are free to write anything you'd like. Write about what you did that day, write about what your challenges and dreams, all of that is fine. What's essential is to write about what's happening right now. Feel free to write about what happened yesterday or what you look forward to tomorrow, but it is important to align it to how you're feeling today. **Option:** If you feel there is too much going on in your mind, you also have the option to "brain-dump"—expelling everything in your mind onto paper as fast as you can, not worrying about proper writing or legibility, just to get it all out. This part is more for writing than it is for reading. Dump out all the emotions—anger, sadness—just write it all out!

After writing your entry, the next step involves completing the entry by naming **five things you are grateful for**. They do not need to be big or significant. They can be as small as "I have a roof over my head" or "I went for a walk today." It is important to avoid any judgment of your answers. What is most crucial, is to put it on paper.

Once you have listed five things that allow you to feel gratitude, notice your body. Breathe in a comfortable way. Did you feel any feelings of relaxation through the body? Any yawning? Sensations of calmness? The exercise is not only about writing how you felt, but also about noticing how you felt. It is a practice to use with intention, to reflect on what happens in that moment when you take the time to acknowledge what's going on.

APPENDIX II

RACIAL TRAUMA RECOVERY: SUMMARY SHEETS

The Binary Complex Trauma Cycle

THE BINARY COMPLEX TRAUMA CYCLE

 The Binary Complex Trauma Cycle describes the influence of whiteness on those who do not identify as white. Whiteness projects its undesirable aspects onto Blackness.

 Doing so causes whiteness to become validated. In order to ensure delegitimization and subjugation, the oppressor must construct a narrative about the oppressed that must be followed at all costs.

Soul Murder
(Intense violence/ projection of negative cognitions)

White Supremacy/Insecurity
Dissociates (distances itself) from Trauma

Black Suffering
Becomes associated (identified with) trauma

Validation of Oppression
(The association of Blackness with suffering feeds into the self-regard of whiteness)

FRANCES CRESS WELSING'S DEFINITION OF WHITE SUPREMACY
A local and global power system of systemic racism conducted in all areas of people activity. The goal: preventing white genetic annihilation on Earth.

ANDREA SMITH'S THREE PILLARS OF WHITE SUPREMACY

 ANTI-BLACK RACISM
Anchoring capitalism: all bodies must be commodified and placed in a racial hierarchy.

 GENOCIDE
Anchoring colonialism: Indigenous people must be relegated to the past.

 ORIENTALISM
Anchoring war: the West must be superior. Foreigners are permanent threats.

Shengold, L. (1991). Soul murder: The effects of childhood abuse and deprivation. BoD–Books on Demand.
Welsing, F. C. (1991). The Isis (Yssis) papers. Chicago, IL: Third World Press
Smith, A. (2012). Indigeneity, settler colonialism, white supremacy. Racial formation in the twenty-first century, 66

The Cycle of Consolidation

THE CYCLE OF CONSOLIDATION

The focus of resolving the internalization of oppression must be on the center rather than the unlimited external triggers or numerous internal experiences of adversity. When we can repair the hub, the rest of the cycle comes to a halt.

CENTRIFUGAL REACTION

Not really a force. Due to inertia. Because the wheel has been moving it continues to move. Survivor has limiting beliefs that the problem will always continue.

CENTRIPETAL FORCE

The force pushing toward the center. Conditions in society encourage the consolidation of negative beliefs and somatic experiences.

NEGATIVE COGNITION

Conscious or preconscious beliefs acquired due to traumatic event.

NEGATIVE SOMATIC EXPERIENCE

The mind and body's involuntary, unpleasant reaction, linked to experiences stored in implicit memory.

Negative Cognition

Negative Somatic Experience

THE HUB

Cycles constantly between the negative cognition and negative feelings about the cognition.

THE SPOKES

Near limitless connections to and from the hub and the internal experiences.

THE TIRE

Internal thoughts, abstract and concrete thought forms connected to trauma reminders.

THE ROAD

Near limitless external events and experiences that can trigger associations to internal experiences.

THE THERAPEUTIC RECONSOLIDATION PROCESS

1. THE ACCESSING SEQUENCE

- Identify the presenting symptom
- Retrieve the emotional learning underlying the symptom (A)
- Present disconfirming knowledge (B)

2. THE TRANSFORMATION SEQUENCE

- Reactivate the emotional learning
- Activate disconfirming knowledge (B), prompting a mismatch with the emotional learning
- Repeat the pairing of A and B

3. VERIFICATION PHASE

- Verify there is no further reactivation of symptoms
- Change is maintained without the need for ongoing maintenance.

The Internalization of Anti-Black Racism

THE INTERNALIZATION OF ANTI-BLACK RACISM

──────── Process of Inferiorization ────────

This consequences of being on the receiving end of violence and exposure to repeated instances of social defeat leads to further delegitimization. The process is initiated by the oppressor.

 Dissociation of undesirable traits by oppressor

 Projection of negative beliefs and violence onto the oppressed

 Vulnerability to violence results in more social delegitimization

──────── Internalized Oppression ────────

Once the oppression becomes internalized, the oppressed person identifies with the negative messages of the perpetrator, consolidating negative cognitions about the self and their cultural group.

 Consolidation of negative beliefs about self and other group

 Reinforces internalization of shame and lack of safety

 Internalization of negative cognitions

 Trauma survivors often engage in substitute actions or negative self-talk to justify the violence and pain. They may generalize beliefs about inferiority to other members of their group.

This prevents people from fully recognizing their potential. Once people regain confidence they can break the cycle of suffering

For a detailed discussion see Archer, D. (2021). Anti-Racist Psychotherapy: Confronting Systemic Racism and Healing Racial Trauma. Each One Teach One Publications.

Rhythm and Processing Technique

RHYTHM AND PROCESSING TECHNIQUE

Setup and Self-Care

The following is the setup for using RAP technique.

Choose a CONTAINER that can be used to contain any stress

- Create a container that is robust enough to contain any stress in the body and mind

Choose a VACUUM that can put your stress in a CONTAINER

- Make sure that it is reliable and large enough to vacuum up any stress

TEST it out

- See if it can work with a mild disturbance (subjective disturbance of less than 3/10)
- Vacuum up the stress (use your hands if that helps or just imagine it)
- Place the container as away as far as it needs to be from you (e.g. visualize it being sent down the street, underground, etc.)
- Check that you feel clear in the body before continuing. If not, upgrade your container or vacuum.

If you're OK with the vacuum/container, go to the next step. Otherwise, return to step 1.

Choose a COM (Calm or Motivating) Video

- Can be anything that makes you feel good or relaxed (e.g. beaches, forests, animals, etc.)
- You can use YouTube or any other streaming video platform. You can also use your immediate environment if there are things (e.g. pets) or sceneries (e.g. nature) that are also COM.
- Video is recommended because it has both audio and visual components, but you can even use an image or a painting if you would like.

Be prepared to blink

- While looking at   ◦ Count to 4 then blink 4-5 times RAPIDLY
  the COM Video   ◦ Count to 5 then blink 4-5 times RAPIDLY
                     ◦ Count to 4 then blink 4-5 times RAPIDLY
                     ◦ Count to 5 then blink 4-5 times RAPIDLY

Check in and notice yourself

- Upgrade the vacuum, container or video to your liking
- Reduce the intensity of the stress to 0.
- Repeat steps 5 and 6 until stress is zero

ENJOY!

- It is highly recommended to do this with a therapist as the effects are stronger when someone else can hold space and do it with you. But it is also a way of self-soothing when used in conjunction with other resources.

RAP Technique: GeneralScan

RHYTHM AND PROCESSING TECHNIQUE
GENERALSCAN

Here are the instructions for using the RAP technique with clients. We start with the GeneralScan to reduce the global level of disturbance. This can help to take the edge off of the problem.

 SETUP (Step #0) Client chooses Vacuum cleaner and container combo

Client chooses video, image, or environmental cue
- Must be COM (Calm or Motivating) and unrelated to any trauma triggers

After SETUP has been completed proceed to the following.

 Step 1
Therapist asks client to select a problem to address

 Step 2
Therapist elicits Subjective Unit of Disturbance (SUD) from client

 Step 4
Utilization of RAP technique

Step 3
Client utilizes vacuum / container to remove the disturbance

Therapist instructs client to attend to the positive focus (play the video through shared screen)

- 1...2...3...4...RAP [client blinks rapidly]
- 1...2...3...4...5...RAP [client blinks rapidly]
- 1...2...3...4...RAP [client blinks rapidly]
- 1...2...3...4...5...RAP [client blinks rapidly]

 Step 5
Therapist asks if client was able to remain calm or feel in the present moment or within window of affect tolerance while watching the video.

If yes Proceed to the step 6

Else Provide them with the options to change the video/positive focus. Then repeat from step 2

Step 6
Therapist asks client to "lightly check in" with the target and determine if there is any remaining disturbance

If disturbance = true then repeat from step 3

If disturbance = false Initiate DeepScan process

RAP Technique: DeepScan

RHYTHM AND PROCESSING TECHNIQUE
DEEPSCAN

Here is the second step. We use the DeepScan typically after using the GeneralScan. This allows us to remove any specific or remaining disturbances in the target memory.

Initiate DeepScan

Step 7

Client is asked to imagine that the problem has a beginning and an end like a movie. Then ask them to scan through every unique scene in the movie to check if there is any remaining disturbance when they imagine the target.

Step 8

Client scans memory searching for any remaining disturbance

If disturbance = true

Begin the following loop

 ❶ Therapist elicits SUD for this specific part of the target

 ❸ Verify the client was calm, present and within window of affect tolerance

 ❷ Vacuum and reinitiate loop

 ❹ Re-evaluate the SUD (Scale of 0 to 10)

 If SUD > 0

Reinitiate this Loop

 If SUD = 0 Exit this Loop

Return to step 8

If disturbance = false

 Re-evaluate the SUD once more when client revisits the whole target.

 If SUD > 0 Because there is still some remaining disturbance, scan again and return to step 8

 Else Now that there is no longer any remaining disturbance, the DeepScan process is complete.

After completing the DeepScan Program, the most difficult part of the target will be completed. The negative cognition has lost its strength

REFERENCES

Adam, E. K., Heissel, J. A., Zeiders, K. H., Richeson, J. A., Ross, E. C., Ehrlich, K. B., Levy, D., Kemeny, M., Brodish A. B., Malanchuk O., & Peck, S. C. (2015). Developmental histories of perceived racial discrimination and diurnal cortisol profiles in adulthood: A 20-year prospective study. *Psychoneuroendocrinology, 62*, 279-291.

Alberini, C. M., & LeDoux, J. E. (2013). Memory reconsolidation. *Current Biology, 23*(17), R746–R750.

American Psychiatric Association. (2013). *Diagnostic and statistical manual of mental disorders: DSM-5.* American Psychiatric Publishing.

Annesley, P., Alabi, A., & Longdon, L. (2019). The EMDR DeTUR protocol for the treatment of self-injury in a patient with severe personality disorder: A case report. *Journal of Criminological Research, Policy and Practice, 5*(2). DOI:10.1108/JCRPP-11-2018-0034

Archer, D. (2020). Racial trauma, neurons, and EMDR: The path towards an anti-racist psychotherapy. *Go With That Magazine, 25*(3), 6-20.

Archer, D. (2021a). *Anti-racist psychotherapy: Confronting systemic racism and healing racial trauma.* Each One Teach One Publications.

Archer, D. (2021b). *Black meditation: Ten practices for self-care, mindfulness, and self-determination.* Each One Teach One Publications.

Belgrave, F. Z., & Allison, K. W. (2018). *African American psychology: From Africa to America.* Sage.

Bor, J., Venkataramani, A. S., Williams, D. R., & Tsai, A. C. (2018). Police killings and their spillover effects on the mental health of black Americans: A population-based, quasi-experimental study. *The Lancet, 392*(10144), 302–310.

Bridge, J. A., Asti, L., Horowitz, L. M., Greenhouse, J. B., Fontanella, C. A., Sheftall, A. H., Kelleher, K. J., & Campo, J. V. (2015). Suicide trends among elementary school–aged children in the United States from 1993 to 2012. *JAMA pediatrics, 169*(7), 673–677.

Brooks, S. K., Webster, R. K., Smith, L. E., Woodland, L., Wessely, S., Greenberg, N., & Rubin, G. J. (2020). The psychological impact of quarantine and how to reduce it: Rapid review of the evidence. *The Lancet, 395*(10227), 912–920.

Brouwers, T. C., de Jongh, A., & Matthijssen, S. J. (2021, December 23). The effects of the Flash technique compared to those of an abbreviated eye movement desensitization and reprocessing therapy protocol on the emotionality and vividness of aversive memories. *Frontiers in Psychology*, DOI: 10.3389/fpsyg.2021.741163.

Bynum, G. (2021). "Race is a fiction; Racism is not"? Understandings of race in antiracist education. *Educational Theory, 71*(2), 223–245.

Comas-Díaz, L., Hall, G. N., & Neville, H. A. (2019). Racial trauma: Theory, research, and healing: *American Psychologist, 74*(1), 1.

Dana, D. (2018). *The Polyvagal theory in therapy: engaging the rhythm of regulation.* Norton.

Dwyer, W. O., & Stanton, L. (1975). Racial differences in color vision: Do they exist? *American Journal of Optometry and Physiological Optics, 52*(3), 224–229.

Ecker, B., Ticic, R., & Hulley, L. (2012). *Unlocking the emotional brain: Eliminating symptoms at their roots using memory reconsolidation.* Routledge.

Fanon, F.. 2008 (1952; 2008). *Black skin, white masks.* Trans. Richard Philcox. Grove Press.

Farrell, D., Kiernan, M. D., de Jongh, A., Miller, P. W., Bumke, P., Ahmad, S., Knibbs, L., Mattheß, C., Keenan, P., & Mattheß, H. (2020). Treating implicit trauma: A quasi-experimental study comparing the EMDR therapy standard protocol with a 'Blind 2 Therapist' version within a trauma capacity building project in Northern Iraq. *Journal of International Humanitarian Action, 5*(1), 1–13.

Farrell, D., Fadeeva, A., Zat, Z., Knibbs, L., Miller, P., Barron, I., Matthess, H., Matthess, C., Gazit, N., & Kiernan, M. D. (2022, July 6). A stage 1 pilot cohort exploring the use of EMDR therapy as a video-conference psychotherapy during COVID-19: A proof of concept study utilising a virtual Blind 2 Therapist protocol. *Frontiers in Psychology.* DOI: 10.3389/fpsyg.2022.901855.

Fisher, A. N., & Ryan, M. K. (2021). Gender inequalities during COVID-19. *Group Processes & Intergroup Relations, 24*(2), 237–245.

French, H. W. (2021). Born in Blackness: Africa, Africans, and the making of the modern world: 1471 to the Second World War. Liveright Publishing.

Gillborn, D. (2016). Softly, softly: Genetics, intelligence and the hidden racism of the new geneism. *Journal of Education Policy, 31*(4), 365–388.

Giotakos, O. (2020). Neurobiology of emotional trauma. *Psychiatriki, 31*(2), 162–171.

Golestaneh, L., Neugarten, J., Fisher, M., Billett, H. H., Gil, M. R., Johns, T., Milagros, Y., Mokrzycki, M. H., Coco, M., Norris, K. C., Perez, H. R., Scott, S., Kim, R. S., & Bellin, E. (2020, August 25). The association of race and COVID-19 mortality. *EClinicalMedicine.* DOI: https://DOI.org/10.1016/j.eclinm.2020.100455.

Grand, D. (2013). *Brainspotting: The revolutionary new therapy for rapid and effective change.* Sounds True.

hooks, b. (2010). *Understanding patriarchy.* Louisville Anarchist Federation.

Howell E. A. (2018) Reducing disparities in severe maternal morbidity and mortality. *Clinical Obstetrics and Gynecology, 61*(2), 387–399. DOI: 10.1097/GRF.0000000000000349

Isobel, S., & Angus-Leppan, G. (2018). Neuro-reciprocity and vicarious trauma in psychiatrists. *Australasian Psychiatry, 26*(4), 388–390.

Karaca-Mandic, P., Georgiou, A., & Sen, S. (2021). Assessment of COVID-19 hospitalizations by race/ethnicity in 12 states. *JAMA internal medicine, 181*(1), 131–134.

Knipe, J. (2005). Targeting positive affect to clear the pain of unrequited love, codependence, avoidance, and procrastination. In Shapiro, R. (Ed.) *EMDR Solutions: Pathways to healing* (pp.189–212). Norton.

Knipe, J. (2009) Dysfunctional positive affect: Codependence or obsession with self-defeating behavior. In Luber, M. (Ed.). *EMDR scripted protocols: Special populations* (pp. 3463–465). Springer.

Korn, D. L., & Leeds, A. M. (2002). Preliminary evidence of efficacy for EMDR resource development and installation in the stabilization phase of treatment of complex posttraumatic stress disorder. *Journal of Clinical Psychology, 58*(12), 1465–1487.

Lee, J. L., Nader, K., & Schiller, D. (2017). An update on memory reconsolidation updating. *Trends in Cognitive Sciences, 21*(7), 531–545.

Leeds, A. M. (2016). *A guide to the standard EMDR therapy protocols for clinicians, supervisors, and consultants.* (2nd ed.). Springer.

Levine, S. (1991). *Guided meditations, explorations, and healings.* Anchor Books Doubleday.

Levine, P. A. (2015). *Trauma and memory: Brain and body in a search for the living past: A practical guide for understanding and working with traumatic memory.* North Atlantic Books.

Manfield, P. E., Lovett, J., Engel, L., & Manfield, D. (2017). Use of the flash technique in EMDR therapy: Four case examples. *Journal of EMDR Practice and Research, 11*(4), 195–205.

Manfield, P. E., Engel, L., Greenwald, R., & Bullard, D. G. (2021). Flash technique in a scalable low-intensity group intervention for COVID-19-related stress in healthcare providers. *Journal of EMDR Practice and Research, 15*(2), 127–139.

Massey, D. S. (2017a). Segregation and stratification: A biosocial perspective. In Beaver, K. M., and Walsh, A. (Eds.).*Biosocial Theories of Crime* (pp. 49-67). Routledge.

Massey, D. S. (2017b). Why death haunts black lives. *Proceedings of the National Academy of Sciences, 114*(5), 800–802.

Mays, V. M., Cochran, S. D., & Barnes, N. W. (2007). Race, race-based discrimination, and health outcomes among African Americans. *Annual Review of Psychology, 58*, 201.

McEwen, B. S. (2006). Protective and damaging effects of stress mediators: Central role of the brain. *Dialogues in clinical neuroscience, 8*(4), 367.

McKenzie, H. A., Varcoe, C., Browne, A. J., & Day, L. (2016). Disrupting the continuities among residential schools, the Sixties Scoop, and child welfare: An analysis of colonial and neocolonial discourses.

International Indigenous Policy Journal, 7(2). DOI: https://DOI.org/10.18584/iipj.2016.7.2.4

Menakem, R. (2021). *My grandmother's hands: Racialized trauma and the pathway to mending our hearts and bodies.* Penguin.

Miller, R. (2012). Treatment of behavioral addictions utilizing the feeling-state addiction protocol: a multiple baseline study. *Journal of EMDR Practice and Research, 6*(4), 159–169.

Miller, P. W. (2015). *EMDR therapy for schizophrenia and other psychoses.* Springer.

Miller, W. R., & Rollnick, S. (2012). *Motivational interviewing: Helping people change.* Guilford press.

Moses, Y. (2017, February 1). Why Do We Keep Using the Word "Caucasian"? *Sapiens.* http://www.sapiens.org/column/race/caucasian-terminology-origin

Mukhopadhyay, C. C. (2016). Getting Rid of the Word "Caucasian." In Kimmel, M. S., and Ferber, A. L. (Eds.). *Privilege: A Reader* (pp. 231–236). Routledge.

Mosquera, D., & Knipe, J. (2017). Idealization and maladaptive positive emotion: EMDR therapy for women who are ambivalent about leaving an abusive partner. *Journal of EMDR Practice and Research, 11*(1), 54–66.

Nijenhuis, E., van der Hart, O., & Steele, K. (2010). Trauma-related structural dissociation of the personality. *Activitas Nervosa Superior, 52*(1), 1–23.

Novak, N. L., Geronimus, A. T., & Martinez-Cardoso, A. M. (2017). Change in birth outcomes among infants born to Latina mothers after a major immigration raid. *International journal of epidemiology, 46*(3), 839–849.

Onibada, (2021, July 22), Sundown towns are still a problem for Black drivers, *BuzzFeed News.* https://www.buzzfeednews.com/article/adeonibada/sundown-towns-racism-black-drivers-tiktok

Panksepp, J. (1998). Affective neuroscience: The foundations of human and animal emotions. Oxford University Press.

Perroud, N., Rutembesa, E., Paoloni-Giacobino, A., Mutabaruka, J., Mutesa, L., Stenz, L., & Karege, F. (2014). The Tutsi genocide and transgenerational transmission of maternal stress: Epigenetics and biology of the HPA axis. *The World Journal of Biological Psychiatry, 15*(4), 334–345.

Pfefferbaum, B., & North, C. S. (2020). Mental health and the Covid-19 pandemic. *New England Journal of Medicine, 383*(6), 510–512.

Piquero, A. R., Jennings, W. G., Jemison, E., Kaukinen, C., & Knaul, F. M. (2021). Domestic violence during the COVID-19 pandemic: Evidence from a systematic review and meta-analysis. *Journal of criminal justice, 74.* [101806]. https://doi.org/10.1016/j.jcrimjus.2021.101806

Popky, A. J. (2005). DeTUR, an urge reduction protocol for addictions and dysfunctional behaviors. In Shapiro, R. (Ed.). *EMDR solutions: Pathways to healing* (pp. 167–188). Norton.

Rutherford, A. (2020). *How to argue with a racist: History, science, race and reality.* Hachette UK.

Schwartz, R. C., & Sweezy, M. (2019). *Internal family systems therapy.* Guilford Publications.

Shapiro, F. (1994). Alternative stimuli in the use of EMD (R). *Journal of Behavior Therapy and Experimental Psychiatry, 25*(1), 89.

Shapiro, R. (2016). *Easy ego-state interventions: Strategies for working with parts.* Norton.

Shapiro, F. (2018). *Eye movement desensitization and reprocessing (EMDR) therapy third edition: Basic principles, protocols, and procedures.* Guilford Press.

Shengold, L. L. (1979). Child abuse and deprivation: Soul murder. *Journal of the American Psychoanalytic Association, 27*(3), 533–559.

Shengold, L. L. (1991). *Soul murder: The effects of childhood abuse and deprivation.* Ballantine Books.

Smith, A. (2012). Indigeneity, settler colonialism, white supremacy. In HoSang, D. M., LaBennett, O., & Pulido, L. (Eds.). *Racial formation in the twenty-first century* (pp. 66–90). University of California Press.

Solomon, R. M., & Shapiro, F. (2008). EMDR and the adaptive information processing model potential mechanisms of change. *Journal of EMDR Practice and Research, 2*(4), 315–325.

Stagoll, B., & Lang, M. (1980). Climbing the family tree: Working with genograms. *Australian Journal of Family Therapy, 1*(4), 161–170.

Tronson, N. C., & Taylor, J. R. (2007). Molecular mechanisms of memory reconsolidation. *Nature Reviews Neuroscience, 8*(4), 262–275.

Trudel, M. (2013) *Canada's forgotten slaves: Two hundred years of bondage.* Trans. George Tombs. Véhicule Press.

Van der Hart, O., Nijenhuis, E. R., & Steele, K. (2006). *The haunted self: Structural dissociation and the treatment of chronic traumatization.* Norton.

Van Egmond, J. J. (2003). Multiple meanings of secondary gain. *The American Journal of Psychoanalysis, 63*(2), 137–147.

White, S. H. (2000). Conceptual foundations of IQ testing. *Psychology, Public Policy, and Law 6*(1), 33–43.

Williams, D. R. (2018). Stress and the mental health of populations of color: Advancing our understanding of race-related stressors. *Journal of Health and Social behavior, 59*(4), 466–485.

Wong, S. L. (2019). Flash technique group protocol for highly dissociative clients in a homeless shelter: A clinical report. *Journal of EMDR Practice and Research, 13*(1), 20–31.

Yasar, A. B., Gundogmus, I., Gunduz, A., & Konuk, E. (2021). Investigation of the effect single session of "Flash Technique" at a group. *Israel Journal of Psychiatry, 58(2),* 41–46.

Yehuda, R., Daskalakis, N. P., Bierer, L. M., Bader, H. N., Klengel, T., Holsboer, F., & Binder, E. B. (2016). Holocaust exposure induced intergenerational effects on FKBP5 methylation. *Biological psychiatry, 80*(5), 372–380

Yokum, N. (2022, June 6). A call for psycho-affective change: Fanon, feminism, and white negrophobic femininity. *Philosophy & Social Criticism*, https://doi.org/10.1177/01914537221103897.

Yousman, B. (2003). Blackophilia and blackophobia: White youth, the consumption of rap music, and white supremacy. *Communication Theory*, *13*(4), 366–391.

INDEX

A

abortion 47, 144, 147, 165
adaptive information processing model 27,
    28, 29, 30, 199, 237
addiction ..ii, 25, 87, 88, 89, 90, 138, 164, 169,
    235, 237
adolescence 9, 34, 157
adulthood 231
Africa 11, 13, 21, 137, 231, 233
African x, 5, 12, 13, 21, 43, 120, 209, 231, 235
Africentric .... xiii, 21, 22, 23, 24, 32, 204
Africentric Psychology .... xiii, 22
allostasis 40, 42, 43, 44, 48
ambivalence 87, 89, 91, 93, 94, 100, 102, 106,
    117, 118, 133, 153, 175, 202
Ambivalence 91, 175
American viii, 7, 10, 13, 15, 21, 26, 28, 37, 41,
    43, 120, 209, 211, 231, 232, 237, 238
American Psychiatric Association ...viii, 7, 37,
    231
American Psychological Association .... viii, 7,
    26
amygdala 37, 38, 39
ancestors ....x, 9, 15, 18, 50, 63, 138, 149, 151,
    153, 206, 208
anglophone..x
anti-Black...ix
anti-racism .... x, 8, 19, 214
anti-racist psychotherapy. xii, xiv, 8, 9, 11, 14,
    17, 32, 37, 70, 77, 85, 136, 148, 153, 205
Anti-racist psychotherapy 19, 36, 206, 231
anti-Semitic 4
Apparently Normal part of personality... 106,
    107, 110, 118, 153, 190, 205
Arab...41
Asian...45, 47
assimilation... 110

B

betrayal...53, 138, 174
biological dysregulation 40
Black male .... xii, 16, 42
Black man.. xii, 16, 42
Black Meditation......... ii, 11, 80, 85, 216, 245
black panthers..xi
Black women .... xi, 7, 40, 45, 95, 149, 171
Black, Indigenous, and People of Color iv, ix
Blackness . 11, 12, 15, 206, 207, 208, 210, 233
Blind2therapist 158
body image... 164
body scan... 195
Borderline.. 107
borderline personality disorder 107
Brainspotting 28, 29, 30
Branispotting .... ii, 28, 29, 32, 233
Bryant C.. 209
burnout 212
butterfly hugs..58, 115

C

Calm or Motivating (COM)59, 115, 127, 128,
    129, 130, 177, 182
Canadian .... x, 13, 120
caucasian 12, 13, 235, 236
Caucasian 235
Center for Epidemiologic Studies
    Depression Scale 79
Centers for Disease Control and Prevention5
centrifugal force 51
child mistreatment....................................... 136
childhood. 15, 34, 35, 140, 157, 163, 201, 237
childhood abuse 15, 237
colonization9, 12, 15, 136, 139, 208, 236, 237
compassion ....xi, 36, 48, 187

complex PTSD 26, 29, 107, 120
copaganda.. 55
cortisol...........................9, 38, 39, 40, 213, 231
Cosby, B..210
counter-conditioning..................................... 54
countertransference 158
critical race theory.......................................4, 14

D

decolonization.. 8
defeat.. 44, 138
depression...6, 23, 35, 90
desensitization26, 27, 58, 59, 61, 88, 232, 237
DeTUR...88, 231, 237
diabetes... 44, 141
disability i
disconfirming information 56
disconfirming knowledge 55, 57, 128, 150
discrimination 8, 51, 138, 206, 235
dissociation106, 107, 108, 118, 120, 139, 153,
238
dorsal vagus............................... 139, 141, 153
dual attention 28
dysfunctional positive affect 91, 101
dysfunctionally stored information......xiii, 65,
197

E

eating disorder 78
economic status 7, 40, 43, 204
ego states... 195
Egyptian.. 11
emancipation... 108
EMDR Therapy......i, ii, xii, 26, 27, 28, 29, 30,
31, 32, 55, 56, 57, 58, 61, 62, 81, 88, 91,
92, 112, 120, 121, 122, 125, 134, 154, 157,
158, 159, 160, 174, 178, 180, 189, 202,
203, 231, 232, 233, 234, 235, 236, 237,
238, 246
emotional freedom technique..................... 167
Emotional part of personality...106, 107, 110,
118, 153, 205
environment.xiv, 23, 44, 51, 80, 95, 109, 111,
120, 136, 138, 139, 140, 141, 142
epigenetics 50
equity ....vii, ix, 10, 13, 42, 47, 160, 176
Eurocentric..207

explicit 52, 56, 148
exploitation... 6
extinction 54

F

family ..x, xiii, 3, 6, 23, 68, 69, 71, 78, 94, 136,
142, 143, 144, 145, 146, 147, 148, 149,
151, 153, 160, 163, 165, 176, 208, 237
family systems 23, 136, 147, 148, 149, 153
family systems context 71
family therapist 143
fictive kin 144
fight, flee, or freeze response........38, 56, 106,
107, 140, 141, 149, 153, 201, 212
fight/flight 149, 153, 208
flash technique 29, 31, 32, 120, 121, 125, 134,
205, 234, 238
Floyd, George 3
four cores of anti-racist psychotherapy70, 71,
72, 80, 85, 174, 205
FSAP...88

G

gaslighting...160
Generalised Anxiety Disorder Questionnaire
....79
generalization 176, 187
genocide 9, 15, 136, 208, 236
genogram ....xii, 23, 142, 143, 144, 145, 146,
147, 148, 149, 150, 175, 176, 237
Google Meet..144
gratitude 117, 174, 200
Greek 37
guided earth meditation 80, 81

H

harmony 22, 24
heterosexism..207
Hispanic 5, 45
homeostasis 24, 38, 40
hypervigilance 35, 37, 48, 55, 56, 206

I

immigrant......................ii, vii, 25, 41, 176, 206
immune system 140, 141

implicit ....ix, 10, 51, 52, 53, 158, 232
Indigenous...ii
indigenous people i
Indigenous people ... i, vii, viii, ix, 5, 8, 10, 12, 136, 137, 138, 235
individual context 71
individual therapy 69, 72
installation 61, 115
integration of the personality 110, 153
Internal family systems (IFS)....................237
internalized oppression.............................212
intrapsychic 36, 53, 102, 105, 106
involuntary/voluntary client 38

J

Jamaican...........................x, 13, 18, 77, 93, 120
Japanese 129
Jewish 13

K

Kanye 10
Kelly, R. 210
King, M. L..14

L

Langevin, H. 137
Latina..41, 236
Latino 41, 43, 47, 211
lynching...209

M

mansplaining.......................................80
marginalized...............................i, 211
meditation 80, 218, 231
memory reconsolidation.. i, xii, 29, 30, 53, 54, 56, 58, 68, 74, 78, 121, 123, 125, 133, 134, 156, 159, 201, 204, 212, 231, 232, 234, 238
mental health ....i, vii, 3, 4, 6, 8, 17, 18, 23, 34, 36, 40, 41, 42, 43, 44, 45, 47, 54, 67, 79, 85, 90, 91, 102, 106, 134, 138, 145, 146, 147, 150, 202, 205, 231, 238
mental illness 45
mental level 109, 110, 111, 112, 117, 118, 171

microaggression.....9, 10, 51, 70, 80, 161, 174, 207
MID-60...79
mindful color breathing 80, 82, 114, 154, 174, 176, 220
mindfulness............ii, xiii, 11, 66, 80, 231, 245
mirror neurons 203
monolith 45
motivational interviewing.....................i, 92
multigenerational transmission 139, 143, 146, 148, 150, 206

N

Native American...................................5
nature..... 12, 22, 24, 29, 31, 34, 45, 46, 50, 55, 59, 68, 123, 128, 129, 138, 150, 157, 170, 174, 175, 186, 208, 212, 221, 238
negative belief... 51, 54, 56, 60, 62, 63, 64, 65, 111, 116, 175, 179, 181, 192, 199, 201, 202, 212
nervous system 9, 24, 29, 34, 35, 38, 39, 41, 44, 48, 50, 56, 64, 105, 111, 112, 116, 118, 139, 140, 141, 142, 153, 202, 207
neurobiology..........................37, 215, 233
neurons 231

O

Obama, B. 41
opioid abuse 145
oppressed.............vii, xiii, 3, 46, 139, 207, 211
oppressor......................149, 208, 215
orientalism......................................208
overturning information..... 56, 57, 58, 59, 63, 85, 111, 112, 115, 128, 148, 183, 189

P

pandemic 3, 4, 5, 6, 7, 8, 30, 35, 58, 121, 233, 234, 235, 236
parasympathetic nervous system ... 38, 39, 48, 116, 139, 140, 141
pathogenic memories 28
PCL-5..79
perceived racial discrimination..............9, 231
phobia 30, 166, 200, 201, 202
physical health 40, 44, 46, 99
police 3, 4, 41, 55, 56

police violence 4, 56
polyvagal theory .... i, xii, xiii, 139, 140, 151
Porges, S. 139, 140
positive engaging focus 122
poverty 6, 7, 43, 44, 45, 137, 149, 163, 201,
   212
pregnant women 9
PROS/CONS 92, 94, 103, 175, 205
psychoanalysis 211
psychotherapy .. vii, viii, x, xii, 3, 8, 25, 26, 28,
   29, 32, 57, 59, 73, 91, 120, 137, 199, 205,
   211, 212, 214, 231, 233
PTSD ...v, 9, 26, 35, 37, 40, 79, 106, 107, 120,
   134

Q

quadrant (for PROS/CONS) 94, 101
Quebec .... x, 138, 175

R

race viii, ix, 2, 4, 5, 7, 9, 12, 13, 14, 15, 23, 32,
   37, 40, 41, 42, 47, 70, 138, 148, 156, 157,
   160, 161, 172, 206, 232, 233, 234, 235,
   237, 238
racial trauma i, ii, iii, iv, v, x, xi, xii, xiii, xiv, 2,
   4, 8, 9, 10, 11, 17, 19, 21, 32, 37, 42, 70,
   133, 139, 142, 151, 153, 156, 161, 168,
   171, 172, 174, 177, 197, 202, 204, 205,
   206, 207, 210, 211, 215
racial trauma target history .... xiii, 154
racism . i, ii, iii, v, viii, ix, x, xiii, 2, 3, 4, 5, 7, 8,
   10, 12, 14, 16, 19, 34, 40, 42, 43, 45, 55,
   95, 138, 149, 160, 161, 204, 206, 207, 208,
   211, 212, 227, 232, 233, 236, 245
reciprocity 80, 111, 142, 203, 207, 234
religion 166
resistance 92, 102, 161
resource development and installation 31,
   112, 113, 118, 234
resource integration 113, 117
rhythm 4, i, vi, x, xii, xiii, 9, 18, 19, 20, 22, 24,
   25, 31, 32, 52, 55, 56, 58, 59, 62, 64, 65,
   67, 68, 74, 80, 85, 92, 94, 113, 115, 118,
   119, 120, 125, 134, 139, 140, 141, 149,
   159, 173, 174, 175, 183, 187, 189, 202,
   205, 215, 218, 220, 228, 232

Rhythm and Processing ..... 4, i, vi, xii, xiii, 18,
   19, 20, 22, 24, 25, 31, 32, 52, 55, 56, 58,
   59, 60, 62, 64, 65, 67, 68, 74, 85, 92, 94,
   113, 119, 120, 125, 126, 128, 129, 130,
   132, 133, 134, 139, 147, 159, 171, 172,
   173, 174, 175, 176, 177, 178, 181, 182,
   184, 186, 187, 188, 189, 190, 192, 193,
   194, 195, 196, 197, 199, 201, 202, 203,
   204, 205, 212, 215, 228, 229, 230, 246

S

Sankofa 24
schizophrenia .... viii, 35, 108, 235
secondary gain 92, 94, 113, 153, 238
segregation 43, 46, 48
self-care 71, 231
self-harm 36, 88, 109, 164, 169
self-love 24, 175
self-soothe 109, 125
sexual violence ... 157, 163, 164, 165, 169, 210
sexuality 71, 77, 148, 160, 163, 172
shame ...95, 125, 137, 139, 147, 153, 158, 164,
   207
sick days 42
social construction ...... i, xiii, 2, 17, 40, 45, 71,
   156, 206, 210
social context 71, 94, 136, 156
social identity 165
social injustice 19, 211
sociodiagnostics 210
soul murder 15
South Asian .... ix, 212
spirituality .... xi, 22, 166
stabilization 78, 110, 150, 234
stereotypes 15
strength 127, 175, 192
stress ..iii, xiii, 9, 26, 34, 37, 38, 39, 40, 43, 57,
   80, 83, 84, 92, 106, 107, 109, 126, 131,
   133, 165, 206, 220, 221, 234, 235, 236,
   238
structural dissociation... i, xii, xiii, 59, 79, 105,
   106, 107, 108, 109, 122, 134, 205, 236
structural violence 42
students .... ix, xi, 41, 121, 137, 163, 164
subjective unit of disturbance .. 59, 60, 61, 63,
   65, 114, 116, 117, 121, 125, 126, 130, 131,
   132, 133, 155, 156, 159, 167, 169, 171,
   176, 178, 179, 182, 186, 190, 194

substance abusers.. 102
substitute action 36, 46, 109, 110, 111, 117,
    118, 148, 149
substitute actions .. 36, 46, 109, 110, 111, 117,
    118, 148, 149
suffering...iv, xi, xii, 3, 5, 7, 17, 19, 22, 23, 24,
    25, 35, 43, 44, 48, 50, 51, 52, 60, 69, 80,
    82, 87, 88, 90, 91, 102, 111, 122, 125, 138,
    160, 170, 172, 188, 190, 202, 203, 204,
    205, 210
suicide.................................... 40, 78, 138
survival responses................................53, 106
sympathetic nervous system ...38, 39, 48, 139,
    141, 151, 153, 202, 207
symptoms .... xiii, 36, 51, 52, 55, 79, 92, 108,
    110, 120, 138, 145, 149, 175, 199, 202,
    232
system...... 5, 6, 8, 14, 38, 39, 40, 45, 105, 110,
    111, 118, 126, 137, 139, 140, 141, 142,
    143, 144, 146, 147, 148, 187, 190, 207,
    210, 211, 212
systemic racism.................... ix, 3, 15, 160, 231

T

technology..xi, 18, 29, 30, 125, 134, 202, 204,
    215
therapeutic reconsolidation.. 55, 65, 117, 125,
    159, 171, 197, 203, 205
Till, E... 209
time orientation.................................23
toxic relationships................................155, 165
transference........................... 24, 125, 158, 160
trauma iv, v, xi, xiii, 7, 8, 9, 11, 13, 14, 15, 18,
    19, 23, 24, 25, 26, 28, 30, 34, 35, 36, 37,
    40, 41, 42, 43, 50, 51, 52, 53, 55, 56, 58,
    60, 64, 65, 70, 76, 78, 80, 85, 87, 91, 102,
    105, 106, 107, 108, 109, 110, 111, 112,
    118, 121, 123, 124, 133, 134, 136, 139,

142, 147, 148, 149, 150, 151, 153, 154,
    155, 156, 157, 158, 159, 160, 161, 162,
    163, 166, 167, 168, 169, 170, 171, 172,
    174, 176, 178, 181, 182, 183, 187, 188,
    190, 196, 197, 199, 203, 204, 205, 206,
    207, 208, 212, 215, 231, 232, 233, 234,
    235
trauma history......78, 150, 151, 153, 154, 155,
    156, 157, 161, 166, 167, 169, 176, 181,
    182
trauma treatment..................... iv, 21, 110, 123
Trump, D. 41

V

ventral vagus41, 111, 139, 140, 141, 151, 153,
    187, 207
verve 22, 24
vicarious....................................42, 234
violence 7, 48, 55, 64, 68, 91, 139, 157, 176

W

West.........................x, 10, 137, 148, 149
white man 137
white supremacy....................................15, 208
White supremacy..... i, viii, 3, 15, 17, 208, 210,
    237
whiteness 11
Whiteness ...viii, 10, 11, 12, 13, 14, 15, 16, 19,
    43, 44, 48, 136, 138, 206, 208
whitesplaining...80, 160

Y

youth protection..68
YouTube.. xii, 31, 59, 129, 130, 178, 197, 202

OTHER BOOKS BY THIS AUTHOR

If you liked *Racial Trauma Recovery*,
you might also like the books that inspired it.

Anti-Racist Psychotherapy: Confronting Systemic
Racism and Healing Racial Trauma

You can get it here: https://amzn.to/3b0iqvT

Black Meditation: Ten Practices for Self-Care,
Mindfulness, and Self-Determination

You can get it here:
https://amzn.to/3JEnhm7

LET'S WORK TOGETHER

David Archer is available for podcasts, presentations, and trainings.

Bring the message of Anti-Racist Psychotherapy to those who need it.

Email me at david@archertherapy.com for more information.

RAP Therapy Trainings, EMDR therapy workshops, and free resources (mailing list, videos, and recorded podcasts) are available at:
http://racialtraumarecovery.com

You are invited to view and download these resources.

Be well, stay healthy, and take care.

Made in the USA
Monee, IL
05 November 2024

69413243R00142